READINGS FROM
AMERICAN PSYCHOLOGICAL SOCIETY

M000080690

Current Directions in SOCIAL PSYCHOLOGY

EDITED BY

Janet B. Ruscher and Elizabeth Yost Hammer

PEARSON
Prentice
Hall

Upper Saddle River, New Jersey 07458

© 2004 by PEARSON EDUCATION, INC.
Upper Saddle River, New Jersey 07458

ISBN 0-13-189583-4

Printed in the United States of America

Contents

The Person in the Situation:
Self-Protection, Self-Evaluation, and Self-Change

Social psychology examines how situational factors influence the individual, as well as how the individual influences the situation. A critical question, then, is who is the person in the situation? Traditionally, social psychologists have addressed this question by considering the Self. The Self comprises beliefs about one's own characteristics, such as abilities, preferences, and possessions, as well as an evaluation of those characteristics (i.e., self-esteem). Beyond these characteristics, the Self also possesses an executive function: it is self-aware, renders decisions, exercises self-control, and executes intentions.

Possessing a relatively favorable view of the Self is associated with being happier, having positive expectations about the future, and initiating the behaviors that may secure a better future. Consequently, when most people feel bad about themselves, they attempt to repair the damage. Behaving hypocritically, hurting another person's feelings, or scoring poorly on an examination, for instance, temporarily reduces positive self-regard, and initiates efforts to restore it. A number of social psychological theories deal with such phenomena, including cognitive dissonance theory, self-affirmation theory, and social comparison theory. Tesser's (2001) article suggests that these varied theories all share the common motive of maintaining positive self-esteem and, consequently, the resolutions to self-threats should be substitutable. For example, dissonance theory predicts that, if you do something at variance with your existing attitudes (e.g., telling a younger sibling to use condoms when you recently have not done so), you later will revise that attitude to remove that terrible feeling of hypocrisy and inconsistency. Tesser's approach, however, suggests that you also might feel better if you engage in self-affirmation (e.g., reminding yourself of your important values and qualities) or social comparison (e.g., outperforming a dorm-mate at billiards or on an exam).

In addition to influencing self-esteem, social comparisons can provide a person with information about the Self. Knowing how one performs relative to classmates provides some information about aptitude in that subject, for example. Scanning an opinion poll in a college newspaper may suggest that one shares the views of others (which, in turn, may enhance feelings that opinions are "correct") or suggest that one is on the "lunatic fringe" of the college population. Beyond comparisons with these larger groups, people often select particular individuals with whom they compare themselves. As Suls, Martin, and Wheeler (2002) demonstrate, people rely upon individuals who possess similar backgrounds or aptitudes to predict their own abilities at ambiguous tasks. (If *she* can do it, so can I!). Possessing relatively accurate views of the Self can, in the long run, maintain self-esteem, insofar as the individual then can seek out situations that enhance self-esteem and avoid situations that threaten self-esteem. In some cases, then, "the person in the situation" actively played a role in selecting the situation itself.

Although people occasionally report the experience of "losing" the Self (e.g., in a huge, emotional crowd; when intoxicated; when overwhelmed by the enormity of the universe), the Self usually is salient to the individual person. People are attentive to their own appearance, their own past actions, and their own true intentions. Egocentrically, we believe that other people are similarly attentive to us: we believe that there is a spotlight upon us. (And, meanwhile, everyone else proceeds as though *he or she* is in the spotlight!!) As Gilovich and Savitsky (1999) suggest, we believe that peers notice changes in our appearance from day to day, and that strangers notice embarrassing qualities such as an unusual t-shirt choice or facial blemish. They don't, at least not to the extent that we expect!

Not all intentions are consciously recognized, of course. But the ones that are recognized at a conscious level may be executed with varying degrees of success: We plan to vote for a particular candidate, decline a party invitation to allocate time to writing a course paper, or resolve to lose weight or to quit smoking. Initiating difficult-to-execute intentions, and carrying them through to the completion, can be mentally and emotionally exhausting. After foregoing the party, one may have difficulty concentrating on one's studies. After an entire week of dieting, one may surrender to the temptation of crème brûlée or an entire bag of Oreo cookies. People occasionally set forth intentions to change themselves, usually in ways that they think ultimately will provide desired outcomes. Unfortunately, as Polivy and Herman (2001) demonstrate, people often are unrealistic with respect to how quickly change occurs, and become disappointed when change does not meet their expectations. Focusing again on their own intentions and desires, people are insensitive to the external factors that they cannot control.

Thus, the person in the situation is an active one: striving to maintain self-esteem, gathering information about the Self, interpreting how others see the Self, and endeavoring to change undesirable characteristics. Active, yes. Perfectly accurate, no. The person in the situation often is egocentric and can be ego-protective to boot. As you progress through other topics of social psychology—most of which focus strongly upon situational forces—try to keep the person in situation in mind.

On the Plasticity of Self-Defense

Abraham Tesser[1]

Department of Psychology, University of Georgia, Athens, Georgia

Abstract

Many qualitatively different mechanisms for regulating self-esteem have been described in the literature. These include, for example, reduction of cognitive dissonance, self-affirmation, and social comparison. The work reviewed here demonstrates that despite their differences, these mechanisms may be substitutable for one another. For example, a threat to self via cognitive dissonance can affect attempts to maintain self-esteem via social comparison. This implies that these mechanisms are serving the same, unitary goal of maintaining self-esteem. Thus, there is surprising generality or flexibility in the processes used to maintain self-esteem. Substitution of one mechanism for another may depend on the transfer of affect. The issue of substitutability across domains is briefly discussed.

Keywords

cognitive dissonance; self-affirmation; self-defense; self-esteem; social comparison

Most psychologists have suggested that persons strive to have or maintain a positive self-evaluation, or positive self-esteem. Compared with other motives like self-consistency and self-accuracy, the self-enhancement motive appears to be particularly strong and robust (Sedikides,1993).

One of the most intriguing aspects of self-evaluation is how it is maintained or defended. Self-defensive and self-augmenting behavior is ubiquitous and easy to observe. For example, Bob explains his good score on the biology test in terms of ability and hard work; he blames his poor score on the chemistry test on bad luck or difficulty of the test. Mary, after being outplayed by her best friend, seems to have lost her enthusiasm for tennis. John insists on talking about his "cousin who got super rich on technology stocks" or his "next-door neighbor who is very important in the state legislature." Self-serving beliefs about the self, flattering social comparisons, and basking in reflected glory are only some of the mechanisms for regulating self-esteem that have been studied. Indeed, the number and diversity of these mechanisms is so great that collectively they have been referred to as the "self-zoo." It is the diversity of these mechanisms that is the focus of this article.

The notion of defending "the self" implies that the self is unitary. However, the mechanisms to defend the self are diverse. The circumstances that call up a particular defense mechanism differ dramatically across mechanisms, and the specific behavioral resolutions that are presumed to restore or increase self-esteem differ just as dramatically across mechanisms. Such qualitative differences raise questions about the unitary nature of the self.

To address these questions, my colleagues and I (Tesser, Martin, & Cornell, 1996) build on the early work of Lewin and his students Zeigarnik and Ovsiankina (Lewin, 1935). The maintenance of self-esteem can be construed as a goal.

If different self-defense mechanisms are serving the same goal, then they should be substitutable for one another (Tesser, 2000). For example, if a dissonant, or inconsistent, behavior threatens self-esteem, then a positive social comparison should reduce the necessity for subsequent dissonance reduction. If, however, the need for consistency is serving an independent goal, then the opportunity for a positive social comparison should have little or no effect on the tendency to reduce cognitive dissonance. Our work (e.g., Tesser & Cornell, 1991) favors the hypothesis that self-esteem is indeed a unitary goal, as we find remarkable substitutability among defense mechanisms.

THREE PROTOTYPICAL DEFENSE MECHANISMS

As noted, there is a self-zoo full of self-defense mechanisms. It is not practical to test all such mechanisms, nor is there a sampling frame from which one can select a few "representative" mechanisms. Therefore, for practicality, we chose three mechanisms to focus on in our work. To make the outcomes of the research relevant to large segments of the literature, we chose mechanisms that have enjoyed substantial research attention. Also, demonstrating substitutability among mechanisms that are quite similar to one another would make a less convincing case than demonstrating substitutability across mechanisms that appear to be qualitatively different from one another. Therefore, we chose mechanisms that are substantially different from one another.

The mechanisms whose substitutability we have explored are cognitive dissonance (e.g., Aronson, 1969), social comparison (e.g., Tesser, 1988), and self-affirmation (e.g., Steele, 1988). These mechanisms differ substantially in their antecedents and consequences. A threat to self via cognitive dissonance is often aroused when an individual freely engages in a behavior that is inconsistent with one of his or her beliefs or attitudes. A typical way of resolving such a threat is to change the relevant attitude or belief in the direction of the behavior. This mechanism is intrapersonal and focused on inconsistency. A threat to self due to social comparison is often the result of being outperformed by another person with whom one compares oneself. Such a threat is inherently interpersonal and has little to do with inconsistency in the dissonance sense. These two kinds of threat also have different resolutions because the resolution of a threat due to social comparison is frequently interpersonal (e.g., distancing oneself from the threatening person). The third mechanism, self-affirmation, refers to a bolstering of self-esteem by simply affirming one's important values. Reaffirming what is important to the self, at least on the surface, is independent of the other two mechanisms. Self-affirmation can happen regardless of consistency between behavior and beliefs or the presence of an interpersonal context.

THE GENERALITY OF SUBSTITUTABILITY

In a seminal study, Steele and Liu (1983) demonstrated that the self-affirmation mechanism can substitute for reduction in cognitive dissonance. Students were induced to write a counterattitudinal essay in favor of raising tuition. To manipulate dissonance, Steele and Liu led half the students to believe they had substantial choice about whether or not they would write the counterattitudinal essay; the other half were led to believe that they had little choice. All participants then filled out a questionnaire concerning economic values. For some participants, economics was an important value domain (high self-affirmation); for others, it was an unimportant value domain (low self-affirmation). An attitude measure was then administered to detect dissonance reduction. The typical dissonance effect was obtained only for the low-self-affirmation participants; that is, in this group, high choice about writing the essay led to more favorable attitudes toward a tuition increase than did low choice. For participants who affirmed an important value, however, there was little difference in attitude regardless of their perceived choice about writing the essay. Self-affirmation appeared to eliminate the threat produced by dissonance. Thus, self-affirmation can substitute for, or "turn off," dissonance reduction.

Self-affirmation also appears to substitute for resolution of threats from social comparison. Cornell and I conducted a study in which, in each session, two pairs of male friends individually filled out a "values inventory" and then engaged in a "password" task in which each participant guessed words on the basis of clues provided by the other 3 participants (Tesser & Cornell, 1991). Different individuals participated in each session. We manipulated whether participants had the opportunity to engage in self-affirmation by varying the content of the values inventories. In the self-affirmation sessions, the values inventory concerned a value that was personally important to the participants; in the remaining sessions, the inventory concerned a value that was personally unimportant to the participants. We also manipulated the operation of social-comparison processes by telling some participants that performance on the password task measured important abilities and telling others that performance was not associated with important abilities. Then, by prearranged feedback, 1 participant from each friendship pair was led to believe that he had not done very well on the task.

According to social-comparison theory, participants who thought they had done poorly and that performance was associated with important abilities would feel threatened by another person's good performance, and especially by a friend's good performance. Thus, to avoid this threat, such participants would give harder clues to their friends than to strangers when the task continued. In contrast, participants who had been led to believe performance was not associated with important abilities had nothing personally important at stake and could bask in the reflected "glory" of a friend's good performance. To accomplish this, they would give easier clues to their friends than to the strangers. This complex prediction was confirmed, but only for participants who had not engaged in self-affirmation. The pattern completely disappeared for participants in the self-affirmation condition. Thus, it appears that self-affirmation can substitute for regulation of self-esteem via social comparison.

Can the arousal of threat via cognitive dissonance affect self-regulation via social comparison? To find out, my colleagues and I induced college students to agree to write a counterattitudinal essay in favor of requiring a senior thesis for college graduation (Tesser, Crepaz, Collins, Cornell, & Beach, 2000). High-dissonance participants were given a "choice" about writing the essay; low-dissonance participants were given no choice. (Agreement to write the essay is suffi-cient to create dissonance, and the participants never actually wrote the essay.) Before they were to write the senior-thesis essay, however, all participants wrote an essay about an experience in which another person outperformed them. Half wrote about a performance domain that was personally important; half wrote about a performance domain that was of little personal importance. Each was then asked a variety of questions intended to measure the psychological distance between him- or herself and the other person in the essay. The social-compari-son prediction was that participants would see the other person as distant if the performance domain was personally important and would see the other person as close if the performance domain was personally unimportant. This prediction was realized, but the effect was strongly moderated by the level of cognitive dis-sonance. Compared with participants in the low-dissonance condition, partici-pants experiencing high dissonance rated the other person as more distant in the important domain and as closer in the unimportant domain. Thus, a threat to self via cognitive dissonance can affect self-regulation via social comparison.

I have described studies in which self-affirmation substituted for reduction of cognitive dissonance and for social comparison, and in which cognitive dissonance affected social comparison. Additional research has also confirmed that cognitive dissonance can affect self-affirmation and that social comparison can affect self-affirmation and cognitive dissonance (Tesser et al., 2000). In short, each of these qualitatively different defense mechanisms substitutes for or affects the others in the way one would expect if there were a single goal of self-esteem maintenance.

How do these mechanisms affect one another? I think the common currency is affect. Affect, in this context, refers to changes in physiological arousal often accompanied by positive or negative feelings. There is substantial research sug-gesting that many self-defense mechanisms (including cognitive dissonance and social comparison) are mediated by affect (see Arndt & Goldenberg, in press, for a review). If someone who perceives a threat to self-esteem is led to believe that the arousal he or she is experiencing is due to something other than the threat, defensive behavior is reduced; if the person experiences arousal from a different source but attributes it to the threat to self-esteem, defensive behavior is increased.

Perhaps substitution works this way as well. Suppose an individual goes through an experience that has an impact on his or her self-esteem. The change in self-esteem is associated with a change in affect. This change in affect, in turn, may help drive the individual's response to a subsequent, but unrelated, situation that is also relevant to self-esteem. For this to happen, however, the individual must be unaware, at least in part, of the change in affect or the con-nection between the affect and the initial causal experience. When the oppor-tunity to engage a substitute mechanism becomes available, the unaccounted—for affect may be transferred—that is, misattributed to the substitute mecha-nism. Just as in other cases of misattribution, this transfer takes place without awareness. The transferred arousal energizes the substitute mechanism, whose completion reduces the affect in the system. For example, an individual who agrees to write a counter-attitudinal essay may experience an increase in arousal and diffuse negative feelings. When a subsequent opportunity to affirm the self arises, unexplained affect from the dissonant behavior adds to the motivation to affirm the self, and the energized affirmation response reduces the negative affect. Maintenance of a positive evaluation of the self is the ultimate goal of this process, and affect plays a key role in how the process unfolds. This account is speculative, and work is clearly needed in this area.

CONTENT DOMAINS

My focus up to this point has been on process, not content. In the experiments summarized, one process substituted for another, but the substitution also crossed content areas. For example, in one of the studies described earlier, dissonance from agreeing to write an essay about a senior thesis affected perceived closeness to other people in performance contexts having nothing to do with senior theses. Substitution across domains is surprising. Why should the perception of closeness of another person in one performance domain be related to the magnitude of dissonance in a totally different domain? It turns out that substitution across domains is not always observed. For example, in a recent set of studies (Stone, Weigand, Cooper, & Aronson, 1997), participants were induced to focus on their own hypocritical behavior regarding condoms. When they were then given an opportunity to contribute to charity or to purchase condoms, they purchased more condoms than control subjects did. That is, they chose to repair the self within the same domain in which the dissonance occurred. At the same time, as in other studies, repair across domains was also observed. When participants did not have the opportunity to purchase condoms, they contributed more to charity than did control subjects.

The resolution to the domain issue might appear straightforward: Repair within a domain is preferred to repair across domains. If only it were that simple. Participants in a recent experiment (Blanton, Cooper, Skurnick, & Aronson, 1997) were threatened and then provided positive information about the self either in the same domain as the threat or in a different domain. The threat to self involved cognitive dissonance: Participants were given either high or low choice to write an essay against increased funding for handicapped students. The feedback to participants affirmed either their creativity (different-domain condition) or their compassion (same-domain condition). Substitution was observed in the different-domain condition: Affirmed participants reduced dissonance less than control participants. However, affirmation in the same-domain condition did not reduce dissonance reduction, but increased it! Although these data do not support the idea that repair within a domain is preferred to repair across domains, they are not difficult to understand. Telling people that they were compassionate shortly after they had agreed to write an essay against funding for the handicapped might simply have exacerbated the inconsistency by reminding them of their recent lapse. Although these data are understandable, they highlight the complexity of the substitutability of self-esteem mechanisms across domains.

CONCLUSION

There are a large number of qualitatively different mechanisms for regulating self-esteem, including cognitive dissonance reduction, self-affirmation, and social comparison. Despite their differences, these mechanisms appear to be substitutable for one another. The self-evaluation system appears to be unitary and surprisingly general and flexible in its processes. At least two major issues have only begun to be addressed. First, although I have suggested that the transfer of affect may play a role in the substitutability of mechanisms, the precise psychological processes by which substitution is accomplished have not yet been established. Second, it is unclear whether substitution is more effective within the same domain or across domains; what little work there is points to an intriguing complexity that previously was not apparent.

Recommended Reading

Harmon-Jones, E., & Mills, J. (Eds.). (1999). *Cognitive dissonance: Progress on a pivotal theory in social psychology.* Washington, DC: American Psychological Association.
Steele, C.M. (1988). (See References)
Tesser, A., Crepaz, N., Collins, J., Cornell, D., & Beach, S. (2000). (See References)
Tesser, A., Martin, L., & Cornell, D. (1996). (See References)

Note

1. This article was written while the author was a visiting faculty member at The Ohio State University. Address correspondence to Abraham Tesser, Department of Psychology, University of Georgia, Athens, GA 30602; e-mail: atesser@arches.uga.edu.

References

Amdt, J., & Goldenberg, J.L. (in press). From threat to sweat: Towards a fuller understanding of the role of physiological arousal in self-esteem maintenance. In A. Tesser, J. Wood, & D. Stapel (Eds.), *Psychology of self: Regulation and group context.* Washington, DC: American Psychological Association.
Aronson, E. (1969). The theory of cognitive dissonance: A current perspective. In L. Berkowitz (Ed.), *Advances in experimental social psychology* (Vol. 4, pp. 2-34). New York: Academic Press.
Blanton, H., Cooper, J., Skurnick, I., & Aronson, J. (1997). When bad things happen to good feedback: Exacerbating the need for self-justification with self-affirmation. *Personality and Social Psychology Bulletin, 23,* 684-692.
Lewin, K. (1935). *A dynamic theory of personality: Selected papers* (D.E. Adams & K.E. Zener, Trans.). New York: McGraw-Hill.
Sedikides, C. (1993). Assessment, enhancement, and verification determinants on the self-evaluation process. *Journal of Personality and Social Psychology, 65,* 317-338.
Steele, C.M. (1988). The psychology of self-affirmation: Sustaining the integrity of the self. In L. Berkowitz (Ed.), *Advances in experimental social psychology* (Vol. 21, pp. 261-302). New York: Academic Press.
Steele, C.M., & Liu, T.J. (1983). Dissonance processes as self-affirmation. *Journal of Personality and Social Psychology, 45,* 5-19.
Stone, J., Weigand, A.W., Cooper, J., & Aronson, E. (1997). When exemplification fails: Hypocrisy and the motive for self integrity. *Journal of Personality and Social Psychology, 72,* 54-65.
Tesser, A. (1988). Toward a self-evaluation maintenance model of social behavior. In L. Berkowitz (Ed.), *Advances in experimental social psychology* (Vol. 21, pp. 181-227). New York: Academic Press.
Tesser, A. (2000). On the confluence of self-esteem maintenance mechanisms. *Personality and Social Psychology Review, 4,* 290-299.
Tesser, A., & Cornell, D.P. (1991). On the confluence of self-processes. *Journal of Experimental Social Psychology, 27,* 501-526.

Tesser, A., Crepaz, N., Collins, J., Cornell, D., & Beach, S. (2000). Confluence of self-esteem regulation mechanisms: On integrating the self-zoo. *Personality and Social Psychology Bulletin, 26*, 1476-1489.

Tesser, A., Martin, L., & Cornell, D. (1996). On the substitutability of self-protective mechanisms. In P.M. Gollwitzer & J.A. Bargh (Eds.), *The psychology of action: Linking motivation and cognition to behavior* (pp. 48-68). New York: Guilford Press.

Critical Thinking Questions

1. The author refers to the self as a zoo, full of self-defense mechanisms; yet he focuses his research on three specific areas. Explain his rationale for focusing on these three to support his argument that there is substitutability among defense mechanisms.

2. Compare and contrast cognitive dissonance, social comparison, and self-affirmation as mechanisms for regulating self-esteem. How do these mechanisms illustrate the active nature of the self?

3. The author argues that the self has a unitary nature and that self-esteem is a unitary goal. What does he mean by this and how does his research support this claim?

Social Comparison: Why, With Whom, and With What Effect?

Jerry Suls,[1] René Martin, and Ladd Wheeler
Department of Psychology, University of Iowa, Iowa City, Iowa (J.S., R.M.), and Macquarie University, Sydney, Australia (L.W.)

Abstract

Social comparison consists of comparing oneself with others in order to evaluate or to enhance some aspects of the self. Evaluation of ability is concerned with the question "Can I do X?" and relies on the existence of a proxy performer. A proxy's relative standing on attributes vis-à-vis the comparer and whether the proxy exerted maximum effort on a preliminary task are variables influencing his or her informational utility. Evaluation of opinions is concerned with the questions "Do I like X?" "Is X correct?" and "Will I like X?" Important variables that affect an individual's use of social comparison to evaluate his or her opinions are the other person's expertise, similarity with the individual, and previous agreement with the individual. Whether social comparison serves a self-enhancement function depends on whether the comparer assimilates or contrasts his or her self relative to superior or inferior others. The kinds of self-knowledge made cognitively accessible and variables such as mutability of self-views and distinctiveness of the comparison target may be important determinants of assimilation versus contrast.

Keywords

social comparison; social influence; opinion formation; self-evaluation

Comparing the self with others, either intentionally or unintentionally, is a pervasive social phenomenon. Perceptions of relative standing can influence many outcomes, including a person's self-concept, level of aspiration, and feelings of well-being (i.e., subjective well-being). Just as comparison of objects and symbols is a core element of human conduct and experience, so too is interpersonal comparison.

In his seminal theory of social comparison, Festinger (1954) hypothesized that other people who are similar to an individual are especially useful to that individual in generating accurate evaluations of his or her abilities and opinions (i.e., in serving the *self-evaluation motive*). However, he did not specify the basis of similarity between the self and the comparison other. Recent decades have seen significant modifications and extensions of Festinger's similarity hypothesis and increasing appreciation that additional motives instigate and direct social comparisons.

Goethals and Darley (1977) integrated key components of attribution theory (i.e., the scientific analysis of lay perspectives about the causes of behavior and performance) with the study of social comparison. They defined similarity in terms of related attributes (i.e., characteristics correlated with or predictive of an ability or opinion); comparing one's own performance with the performance of someone possessing similar related attributes could answer the question "Am

I as good as I ought to be?" For example, if one man swims as well as another man of the same age and physical condition, this implies that he is as good a swimmer as he ought to be. Comparing one's performance with the performance of someone with superior or inferior related attributes is not as informative because any performance difference could be attributed to differential standing on the attributes rather than to differences in inherent ability.

Two decades of research have shown that social comparisons are more complex and that people play a more active role in making use of comparison information than initially thought. Concepts from social cognition, emotion research, cognitive psychology, self-theory, and the study of naturalistic experience have yielded insights into the process of social comparison and the motives that underlie it (Suls & Wheeler, 2000).

SELF-EVALUATION OF ABILITIES AND OPINIONS

An important advance involved recognizing that self-evaluation can have different meanings. For example, "Can I make a hole-in-one?" is a different question than "Do I play golf as well as I ought to?" Two recent theories demonstrate how comparison processes in the domains of ability and opinion vary depending on the type of self-evaluative question.

Social Comparison of Ability: The Proxy Model

The proxy model (Wheeler, Martin, & Suls, 1997) pertains to the use of social comparison to gain information for anticipating one's likely success at some unfamiliar task (i.e., "Can I do X?"). For example, imagine someone is contemplating whether to pursue graduate study; the wrong decision would be costly in time, effort, and self-esteem. The model proposes that one can expect to perform at the level of an experienced other (a *proxy*) on a new task (Task 2; graduate school) if one's history of performance on some initial relevant task (Task 1; e.g., college) is similar to the proxy's history of performance on that task and the proxy is known to have exerted maximal effort on that preliminary endeavor. In contrast, comparing oneself with someone who performed dissimilarly on Task 1 or whose Task 1 effort is unknown or ambiguous will not yield a clear sense of how one is likely to fare on the novel undertaking. The proxy model is unique in its treatment of related attributes. According to the model, when the proxy's Task 1 effort is known, related attributes are irrelevant and likely to be disregarded in predicting performance. However, the model posits that related attributes will be factored into performance predictions when information about the proxy's effort is ambiguous.

We have found support for the basic premises of the proxy model, using both physical strength and intellectual problem-solving tasks (Martin, Suls, & Wheeler, 2002). For example, when asked to anticipate performance on a grip strength task, participants factored the proxy's standing on a related attribute (i.e., hand size) into their predictions, but only when the proxy's effort on an initial task had been ambiguous. When the proxy was known to have produced maximal effort on Task 1 and performed similarly to the participant on that task, participants expected to match the proxy's Task 2 performance, regardless of

11

relative hand size (see Fig. 1). With its unique attention to the interaction of related attributes and effort, the proxy model is a potentially rich resource for researchers interested in studying people's aspiration and goal setting.

Opinion Formation: The Triadic Model

Goethals and Darley (1977) differentiated between beliefs and values. We (Suls, Martin, & Wheeler, 2000) extended this view to posit three types of opinions: current preferences, beliefs, and future preferences. Current preferences ("Do I like X?") are personal opinions concerning liking or appropriateness (e.g., "Do I hate mimes?"). The model proposes that people sharing similar related attributes (e.g., background, general worldview) will be seen as personally relevant and therefore will be most influential for preference evaluation. Similar others also suggest which preferences one's peers will accept.

Belief evaluation ("Is X correct?") pertains to verifiable facts (e.g., "Am I correct in expecting terrorists to attack again?"). Obviously, others possessing expertise (i.e., people who are superior to oneself on related attributes) can answer such comparative questions. An expert's response on an issue is likely to

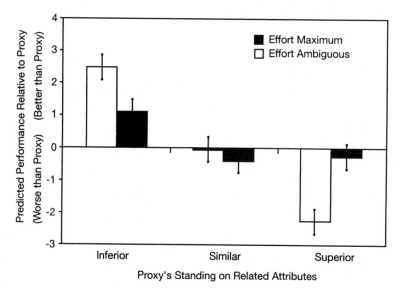

Fig. 1. Average predicted performance difference between the self and a proxy in a study of expected grip strength. Results are shown separately for six conditions defined by whether the proxy's effort on a previous relevant task was ambiguous or maximum and whether the proxy's related attributes were inferior, similar, or superior to the self's related attributes. Positive scores represent expectations of greater grip strength than the proxy (better performance), whereas negative scores reflect the anticipation of weaker grip strength than the proxy (poorer performance). From "Ability Evaluation by Proxy: Role of Maximum Performance and Related Attributes in Social Comparison," by R. Martin, J. Suls, and L. Wheeler, 2002, *Journal of Personality and Social Psychology: Interpersonal Relations and Group Processes*, 82, p. 786. Copyright 2002 by the American Psychological Association. Adapted with permission.

be rejected, however, unless that person shares one's fundamental religious, political, and social values. Thus, the model assigns considerable importance to the role of the *similar expert* (someone who is similar in some ways but not others) in belief evaluation.

In a study comparing preference and belief evaluations, we (Suls et al., 2000) obtained results consistent with the model, finding that the preferred comparison other varied as a function of the evaluative question. Specifically, comparison others with similar related attributes were selected for preference questions. However, when belief questions were formulated for the same attitudinal stimulus, participants opted to compare with a more knowledgeable other. Field research on opinion leaders and innovators confirms the similar-expert hypothesis. For example, gay men are more likely to adopt safe-sex practices if such practices are advocated by someone who both is more knowledgeable than them and shares their sexual orientation.

The third type of opinion question concerns predictions about future preferences ("Will I like X?"). Knowing that a proxy enjoyed a particular book does not allow someone to anticipate his or her own response, unless the pattern of the proxy's past preferences, relative to the self, is known. If the self and the proxy have agreed about books in the past, the proxy's feedback about a book currently in question has informational utility. (This intuitive strategy used by laypeople is formally implemented by marketers and is referred to as *collaborative filtering*. For example, Amazon.com uses shared shopping patterns as a basis for formulating customer recommendations.) If the proxy's past relative preferences are unknown, related attributes can provide a basis for comparison, as has been demonstrated in several experiments (Suls et al., 2000).

SELF-ENHANCEMENT: UPWARD OR DOWNWARD?

In the 1980s and 1990s, researchers found that comparisons with dissimilar others may be used to enhance or protect subjective well-being, and thereby satisfy the *self-enhancement motive*. Wills's (1981) influential downward-comparison theory proposed that (a) threatened people are more likely to compare with others who are worse off than themselves than with others who are better off and (b) exposure to a less fortunate other (i.e., a downward target) boosts subjective well-being. Breast cancer patients (Wood, Taylor, & Lichtman, 1985) and other threatened individuals seemed to benefit from strategic downward comparisons, indicating that some people spontaneously make such comparisons to cope and that interventions by health and clinical psychologists might use downward comparisons to help patients. Downward-comparison theory emphasized the positive effects of downward comparisons (e.g., "I only had a lumpectomy, but those other women lost a breast"), which implied that upward comparisons invariably have a negative impact. The active use of comparison as a coping strategy and of self-enhancement via downward comparison, in particular, were dominant themes of social and health psychology research for more than a decade, but recent findings have raised serious questions about the benefits of downward comparison.

First, although correlational survey and interview studies supported the idea that threatened individuals buttress their subjective well-being through downward comparison, experimental evidence comparing upward and downward comparison was inconsistent, and studies often failed to include no-comparison control groups. Without a baseline condition, it was not possible to determine whether upward comparisons decreased well-being or downward comparisons increased this feeling. Second, studies of spontaneous social comparisons in daily life (Wheeler & Miyake,1992) found that people made downward comparisons when they felt happy, rather than unhappy; in addition, contrary to Wills's perspective, high rather than low self-esteem predicted downward comparison. Such results are consistent with affect-cognition theories in which particular kinds of affect elicit congruent cognitions about the self (e.g., negative affect elicits negative self-thoughts, leading to a contrastive upward comparison and further feelings of inferiority).

Third, the idea that upward comparison invariably is aversive was reconsidered. Collins (2000) reviewed research showing that people intentionally compare themselves with superior others (i.e., upward targets) and that such comparisons can make self-views more positive. This is because people want, and believe they have, positive characteristics, so they perceive similarity with upward targets and conclude "that they are among the better ones" (Collins, 2000, p. 170).

Wood (1989) proposed that there is a *self-improvement motive*, which directs comparisons in the interest of improving the self. Upward comparison with superior role models can provide hope and inspiration. Whether self-improvement should be considered a third distinct motive in addition to self-evaluation and self-enhancement is debatable. It may be a variant of self-enhancement provided by the inspiration of an upward target's success. Lockwood and Kunda (1997) showed that exposure to upward targets increased self-evaluations of competence and motivation when individuals believed in the possibility of change in their status.

Not only can upward comparisons produce positive evaluations in some cases, but also downward comparisons can produce negative evaluations (Buunk, Collins, Taylor, Van Yperen, & Dakof, 1990). Thus, it is clear that the affective outcome of a comparison is not determined by its direction. Exposure to someone who is less fortunate than oneself can lead to either positive or negative evaluations because such exposure potentially communicates two things: (a) that one's standing is relatively advantaged and (b) that one's status could decline. In parallel fashion, exposure to someone who is superior to oneself can lead to either positive or negative evaluations because such exposure suggests (a) that one is relatively disadvantaged and (b) that one could improve. The salient implication of a comparison will determine its affective consequences. Hence, comparison sometimes produces an evaluation that is displaced toward the comparison target (i.e., an assimilative outcome) rather than an evaluation that is displaced away from the target (i.e., a contrastive outcome).

ASSIMILATION AND CONTRAST IN SOCIAL COMPARISON

Assimilation is promoted by the belief that one could obtain the same status as the target (Lockwood & Kunda, 1997), by psychological closeness (i.e., perceiving an identification or connection to the other person), by having related attributes similar to those of the comparison target (Collins, 2000), and by the salience of one's connection with other people ("we"). Contrast is facilitated by the personal relevance of the attributes one has in common with the other person, by one's extremity on those attributes, and by the salience of the individual self ("I").

Mussweiler (2001) proposed that the moderators just mentioned may produce assimilation or contrast through a common process. Each moderator tends to make more cognitively accessible certain kinds of information about the self that are either congruent (leading to assimilation) or incongruent (leading to contrast) with the comparison target. Because there are many facets to the self, in most cases, people can remember or construe self-knowledge in such a way that comparison outcomes are consistent with their expectations. For example, people typically expect to be similar to those with whom they feel psychologically close. Thus, if someone compares him- or herself with a friend, shared attributes or experiences should be highly accessible, (e.g., "we both like to play chess"). This differential accessibility of self-knowledge that highlights similarity should facilitate the displacement of personal judgments toward the comparison target, producing assimilation. However, in the absence of psychological closeness, differences with the comparison target will be more accessible (e.g., "he likes sherry, but I like domestic beer"). In the latter case, self-judgments will be displaced away from the target, leading to contrast. In sum, the various moderators make certain kinds of self-knowledge highly accessible, and this, in turn, produces assimilation or contrast.

Two additional factors, distinctness and mutability, have been proposed by Stapel and Koomen (2000) to influence whether assimilation or contrast results after exposure to an upward or downward target. Distinctness refers to the extent to which the comparison target is seen to have clear boundaries. Mutability refers to the degree to which the image of the self is unclear and there is room for inclusion of additional information. Very distinct targets should discourage "spillover," so that the target serves as an anchor and displaces self-evaluations away from the target, producing contrast. When the target has vague boundaries and self-views are mutable, however, assimilation is facilitated. Recent laboratory research manipulating perceived mutability and distinctness provides support for these predictions (Stapel & Koomen, 2000).

Approaches that emphasize knowledge accessibility and constructs such as mutability and distinctness integrate comparison processes with the broader literature on social cognition. Further, this work is developing an overarching framework to help organize the growing catalogue of moderators of assimilation versus contrast.

CONCLUSIONS

Advances in social comparison initially drew on concepts from attribution theory. More recently, concepts such as knowledge accessibility and motivated reasoning also have proved useful. Evaluation via social comparison now is seen to involve a large set of self-evaluative questions and self-motivations. Comparison is used not just to evaluate past and current outcomes but also to predict future prospects. Assessing preferences and beliefs involves different kinds of comparisons, and validation does not always derive from comparison with similar others.

Another important insight is that the effects of social comparison on self-evaluations are not intrinsically linked to the direction of the comparison. Comparison can produce positive and negative contrastive and assimilative effects, which have implications for any setting where relative standing is salient (e.g., schools, playing fields).

Several issues relating to upward and downward comparison remain to be investigated. For example, it remains unclear which variables are most important in determining whether responses are assimilative or contrastive. Learning more about such variables will be important if research on social comparison is to be useful for understanding coping with medical and other threats.

Cognitive and emotional responses to comparison have been extensively studied, but less is known about the effects of comparison on behavior. Social comparison, of course, is only one source of self-evaluative information. Its relative place among direct feedback, comparisons with past selves, and other sources of information used for self-evaluation remains to be determined. Contemporary theories and research suggest some ways that people are able to benefit from certain comparisons for predicting their performance, validating their opinions, and enhancing their self-image. It seems likely that, in the not-too-distant future, continued research on social comparison will have the potential to inform social policy and inspire interventions targeted at improving well-being.

Recommended Reading

Buunk, B., & Gibbons, F.X. (Eds.). (1997). *Health and coping: Perspectives from social comparison theory.* Mahwah, NJ: Erlbaum.
Buunk, B., & Mussweiler, T. (Eds.). (2001). New directions in social comparison research [Special issue]. *European Journal of Social Psychology, 31*(5).
Suls, J., & Wheeler, L. (Eds.). (2000). (See References)
Wood, J. (1996). What is social comparison and how should we study it? *Personality and Social Psychology Bulletin, 22,* 231-248.

Acknowledgments—Preparation of this article was partly supported by National Science Foundation Grant BCS-9910592.

Note

1. Address correspondence to Jerry Suls, Department of Psychology, University of Iowa, Iowa City, IA 52242; e-mail: jerry-suls@uiowa.edu.

References

Buunk, B.P., Collins, R.L., Taylor, S.E., Van Yperen, N., & Dakof, G.A. (1990). The affective consequences of social comparison: Either direction has its ups and downs. *Journal of Personality and Social Psychology, 59,* 1238-1249.
Collins, R.L. (2000). Among the better ones: Upward assimilation in social comparison. In J. Suls & L. Wheeler (Eds.), *Handbook of social comparison* (pp. 159-172). New York: Kluwer Academic/Plenum.
Festinger, L. (1954). A theory of social comparison processes. *Human Relations, 7,* 117-140.

Goethals, G.R., & Darley, J. (1977). Social comparison theory: An attributional approach. In J. Suls & R.L. Miller (Eds.), *Social comparison processes: Theoretical and empirical perspectives* (pp. 259-278). Washington, DC: Hemisphere Publishing.

Lockwood, P., & Kunda, Z. (1997). Superstars and me: Predicting the impact of role models on the self. *Journal of Personality and Social Psychology, 73*, 91-103.

Martin, R., Suls, J., & Wheeler, L. (2002). Ability evaluation by proxy: Role of maximum performance and related attributes in social comparison. *Journal of Personality and Social Psychology: Interpersonal Relations and Group Processes, 82*, 781-791.

Mussweiler, T. (2001). 'Seek and ye shall find': Antecedents of assimilation and contrast in social comparison. *European Journal of Social Psychology, 31*, 499-509.

Stapel, D., & Koomen, W. (2000). Distinctness of others, mutability of selves: Their impact on self-evaluations. *Journal of Personality and Social Psychology, 79*, 1068-1087.

Suls, J., Martin, R., & Wheeler, L. (2000). Three kinds of opinion comparison: The Triadic Model. *Personality and Social Psychology Review, 4*, 219-237.

Suls, J., & Wheeler, L. (Eds.). (2000). *Handbook of social comparison*. New York: Kluwer Academic/Plenum.

Wheeler, L., Martin, R., & Suls, J. (1997). The Proxy social comparison model for self-assessment of ability. *Personality and Social Psychology Review, 1*, 54-61.

Wheeler, L., & Miyake, K. (1992). Social comparisons in everyday life. *Journal of Personality and Social Psychology, 62*, 760-773.

Wills, T.A. (1981). Downward comparison principles in social psychology. *Psychological Bulletin, 90*, 245-271.

Wood, J.V. (1989). Theory and research concerning social comparisons of personal attributes. *Psychological Bulletin, 106*, 231-248.

Wood, J.V., Taylor, S.E., & Lichtman, R. (1985). Social comparison in adjustment to breast cancer. *Journal of Personality and Social Psychology, 49*, 1169-1183.

Critical Thinking Questions

1. Traditionally, downward social comparison is associated with positive consequences for the self, while upward social comparison has been linked with negative consequences. Discuss some of the research that goes against this pattern.

2. Distinguish among self-evaluation, self-enhancement, and self-improvement. Explain how social comparison is used in each of these active processes.

3. The authors assert that further research in the area of social comparison could be used to "inform social policy and inspire interventions targeted at improving well-being." Speculate on some applications of this research to these areas.

The Spotlight Effect and the Illusion of Transparency: Egocentric Assessments of How We Are Seen by Others

Thomas Gilovich and Kenneth Savitsky[1]

Department of Psychology, Cornell University, Ithaca, New York (T.G.), and Department of Psychology, Williams College, Williamstown, Massachusetts (K.S.)

Abstract

We review a program of research that examines people's judgments about how they are seen by others. The research indicates that people tend to anchor on their own experience when making such judgments, with the result that their assessments are often egocentrically biased. Our review focuses on two biases in particular, the spotlight effect, or people's tendency to overestimate the extent to which their behavior and appearance are noticed and evaluated by others, and the illusion of transparency, or people's tendency to overestimate the extent to which their internal states leak out and are detectable by others.

Keywords

egocentrism; spotlight effect; transparency

Everyday social interaction often requires that people try to anticipate how they are seen by others. "Does my boss know how hard I've worked?" "Did I come across as badly as I fear?" The accuracy of such judgments and the processes by which they are made have recently sparked strong interest among social psychologists (Kenny & DePaulo,1993). In this article, we describe our own work on the topic. The overriding theme of our research is that people's appraisals of how they appear to others tend to be egocentrically biased. Because people are so focused on their own behavior, appearance, and internal states, they overestimate how salient they are to others. Thus, others are less likely than one suspects to notice an embarrassing faux pas or a meritorious personal triumph, and one's internal states, such as nervousness, disgust, or alarm, seldom leak out as much as one thinks.

THE SPOTLIGHT EFFECT

In a memorable scene from the not-so-memorable film *The Lonely Guy*, the comedian Steve Martin arrives at a restaurant and is asked by the maitre d', "How many in your party, sir?" When Martin replies that he is dining alone, the maitre d' raises his voice and asks with astonishment, "Alone?" The restaurant falls silent as everyone stares at Martin in disbelief. To make matters worse, a spotlight suddenly appears from nowhere and follows Martin as he is escorted to his seat.

Although farcical, the scene captures the fear many people have of how their awkward moments look to others. Whether dining out alone, fumbling with change at the front of the bus, or momentarily having no one to talk to at a cocktail party, people are typically afraid that they will stick out like a sore thumb. How realistic are these fears? We maintain that they tend to be overblown that people often overestimate the extent to which others notice them. They do so, furthermore, not just for their mishaps and awkward moments, but for their triumphs as well. The efforts that an individual views as extraordinary whether a brilliant comment after a scholarly presentation or a no-look bounce pass on the basketball court often go unnoticed or underappreci-ated by others. We have dubbed this phenomenon the spotlight effect (Gilovich, Medvec, & Savitsky, in press). People tend to believe that the social spotlight shines more brightly on them than it actually does. We have documented the spotlight effect in a number of contexts. In one study, individual participants were asked to don a T-shirt featuring a picture of pop singer Barry Manilow (a figure of dubious renown among college students). In each session, one such par-ticipant was escorted to another room in the laboratory and instructed to knock on the door. A second experimenter answered and ushered the participant into the room, where 4 to 6 other (normally dressed) participants were seated filling out questionnaires. After a brief interchange, the second experimenter escorted the participant back out of the room and into the hallway. There, the participant was asked to estimate how many of those seated in the room would recall who was pictured on his or her shirt. As expected, participants overestimated the actual accuracy of the observers (by a factor of 2). The T-shirt wearers were noticed far less than they suspected (Gilovich et al., in press).

We have also demonstrated this effect in a number of other experiments. We have shown, for example, that participants tend to overestimate the salience of their own contributions both positive and negative to a group discussion. And we have shown that participants who were absent for a portion of an experiment expected their absence to be more apparent to the other participants than it actually was. Once again, people expected others to notice them (even their absence) more than was actually the case (Gilovich et al., in press; Savitsky & Gilovich, 1999).

Finally, we have explored a corollary of the spotlight effect: We propose that beyond overestimating the extent to which others are attentive to their momen-tary actions and appearance, people also overestimate the extent to which others are likely to notice the variability of their behavior and appearance over time. For the individual performer, it is often the differences in performance across time that are salient, with the constancies relegated to the background. For observers, the pattern is often reversed. To examine this issue, we have asked participants to estimate how they would be judged on successive occasions and then com-pared the variations in those predictions with variations in how they were actu-ally rated by their peers. Thus, we asked college students to predict, on a number of occasions, how their personal appearance would be judged, relative to their usual appearance (were they having a good or bad day on that occasion?). We also asked collegiate volleyball players to rate how their performance would be judged by their teammates after numerous scrimmages. In both studies, partic-ipants expected their peers ratings of them to be more variable than they actu-ally were. What one takes to be an outstanding performance or a bad hair day, for instance, and expects others to notice, may be largely indistinguishable from what others perceive to be one's typical performance or appearance (Gilovich, Kruger, Medvec, & Savitsky, 1999).

Having established the existence of the spotlight effect, we examined the obvious next question: Why do people overestimate the salience of their own appearance and behavior? Our answer emphasizes the difficulty of getting beyond one's own phenomenological experience. To be sure, people are often aware that others are less focused on them than they are on themselves, and that some adjustment from their own experience is necessary to capture how they appear in the eyes of others. Even so, it can be difficult to get beyond one's own perspective. The adjustment that one makes from the anchor of one's own phenomenology (Jacowitz & Kahneman, 1995), or, in Gilbert's (1989) terms, the correction from an initial characterization, tends to be insufficient. The net result is that estimates of how one appears to others are overly influenced by how one appears to oneself (Kenny & DePaulo, 1993).

We have obtained support for this interpretation in a number of ways. In one experiment, some participants were given an opportunity to acclimate to wearing an embarrassing shirt prior to confronting their audience. Others were not. Because the habituation period tended to decrease the extent to which participants were themselves focused on the shirt, the estimates of participants who became accustomed to wearing the shirt began from a less powerful internal state or a lower anchor than the estimates of participants who had no habituation period, and their predictions of the number of observers who had noticed their shirt were diminished. Note that the objective nature of the stimulus was unchanged across conditions it was, after all, the same shirt. But because participants phenomenological experience of wearing the shirt had changed, so did their sense of being in the spotlight (Gilovich et al., in press).

ANTICIPATING HOW ONE WILL BE JUDGED BY OTHERS

Recall the predicament of individuals who must dine alone in a restaurant. They are made anxious not simply by the prospect that they will be noticed, but by the anticipation that, once spotted, they will be judged harshly as outcasts who lack social appeal. Our current research suggests that these concerns, too, are overblown. We have demonstrated that after a failure (whether a social faux pas or an intellectual downfall), individuals expect others to judge them more harshly than they actually do. Participants who fail to perform well at solving anagrams, for instance, expect their faulty performance to garner more condemnation than it actually does, and expect observers to rate them more harshly on attributes such as intelligence and creativity than they actually do (Savitsky, Epley, & Gilovich, 1999).

Anchoring and adjustment may be at work here, too. There is evidence that individuals often condemn themselves more harshly for a failure than they expect others to, and such harsh self-recriminations can then serve as their starting point in attempting to discern how harshly they will be judged by others. Even if individuals realize that their self-recriminations are more acute than what they will receive from others, their adjustments from their own feelings are typically insufficient. Consequently, there may be some residual effect of how individuals judge themselves when they anticipate how they will be judged by others.

We suspect, however, that people's excessive concern about the severity of others judgments is also due to a failure to anticipate a particular type of judgmental charity on the part of observers the charity that comes with having experienced similar failures themselves. People often commiserate with those they witness dining alone, losing their train of thought during a presentation, or forgetting the name of an acquaintance in part because they have suffered similar embarrassments themselves.

We have collected evidence indicating that, on average, people think they are more prone to such embarrassing episodes than their peers, and that they fail to appreciate the extent to which those who have been there, done that are likely to empathize with their misfortune and withhold judgment. In one study, participants attempted challenging word problems and failed in view of two observers. One of the observers possessed (and was known by the participants to possess) the answers to the word problems; the other did not. Not surprisingly, the observers who were given the answers considered the questions to be easier than did those who were not, and thus judged the participants more negatively. But this difference was lost on the participants, who expected the two observers to judge them equally harshly. The participants apparently failed to anticipate the extent to which the uninformed observers would simply conclude that the problems were difficult. We suspect that this failure to anticipate the extent to which others will empathize with one's plight is at work in many situations in which individuals expect to be judged more harshly than they actually are (Eply, Savitsky, & Gilovich, 1999).

THE ILLUSION OF TRANSPARENCY

In addition to being acutely aware of their own appearance and behavior, individuals are often quite focused on their internal states and emotional sensations. Sometimes these states are apparent to others, but other times they are well hidden and it is often important to know whether such states are apparent to others or not. "Can he tell I'm not interested?" "Was my nervousness apparent?" We propose that in making these determinations, people are likewise egocentrically biased. Once again, people realize that others are less aware of their sensations than they are themselves; they know that others cannot read their minds. But the adjustments that individuals make to try to capture other people's perspectives tend to be insufficient. As a result, people tend to overestimate the extent to which their internal sensations leak out and are apparent to others. We refer to this as the illusion of transparency (Gilovich, Savitsky, & Medvec, 1998).

We have shown in a number of investigations that individuals are typically less transparent than they suspect. In one study, participants were asked to conceal their disgust over a foul-tasting drink, and then to estimate how successfully they had done so. Specifically, we asked participants to taste five specially prepared drinks while we videotaped their reactions. Four of the drinks were pleasant tasting and one randomly placed amidst the other four was decidedly unpleasant. After tasting all five, participants estimated how many of 10 observers would be able to guess which drink had been the foul-tasting one after watching a videotape of their facial expressions. As expected, tasters overestimated the extent to which their disgust was transparent: The observers were far less accurate than the tasters predicted (Gilovich et al., 1998).

We have demonstrated the illusion of transparency in a host of other paradigms as well. We have shown, for example, that people tend to think that their nervousness over telling lies leaks out more than it actually does, and so they overestimate the extent to which their lies are detectable. We have also shown that witnesses to a staged emergency believe their concern about the situation is more apparent than it actually is, and that negotiators overestimate the extent to which their negotiation partners can discern their preferences (Gilovich et al., 1998; Van Boven, Medvec, & Gilovich,1999). In these studies, we have employed a number of control conditions to rule out various alternative interpretations, such as the curse of knowledge (i.e., the belief that what one knows is known to others as well) or the fact that people may have inaccurate abstract theories about how easily internal states not just one's own, but anyone's can be detected. The results have consistently supported the critical role of the illusion of transparency.

CONCLUSION

Across three lines of inquiry, we have demonstrated that individuals have difficulty anticipating how they appear in the eyes of others. When it comes to predicting whether one will be noticed, how one will be judged, or whether one's internal sensations are detectable, there is often a considerable gap an egocentric gap between one's intuitions and the actual judgments of others. Much work, of course, remains to be done. Although our research has shown that the spotlight effect and illusion of transparency exist for both positive and negative experiences, there surely are differences in how the two phenomena are played out for positive versus negative experiences, and an understanding of these differences should increase understanding of both phenomena. It is also important to determine whether the spotlight effect and illusion of transparency vary with development, as has been shown for egocentrism more generally. Finally, there are a host of applied implications that await exploration. Does the illusion of transparency contribute to marital miscommunication? Can the spotlight effect shed light on social phobia and anxiety? Does the spotlight effect contribute to the perception that one has lost face, and to the humiliation and violence that such a perception engenders? We hope that it is not too egocentric to suggest that these are important questions waiting to be addressed.

Recommended Reading

Gilovich, T., Savitsky, K., & Medvec, W.H. (1998). (See References).
Kenny, D.A., & DePaulo, B.M. (1993). (See References).
Keysar, B., Barr, D.J., & Horton, W.S. (1998). The egocentric basis of language use: Insights from a processing approach. *Current Directions in Psychological Science, 7*, 46-50.
Vorauer, J.D. (in press). Transparency estimation in social interaction. In G.B. Moskowitz (Ed.), *Future directions in social cognition*. Mahwah, NJ: Erlbaum.

Acknowledgments—This research was supported by Research Grants SBR9319558 and SBR9809262 from the National Science Foundation.

Note

1. Address correspondence to Thomas Gilovich, Department of Psychology, Cornell University, Ithaca, NY 14853, e-mail: tdg1@cornell.edu, or to Kenneth Savitsky, Department of Psychology, Bronfman Science Center, Williams College, Williamstown, MA 01267, e-mail: kenneth.k.savitsky@williams.edu.

References

Eply, N., Savitsky, K., & Gilovich, T. (1999). *Anticipating overly harsh judgments of the self: On the failure to anticipate the empathic discounting of others.* Unpublished manuscript, Cornell University, Ithaca, NY.

Gilbert, D.T. (1989). Thinking lightly about others: Automatic components of the social inference process. In J. Uleman & J.A. Bargh (Eds.), *Unintended thought* (pp. 189-211). New York: Guilford Press.

Gilovich, T., Kruger, J., Medvec, V.H., & Savitsky, K. (1999). *Biased estimates of how variable we look to others.* Unpublished manuscript, Cornell University, Ithaca, NY.

Gilovich, T., Medvec, V.H., & Savitsky, K. (in press). The spotlight effect in social judgment: An egocentric bias in estimates of the salience of one's own actions and appearance. *Journal of Personality and Social Psychology.*

Gilovich, T., Savitsky, K., & Medvec, V.H. (in 1998). The illusion of transparency: Biased assessments of others ability to read our emotional states. *Journal of Personality and Social Psychology, 75,* 332-346.

Jacowitz, K.E., & Kahneman, D. (1995). Measures of anchoring in estimation tasks. *Personality and Social Psychology Bulletin, 21,* 1161-1166.

Kenny, D.A., & DePaulo, B.M. (1993). Do people know how others view them? An empirical and theoretical account. *Psychological Bulletin, 114,* 145-161.

Savitsky, K., Epley, N., & Gilovich, T. (1999). *The spotlight effect revisted: Overestimating the extremity of how we are judged by others.* Unpublished manuscript, Cornell University, Ithaca, NY.

Savitsky, K., & Gilovich, T. (1999). *Is our absence as conspicuous as we think?* Unpublished manuscript, Cornell University, Ithaca, NY.

Van Boven, L., Medvec, V.H., & Gilovich, T. (1999). *The illusion of transparency in negotiations.* Unpublished manuscript, Cornell University, Ithaca, NY.

Critical Thinking Questions:

1. This line of research focuses on our egocentric bias in judging how others see us. Explain how both the spotlight effect and the illusion of transparency are egocentrically biased.

2. The authors claim that the spotlight effect holds for both positive and negative occurrences. Explain this and describe some research evidence that supports this claim.

3. The fact that we overestimate the extent to which others notice our shortcomings seems to contradict the self-defense strategies discussed in the Tesser article included in this section. How can these two approaches to the self be reconciled?

The False-Hope Syndrome: Unfulfilled Expectations of Self-Change

Janet Polivy[1] and C. Peter Herman

Department of Psychology, University of Toronto, Mississauga, Ontario, Canada

Abstract

Why do people persist in attempting to change themselves, despite repeated failure? Self-change is often perceived as unrealistically easy to achieve, in an unreasonably short period of time. Moreover, embarking on self-change attempts induces feelings of control and optimism that supersede the lessons of prior experience. Finally, people tend to expect an unrealistically high payoff from successful self-change. Some sorts of self-change are feasible, but we must learn to distinguish between realistic and unrealistic self-change goals, between confidence and overconfidence. Overconfidence breeds false hope, which engenders inflated expectations of success and eventually the misery of defeat.

Keywords

false hope; self-change; self-improvement; expectations

Who among us has not attempted to change something about himself or herself? Whether we make a New Year's resolution, or go on a diet, or work to improve our golf swings, we begin each new endeavor with high hopes of success, and of the positive impact the alteration will have on our lives (Polivy & Herman, 1999). Some of these self-change efforts work—we all know someone who has lost weight, quit smoking, or taken up jogging. This convinces us that it is possible to alter ourselves, and that our new selves will be more popular, successful, or attractive. Indeed, when we attempt to change, we often meet with some success, at least initially. Unfortunately, these early successes are usually followed by "relapses," when boredom or difficulty undermines our efforts.

What happens when we hit these "walls" blocking successful self-change? Generally, we blame ourselves and our lack of "willpower," developing feelings of guilt and hopelessness about ourselves and our ability to change. But soon the next program appears, bringing renewed hope that this time we will finally improve. The ever-expanding market of self-help and other "change" programs attests to the sad fact that desire for self-modification outstrips its attainment. Given the high failure rate of self-change attempts, why do we keep trying to alter those recalcitrant bad habits? This article addresses the false hope offered by self-change attempts, that is, the oft-broken promise that we will succeed at changing ourselves, and in doing so reap all sorts of rewards.

WHY EMBARK ON SELF-CHANGE?

Why do we try to change? We expect to receive benefits secondary to the change itself. We want to lose weight because we believe that weighing less will make us more attractive, healthier, and more likely to achieve other goals. In general, we expect that modifying some aspect of ourselves will bring us admiration or appreciation, and internal advantages such as pride, confidence, or improved health or functioning. The major attraction of self-change is thus the anticipated outcome. Moreover, altering something about ourselves may also be a way of attempting to gain control over these rewards.

In addition, we try to improve ourselves in ways in which we believe we can succeed. Weight is perceived as malleable, and thus is something that people attempt to change, whereas height is seen as immutable (except perhaps through surgery), so people do not spend time stretching in an attempt to become taller. Some changes are perceived as being relatively easy (e.g., changing hair color), whereas others are seen as being more difficult (e.g., changing body shape). Presumably, one is more likely to embark upon a change that is believed to be not only possible but also easy to effect, though often the expected payoffs (and motivators) are greater for the more difficult modifications.

Advantages of Feeling in Control

Individuals prefer to feel in control of their lives, and resolving to change oneself promotes such feelings. Even when participating in chance activities, people who take an active role develop an exaggerated sense of control. For example, those who select their own lottery tickets instead of having the experimenter assign one to them feel more in control and more confident of a favorable outcome, as do those who choose a marble out of a hat rather than being given one randomly by an experimenter (Wortman, 1975).

A study of cancer patients found that the more the patients perceived they had some control over their disease, the less depressed they were, even after the researchers eliminated the effects of variables such as physical functioning and marital satisfaction (Thompson, Sobolew-Shubin, Galbraith, Schwankovsky, & Cruzen, 1993). Even so minor an effort at controlling one's problems as phoning to schedule an appointment with a psychotherapist produces measurable improvement in distressed individuals (Howard, Kopta, Krause, & Orlinsky, 1986).

Beginning a diet may be a further example of control enhancement, just as breaking a diet seems to involve lack of control. North Americans generally believe that individuals control their weights and body shapes, and are responsible for being overweight (Crandall & Martinez, 1996). Merely committing to a diet may make people feel more in control, more responsible for their weight, and, potentially, more likely to achieve their goals than they felt before making the commitment.

Succeeding at dieting is treated by current Western society as not simply a means to personal goals such as greater attractiveness and longevity (Brownell, 1991). It has come to stand for much more: self-control, ambition, and success in life. This symbolism is based on the idea that individuals control their behavior, which in turn controls weight. People whose bodies conform to the societal ideal are assumed to have other positive attributes, but those with less than perfectly slim bodies are derogated. People overestimate the degree of control they and others actually have over their body shape, and discount the influence of physiological constraints.

Realistic Versus Unrealistic Expectations

Are the expected outcomes realistically connected to the changes people plan to make? For some changes, the predicted benefit is likely to result from the alteration. For example, quitting smoking should make the individual healthier, more able to exercise, less noxious smelling, slightly wealthier (from not buying cigarettes), and better able to taste and enjoy food and drink. However, it is not likely to produce a winning lottery ticket, a better personality, or higher grades. Many desired outcomes are linked unrealistically to self-changes. Often desired outcomes are not actually attainable, yet people are convinced that changing themselves will yield the desired benefit. Many people embarking upon self-change exercises are doomed to fail because their expectations are overinflated. Brownell (1991) has described the assumption that changes such as weight loss will convey major rewards; there is little evidence to support this.

Of course, evaluating the benefits of self-change is not the only domain in which expectations are unrealistic. Overinflated expectations are also likely with regard to the amount of change that will be achieved, the speed with which the change will be accomplished, and the ease of accomplishing the change.

People frequently expect to change more than is feasible. For example, Foster, Wadden, Vogt, and Brewer (1997) assessed obese patients' goals, expectations, and evaluations of various weight-loss outcomes. Before treatment, patients defined their goal weight and their "dream," "happy," "acceptable," and "disappointed" weights. By the end of treatment, the average weight loss was 16 kg (more than 35 lb), and almost half the patients had not even reached what they had previously defined as a "disappointed weight." This illustrates the degree to which patients' expectations exceed what is possible, and lead them to reject more achievable goals.

People also anticipate that they will change more quickly and more easily than is feasible. There is an optimistic bias in how people predict their speed at accomplishing any goal (Buehler, Griffin, & Ross, 1994), including self-change. Furthermore, people believe that the changes they desire are easy to attain. Brownell (1991) discussed the tendency of overweight dieters to believe that weight is highly malleable, despite the difficulty most individuals encounter in attempting to lose weight. Prochaska, DiClemente, and Norcross (1992) reported that even individuals who are eventually successful at changing addictive behaviors must make many attempts, and pass through five stages of change repeatedly before they succeed. Unfortunately, most self-changers are not familiar with this psychological literature, and are largely oblivious to the experiences of those around them, and indeed, even to their own prior experiences.

WHEN SELF-CHANGE EFFORTS FAIL—THE FALSE-HOPE SYNDROME

When unreasonable expectations for self-change are not met, people are likely to feel frustrated and despondent, and to give up trying to change. The unrealistic beliefs with which they begin self-change attempts—and the corresponding unattainable criteria for success—may thus be responsible for the failure of the attempts, creating false hope and then dashing it. This phenomenon of beginning self-change attempts with high hopes and expectations of successful outcomes is illustrative of a phenomenon we call the *false-hope syndrome*. The increased perception of control induced by making the resolution to improve themselves leads many people to feel a false sense of confidence in their likelihood of achieving this resolve, and engenders distorted beliefs about the effects that this success will have on other aspects of their lives. When these expectations are not met, the outcome of attempted self-modification is often disappointment, discouragement, and perception of oneself as a failure (Polivy & Herman, 1999).

The false-hope syndrome is in many respects a problem of overconfidence. One cause of overconfidence or unrealistic expectations may be the inflated promises of change programs. Groups, books, and other sources of help with changing often play into people's fantasies that they can change enormously, and do so effortlessly and quickly, acquiring tremendous benefits. These outcomes are routinely promised, despite the fact that few people, if any, achieve them.

Another source of overconfidence is the individual him- or herself. Baumeister, Heatherton, and Tice (1993) observed, "When people make decisions involving committing themselves to a particular goal or contingency structure, their positive illusions or overconfidence should create a tendency to set goals too high for themselves, with the result that their likelihood of eventual failure increases" (p. 142). Similarly, people tend to overestimate their likelihood of completing tasks (Buehler et al., 1994), and they underestimate how long it will take themselves, but not other people, to complete tasks. Given the literature indicating that positive illusions abound in non-depressed individuals, it is not surprising that such illusions pervade a domain so prone to cognitive distortion as expectations about self-change.

Other cognitive distortions contribute to unrealistic expectations as well. People who attempt to change have often made similar efforts in the past, and are more likely to remember previous successes than failures. Unfortunately, however, the optimism and positive affect that accompany the beginning of a change attempt tend to dissipate with the vicissitudes of actually working to effect the change (Polivy & Herman, 1999). As negative emotions build, the self-control required for further success gives way to overindulgence, and behavior may spiral out of control.

Heatherton and Nichols (1994) analyzed stories about successful and failed life-change experiences to determine what factors are associated with successful change. Compared with failure stories, success stories showed higher levels of social support, increased perceptions of being in control, and a tendency to blame external events for relapses. Success stories also reflected an apparently greater investment of effort in the attempt to change, and were characterized by higher self-esteem and satisfaction. Failure stories, however, described change as being dependent on willpower and external factors, and described change as being intrinsically more difficult than success stories did. People who failed claimed to have been seeking something by changing, but apparently did not find what they sought. In another study, participants undergoing self-change efforts were likely to fail, and felt worse about themselves and saw themselves as failures after an attempt (Polivy & Herman, 1999).

Difficulties encountered during a self-change effort may unleash factors making the modification even harder to achieve. For example, under conditions of stress or mental effort, thoughts of an unwanted mood or action are more accessible, and self-reports of mood opposite to the one intended increase (Wegner, Erber, & Zanakos, 1993). The process of trying to change thoughts or behaviors may be, by its very nature, an uphill battle. Wegner (1997) pointed out that people may unintentionally create the very problems they are trying to overcome by monitoring themselves for thoughts indicating failure to maintain the desired ideational state; as a result, the monitoring process itself occupies the mind with the "wrong" thoughts. Attempts to suppress thoughts can thus make the unwanted thoughts even more salient, resulting in their eventual supremacy. Shoham and Rohrbaugh (1997) concurred, pointing out that the more one focuses on what one wishes to change, the more salient that issue becomes. Thus, the mere focus on the intended alteration may undermine attempts at self-change and produce failure, especially if the self-change involves suppression of thoughts or behaviors.

Baumeister, Tice, and their colleagues (Baumeister, Bratslavsky, Muraven, & Tice, 1998; Muraven, Tice, & Baumeister,1998) proposed that attempts to regulate oneself (and one's behavior) utilize mental energy, which can become depleted. They demonstrated this experimentally, and showed that people who use their energy to control themselves in one situation have less energy for subsequent situations. One cannot inhibit a later behavior if one has spent one's energy on something else.

Self-modification efforts thus appear to require more than has been acknowledged by either the programs or the participants. Self-confidence and elevated self-efficacy may be helpful when the outcome is achievable; hope, or the belief that one can change, appears to be a powerful curative factor. However, when the alteration is too difficult, or one's expectations are unrealistic, self-confidence may become overconfidence, leading from hope to false hope. This raises the question, however, of how self-efficacy, which appears to predict successful self-modification, relates to overconfidence and false hope. Is there an inconsistency in the potential effects of self-efficacy, or can improvements in self-efficacy protect against overconfidence? In order to replace false hopes with real hope, we must learn to determine accurately the difficulty of self-change, to establish realistic goals, to keep our expectations reasonable, and to develop coping skills to help us contend with the setbacks that are normal with efforts to change.

Recommended Reading

Cohen, S., Lichtenstein, E., Prochaska, J.O., Rossi, J.S., Gritz, E.R., Carr, C.R., Orleans, C.T., Schoenbach, V.J., Biener, L., Abrams, D., DiClemente, C., Curry, S., Marlatt, G.A., Cummings, K.M., Emont, S.L., Giovino, G., & Ossip-Klein, D. (1989). Debunking myths about self-quitting: Evidence from 10 prospective studies of persons who attempted to quit smoking by themselves. *American Psychologist, 44,* 1355-1365.

Heatherton, T.F., & Nichols, P.A. (1994). (See References)
Polivy, J., & Herman, C.P. (1991). Good and bad dieters: Self-perception and reaction to a dietary challenge. *International Journal of Eating Disorders, 10,* 91-99.
Polivy, J., & Herman, C.P. (1993). Etiology of binge eating: Psychological mechanisms. In C.G. Fairburn & G.T. Wilson (Eds.), *Binge eating: Nature, assessment and treatment* (pp. 173-205). New York: Guilford Press.
Polivy, J., & Herman, C.P. (1999). (See References)

Acknowledgments—This research was supported by a grant from the Social Sciences and Humanities Research Council of Canada.

Note

1. Address correspondence to Janet Polivy, Department of Psychology, University of Toronto at Mississauga, Mississauga, Ontario, L5L 1C6, Canada.

References

Baumeister, R.F., Bratslavsky, E., Muraven, M., & Tice, D.M. (1998). Ego depletion: Is the active self a limited resource? *Journal of Personality and Social Psychology, 74,* 1252-1265.
Baumeister, R.F., Heatherton, T.F., & Tice, D.M. (1993). When ego threats lead to self-regulation failure: Negative consequences of high self-esteem. *Journal of Personality and Social Psychology, 64,* 141-156.
Brownell, K.D. (1991). Personal responsibility and control over our bodies: When expectation exceeds reality. *Health Psychology, 10,* 303-310.
Buehler, R., Griffin, D., & Ross, M. (1994). Exploring the "planning fallacy": Why people underestimate their task completion times. *Journal of Personality and Social Psychology, 67,* 366-381.
Crandall, C.S., & Martinez, R. (1996). Culture, ideology, and antifat attitudes. Personality and Social Psychology Bulletin, 22, 1165-1176.
Foster, G.D., Wadden, T.A., Vogt, R.A., & Brewer, G. (1997). What is a reasonable weight loss? Patients' expectations and evaluations of obesity treatment outcomes. *Journal of Consulting and Clinical Psychology, 65,* 79-85.
Heatherton, T.F., & Nichols, P.A. (1994). Personal accounts of successful versus failed attempts at life-change. *Personality and Social Psychology Bulletin, 20,* 664-675.
Howard, K.I., Kopta, S.M., Krause, M., & Orlinsky, D.E. (1986). The dose-response relationship in psychotherapy. *American Psychologist, 41,* 159-164.
Muraven, M., Tice, D.M., & Baumeister, R.F. (1998). Self-control as limited resource: Regulatory depletion patterns. *Journal of Personality and Social Psychology, 74,* 774-789.
Polivy, J., & Herman, C.P. (1999). Effects of resolving to diet on restrained and unrestrained eaters: The "False Hope Syndrome." *International Journal of Eating Disorders, 26,* 434-447.
Prochaska, J.O., DiClemente, C.C., & Norcross, J.C. (1992). In search of how people change: Applications to addictive behaviors. *American Psychologist, 47,* 1102-1114.
Shoham, V., & Rohrbaugh, M. (1997). Interrupting ironic processes. *Psychological Science, 8,* 151-153.
Thompson, S.C., Sobolew-Shubin, A., Galbraith, M.E., Schwankovsky, L., & Cruzen, D. (1993). Maintaining perceptions of control: Finding perceived control in low-control circumstances. *Journal of Personality and Social Psychology, 64,* 293-304.
Wegner, D.M. (1997). When the antidote is the poison: Ironic mental control processes. *Psychological Science, 8,* 148-150.
Wegner, D.M., Erber, R., & Zanakos, S. (1993). Ironic processes in the mental control of mood and mood-related thought. *Journal of Personality and Social Psychology, 65,* 1093-1104.
Wortman, C.B. (1975). Some determinants of perceived control. *Journal of Personality and Social Psychology, 31,* 282-294.

Critical Thinking Questions

1. The authors claim that one reason why we have high hopes for self-change is because we can remember cases in which self-change has worked for others. Relate this claim to upward social comparison.

2. Explain how feelings of control can lead to both the initiation of self-change and the false-hope syndrome.

3. Discuss some of the cognitive distortions that lead the false-hope syndrome. Given that research shows that we are motivated to protect our self-esteem, why then do we have these distortions that seemingly set us up for failure?

Influences on Social Knowledge:
Unconscious Processes, Biases, and Culture

Considering an ancient volcano like the one that created the unique shape of Santorini Island, an earth scientist may examine the landscape, life, and weather impacted by its eruption, as well as the factors that precipitate eruption in active volcanoes. A contemporary earth scientist does not, however, posit *social* aspects of the volcano's activity. For instance, he does not infer the intent of the volcano or posit the existence and ire of a sentient entity that controls the volcano's activity. Aspects of the physical world can be active, but they obviously are distinct from the social world: Not only do other people have intentions and cause things to happen, they also can mask those intentions and deflect responsibility for events that they have caused. As Shakespeare observed, a villain who smiles is still a villain. Which other humans are safe, and which other humans are smoldering volcanoes?

Many influences on what people believe about the other people and their social world are relatively nonconscious. A person may recognize, for example, that she holds stereotypic beliefs about a group, but may not be aware that she nonconsciously is applying the stereotype when forming an impression of a member of that group. People also may provide reasons for why they like a particular person, but these reasons simply may reflect the salient reasons that are easy to put into words (e.g., one may dislike a new instructor because her mannerisms are reminiscent of a hated 3rd grade teacher, but one may be unable to make this connection consciously). Some preferences are simply the result of repetition: familiarity breeds liking. Zajonc (2001) describes this mere exposure effect with faces, showing that even familiar faces that are presented too quickly to be recognized consciously are preferred. Zajonc speculates that the preference for the familiar may be an evolutionary adaptation: a familiar face that is not associated with harmful consequences is, at least, safe. [Ancient hominids who preferred familiar and safe faces presumably were more likely to survive, and subsequently pass their genes along to the next generation.]

The preference for familiar (and safe) faces may be related conversely to our adaptation to react to faces that are threatening. As Öhman (2002) argues, humans are adapted to detect threat in faces. Cutting-edge technologies that examine electrical activity in the facial muscles (EMG) or blood-flow in the brain (fMRI) reveal that affective reactions to such faces are relatively automatic. Again, ancient hominids who quickly detected which other hominids were threatening presumably were more likely to pass along their genes: they appeased the threatening conspecific, found a better weapon, or ran. Similarly, ancient hominids who recognized fear in others could use that fear as a social cue to flee from danger.

As a social species, humans are extraordinarily adept at recognizing a core set of facial expressions. Consistent with the proposition that recognition of facial expressions is universal, people from remote developing countries can recognize the core emotions conveyed by people in crowded industrialized nations and vice versa. Although this recognition is well beyond chance, facial expressions do not simply and uniformly convey the person's true emotional experience. In some cases, an individual may wish to mask the true emotion (e.g., upon receiving a hideous gift from a beloved aunt or one's boss). EMG or slow-motion replay on a video camera may reveal the true and original emotional expression, but otherwise it may not be noticed consciously by an observer. Alternatively, emotional display rules vary across cultures. Anger or happiness may be displayed intensely in one culture, but appear more subdued in another culture. Elfenbein and Ambady (2003) argue that ability to recognize emotions is superior when the person displaying the emotion is from one's own culture. Some of the awkwardness that people may experience in cross-cultural interactions may derive from difficulty in "reading" each other's emotional cues. Ironically, we perhaps focus on the purported inability of persons from other cultures to "act normal" or to transmit emotions in ways that we can understand, rather than recognizing that our own cultural background is interfering with our ability to decode their emotions.

Social scientists have come to recognize that cultural experience influences how people think about a unique quality of human activity: intent and underlying dispositional causes. Relative to his consideration of a volcano, a perceiver considering human activity may wonder whether an actor should be held accountable for an event, elected to put elements into motion that caused the event, and has characteristics that explain why the event happened. The process by which people ascertain the causes of social events is called attribution. For decades, social psychologists theorized that people drawing attributions were likely to make the fundamental attribution error (also known as the correspondence bias or overattribution bias), which involves an over-reliance upon dispositional factors and under-reliance upon situational factors. For instance, if one witnesses a mother scolding her child, one quickly may infer that the mother is impatient or unkind, rather than observing that the child had been pulling the tail of an angry sharp-clawed feline. This tendency to focus first on dispositional explanations, though, varies across cultures. Norenzayan and Nisbett (2000) detail a number of studies that show how East Asians are much more sensitive to situational explanations (i.e., less likely to make the fundamental attribution error) than are Westerners. [East Asians can and do recognize intent and personality, of course, just as Westerners can recognize situational factors. Each group simply has a different default that has priority in attribution.]

How we think about other people therefore derives in part from factors about which we scarcely surrender a thought in daily life. Evolution has adapted us to be sensitive to what is familiar and safe, as well as to recognizing which faces are threatening. Moreover, these sensitivities appear to be automatic and nonconscious. Embeddedness in our own culture renders certain behaviors, facial expressions, and explanations normal, and these are neither noticed nor questioned. As a consequence, we have greater ease in decoding the emotional displays of members from our own familiar culture, and explain their behavior in ways that seem natural to our own culture. What we know—or rather what we believe—is as much a consequence of the nonconscious workings of our minds as of the attributes of the social event and the context within it is perceived.

Mere Exposure: A Gateway to the Subliminal

R.B. Zajonc[1]

Department of Psychology, Stanford University, Stanford, California

Abstract

In the mere-repeated-exposure paradigm, an individual is repeatedly exposed to a particular stimulus object, and the researcher records the individual's emerging preference for that object. Vast literature on the mere-repeated-exposure effect shows it to be a robust phenomenon that cannot be explained by an appeal to recognition memory or perceptual fluency. The effect has been demonstrated across cultures, species, and diverse stimulus domains. It has been obtained even when the stimuli exposed are not accessible to the participants' awareness, and even prenatally. The repeated-exposure paradigm can be regarded as a form of classical conditioning if we assume that the absence of aversive events constitutes the unconditioned stimulus. Empirical research shows that a benign experience of repetition can in and of itself enhance positive affect, and that such affect can become attached not only to stimuli that have been exposed but also to similar stimuli that have not been previously exposed, and to totally distinct stimuli as well. Implications for affect as a fundamental and independent process are discussed in the light of neuroanatomical evidence.

Keywords

affect; preference; mere exposure; classical conditioning

Preferences constitute one of the fundamental sources of social and individual stability and change. They give our lives direction and our actions meaning. They influence ideological values, political commitments, the marketplace, kinship structures, and cultural norms. They are sources of attachment and antagonism, of alliance and conflict. No species would evolve if it could not actively discriminate between objects, events, and circumstances that are beneficial and those that are harmful.

Preferences are formed by diverse processes. Some objects, by their inherent properties, induce automatic attraction or aversion. Sucrose is attractive virtually at birth, whereas bitter substances—quinine, for example—are universally aversive. Preferences may also be established by classical or operant conditioning. If a child is rewarded when she sits in a particular corner of the crib, that corner will become a preferred location for her. An office worker whose colleagues notice his new tie will develop a preference for similar ties. Preferences can also be acquired by virtue of imitation, a social process that emerges in fashions. Preferences also arise from conformity pressures. In economics, preference is regarded as the product of rational choice—a deliberate computation that weighs the pros and cons of alternatives.

But among the many ways in which preferences may be acquired, there is one that is absurdly simple, much simpler than rational choice. I discuss here this very primitive way—conscious and unconscious—of acquiring preferences, namely, the mere repeated exposure of stimuli, and I explain the process whereby repeated exposure leads to the formation of preferences.

THE MERE-REPEATED-EXPOSURE PHENOMENON

The repeated-exposure paradigm consists of no more than making a stimulus accessible to the individual's sensory receptors. There is no requirement for the individual to engage in any sort of behavior, nor is he or she offered positive or negative reinforcement. The exposures themselves are sometimes so degraded that the individual is not aware of their occurrence. Their effects are measured by the resulting changes in preference for the object. In contradiction to some early contentions (Birnbaum & Mellers, 1979; Lazarus, 1982), it can now be claimed that no cognitive mediation, rational or otherwise, is involved in these effects.

It is well known that words with positive meanings have a higher frequency of usage than words with negative meanings (Zajonc, 1968). The relationship holds over all parts of speech. Not only is *good* (5,122 occurrences in a random sample of 1,000,000 English words) more frequent than *bad* (1,001), and *pretty* (1,195) more frequent than *ugly* (178), but also *on* (30,224) is more frequent than *off* (3,644), *in* (75,253) is more frequent than *out* (13,649), and even *first* (5,154) is more frequent than *last* (3,517). In fact, the words in nearly every semantic category, and even letters and numbers, show a strong correlation between ratings for preference and frequency of usage, and not only words but all kinds of stimuli have been found to increase in attractiveness with repeated exposures. This seemingly innocent finding (Zajonc, 1968) has stimulated decades of research on the relation between cognition and affect.

Obviously, the first question to ask is that of causality, that is, whether we are more likely to seek out positive than negative experiences, and therefore favor positive stimuli, or whether aspects of the world that we experience often acquire thereby positive valence. The finding that frequently occurring numbers and letters are better liked than less frequent numbers and letters favors the latter possibility. It has been demonstrated that the mere repeated exposure of a stimulus is entirely sufficient for the enhancement of preference for that stimulus. This mere-repeated-exposure effect is found in a variety of contexts, for a wide assortment of stimuli, using diverse procedures, and among both humans and nonhuman animals. In the extreme, an exposure effect was obtained prenatally (Rajecki, 1974). Tones of two different frequencies were played to two sets of fertile chicken eggs. When the hatched chicks were then tested for their preference for the tones, the chicks in each set consistently chose the tone that was played to them prenatally. Similarly, one group of rats was exposed to music by Schonberg and another to music by Mozart to see if they could acquire corresponding preferences. They did, slightly favoring the latter composer. And Taylor and Sluckin (1964) found that domestic chicks that were exposed either to their conspecific age peers or to a matchbox preferred the object to which they were previously exposed.

The earliest explanation of the effect was offered by Titchener. It proposed a virtual tautology, namely, that we like familiar objects because we enjoy recognizing familiar objects. But Titchener's hypothesis had to be rejected because in numerous studies, the enhancement of preferences for objects turned out not to depend on individuals' subjective impressions of how familiar the objects were (Wilson, 1979).

SUBLIMINAL INDUCTION OF AFFECT

The cumulative results lead to the inescapable conclusion that the changes in affect that accompany repeated exposures do not depend on subjective factors, such as the subjective impression of familiarity, but on the objective history of exposures (Zajonc, 2000). Even when exposures are subliminal, and subjects have no idea that any stimuli at all have been presented, those subliminal stimuli that are flashed frequently are liked better than those flashed infrequently (Murphy, Monahan, & Zajonc, 1995; Zajonc, 1980).[2] In fact, exposure effects are more pronounced when obtained under subliminal conditions than when subjects are aware of the repeated exposures.

ABSENCE OF AVERSIVE EVENTS AS AN UNCONDITIONED STIMULUS

Careful experiments have ruled out explanations of this phenomenon based on ease of recognition, an increased perceptual fluency, or subjective familiarity. But mere-exposure effects cannot take place in a total vacuum. What, then, is the process that induces preferences by virtue of exposures? One possibility that cannot be ruled out is that we have here a form of conditioning, unique to be sure, but nevertheless a form that features the essential conditioning factors. The classical paradigm of classical conditioning requires that the conditioned stimulus (CS) be followed by an unconditioned stimulus (US), preferably within 500 ms. The paradigm also requires that this joint occurrence be repeated several times in very much the same form. It is taken as given that the US has an innate capacity of eliciting the unconditioned response (UR). Thus, a dog will salivate (UR) when presented with food (UC), and if a bell is rung (CS) during the dog's feeding time, then after several repetitions of this joint event, the bell alone will make the dog salivate. The elicitation of salivation by the bell alone is evidence that conditioning has been successful, and salivation has become a conditioned response (CR). Although the connection between the response and the US is innate, the new relationship between the CS and the CR is acquired.

In the mere-repeated-exposure paradigm, the repeatedly exposed stimuli can be viewed as CSs. We can also think of the preference response as the CR. But where is the US? The mere-exposure paradigm requires that no positive or negative consequences follow exposures. And no response other than maintaining sensory access to the exposed stimulus is required of the participant. But just because the experimenter does not provide a US does not mean that there is no event that, from the point of view of the participant, could constitute a US. In fact, there is such an event. Contiguous with exposures (i.e., the presentations of the CS) are events characterized by a conspicuous absence of noxious or aversive consequences. Hence, the very absence of a noxious consequence could well act as a US. The absence of aversive consequences constitutes a safety signal that is associated with the CS. As in classical conditioning, after several CS-US occurrences, in which the US is simply the fact that the individual does not suffer any untoward experiences, the CR—an approach tendency—becomes attached to the CS, now communicating that the current environment is safe.

On the initial presentations, when the stimulus is novel, both avoidance and approach responses are elicited, and the tendency to explore (approach) is tentative. But because the aftermath of the CS is invariably benign, avoidance and escape drop out to leave only approach responses. It is thus that positive affect can be attached to a stimulus by virtue of mere repeated exposures. Some forms of imprinting (Zajonc, 2000) can be conceptualized in the very same manner.

REPEATED EXPERIENCES AS A SOURCE OF POSITIVE AFFECT

How can we inquire into the dynamics of this conditioning paradigm in which even the CS is inaccessible to awareness and the very presence of the US is a matter of conjecture? We can assume that the absence of an aversive event that engenders approach behavior to the exposed object generates positive affect. Therefore, because a condition such as an absence of an aversive event is diffuse and unattached to any particular object in the immediate environment, not only should the exposed object become more attractive, but the overall affective state of the individual should become more positive. We should expect an enhancement of the individual's general affect and mood state just by virtue of the repeated exposures themselves. Monahan, Murphy, and I (Monahan, Murphy, & Zajonc, 2000) inquired into the effects of sheer stimulus repetition by subliminally exposing two groups to Chinese ideographs. One group was exposed to 5 ideographs, five times each in random order. The other group was exposed to 25 different ideographs, each shown but once. All exposures lasted 4 ms. Following the exposures, the participants in the repeated-exposures condition were in better moods and felt more positive than the participants who were exposed to 25 different ideographs.

Thus, repetitions of an experience in and of themselves are capable of producing a diffuse positive affective state. And if that is one of the consequences of repeated exposures, then the changed mood, although diffuse and unspecific, could well become attached to stimuli that are presented just afterward. Previous research has demonstrated that repeated exposures enhance preferences for the exposed stimuli. The exposures can also generate positive affect in response to additional stimuli that are similar in form or substance—even though they were not previously exposed. But if the affect generated by repetition of exposures is diffuse, and nonspecific, then any stimulus, if it follows a benign repetition experience, would become infused with positive affect. In a new experiment (Monahan et al., 2000), we again presented 5 stimuli five times each to one group of participants and 25 different stimuli once each to another group. Afterward, however, instead of measuring the participants' overall mood, we asked them to rate three categories of stimuli: Chinese ideographs that were previously shown, Chinese ideographs that were similar to those previously shown but novel, and totally distinct stimuli—random polygons. In all cases, the group that was exposed to repeated ideographs rated the stimuli more positively than the group exposed to 25 ideographs one time each. Also in all cases, the ratings of the repeated-exposure group were more positive than those obtained from a control group that had not experienced any prior exposures of the stimuli (see Fig. 1).

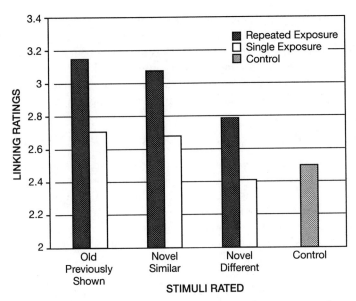

Fig. 1. Preferences for diverse stimuli as a function of exposure condition (adapted from Monahan, Murphy, and Zajonc, 2000).

THE INDEPENDENCE OF AFFECT AND COGNITION

This array of findings supports not only the proposition that affect may be elicited without a prior cognitive appraisal, but also the contention that affect and cognition may well be independent processes, because in the context of exposure effects, prototypical cognition is measured by recognition memory, whereas prototypical affect is measured by preference judgments. (For a more detailed discussion of the distinction, see Zajonc, 2000, pp. 46-47.) When I first published this hypothesis (Zajonc, 1980), claiming that affective reactions may precede cognitive reactions, and thus require no cognitive appraisal, there was no neuroanatomical or neurophysiological evidence to support it. Eventually, however, LeDoux (1996); Zola-Morgan, Squire, Alvarez-Royo, and Clower (1991); and other investigators published results confirming the original hypothesis that affect and cognition, although participating jointly in behavior, are separate psychological and neural processes that can be influenced independently of one another. Especially important is the work of Zola-Morgan and his colleagues, who have conducted experiments with monkeys, showing that lesions to the amygdala (a brain structure that is responsive to affective qualities of stimulation) impair emotional responsiveness but leave cognitive functions intact, whereas lesions to the hippocampus (a brain structure that plays an important role in memory) impair cognitive functions but leave emotional responsiveness intact.

Other neuroanatomical studies have confirmed that affect can be induced unconsciously. Thus, Elliott and Dolan (1998), taking PET (positron emission tomography) measures, examined preference acquisition as a function of subliminal repeated exposures and inquired into the neuroanatomical correlates of these effects. They found that different regions of the brain were activated during subjects' affective reactions and memory judgments. Recognition judgments were localized in the frontopolar cortex and the parietal areas, whereas preference reactions showed right lateral frontal activation. This finding that recognition and preference are associated with different brain structures further supports the hypothesis that cognition and affect are independent systems.

Given the independence of affect, we can explain why it is that repeated-exposure effects are clearer and stronger when the exposures are subliminal than when subjects are aware of them. If a given process depends on cognitive appraisal, different individuals will access different cognitive content and attach different meanings to the same stimuli. Hence, the between-participants variability in reactions will be increased. If cognitive processes are not involved in a behavior, however, affective influences, which are necessarily less diverse than cognitive influences, will dominate the behavior, yielding a more homogeneous array of reactions.

CONCLUSION

The mere-exposure effect, when viewed as classical conditioning with the US consisting of the absence of aversive consequences, is a very simple yet effective process for acquiring behavioral tendencies of adaptive value. The mere-exposure effect provides a flexible means of forming selective attachments and affective dispositions, with remarkably minimal investment of energy, even when exposures are not accessible to awareness.

The consequences of repeated exposures benefit the organism in its relations to the immediate animate and inanimate environment. They allow the organism to distinguish objects and habitats that are safe from those that are not, and they are the most primitive basis of social attachments. Therefore, they form the basis for social organization and cohesion—the basic sources of psychological and social stability. Imprinting effects manifest substantial permanence. It remains to be demonstrated, however, how permanent are preferences induced by mere repeated exposures, under supra- and subliminal conditions. It is also not yet known if repeated-exposure effects are more readily established in younger than in older organisms, and what processes can reverse or extinguish them.

Recommended Reading

Bornstein, R.F., Leone, D.R., & Galley, D.J. (1987). The generalizability of subliminal mere exposure effects: Influence of stimuli perceived without awareness on social behavior. *Journal of Personality and Social Behavior, 53*, 1070-1079. Harrison, A.A. (1977). Mere exposure. In L. Berkowitz (Ed.), *Advances in experimental social psychology* (Vol. 10, pp. 39-83). New York: Academic Press.

Jacoby, L.L. (1983). Perceptual enhancement: Persistent effects of an experience. *Journal of Experimental Psychology: Learning, Memory, and Cognition, 9*, 21-38.

Acknowledgments-I am grateful to Hazel Markus for her helpful suggestions.

Notes

1. Address correspondence to R.B. Zajonc, Department of Psychology, Stanford University, Stanford, CA 94305-2130; e-mail: zajonc@psych.stanford.edu.

2. The fact that the stimuli were actually below participants' awareness was tested by a forced-choice method developed by Eriksen (1980).

References

Birnbaum, M.H., & Mellers, B.A. (1979). Stimulus recognition may mediate exposure effects. *Journal of Personality and Social Psychology, 37,* 1090-1096.

Elliott, R., & Dolan, R.J. (1998). Neural response during preference and memory judgments for subliminally presented stimuli: A functional neuro-imaging study. *Journal of Neuroscience, 18,* 4697-4704.

Eriksen, C.W. (1980). Discrimination and learning without awareness: A methodological survey and evaluation. *Psychological Review, 67,* 279-300.

Lazarus, R.S. (1982). Thoughts on the relations between emotion and cognition. *American Psychologist, 46,* 352-367.

LeDoux, J. (1996). *The emotional brain.* New York: Simon and Schuster.

Monahan, J.L., Murphy, S.T., & Zajonc, R.B. (2000). Subliminal mere exposure: Specific, general, and diffuse effects. *Psychological Science, 11,* 462-466.

Murphy, S.T., Monahan, J.L., & Zajonc, R.B. (1995). Additivity of nonconscious affect: Combined effects of priming and exposure. *Journal of Personality and Social Psychology,69,* 589-602.

Rajecki, D.W. (1974). Effects of prenatal exposure to auditory or visual stimulation on postnatal distress vocalizations in chicks. *Behavioral Biology,11,* 525-536.

Taylor, K.F., & Sluckin, W. (1964). Flocking in domestic chicks. *Nature, 201,* 108-109.

Wilson, W.R. (1979). Feeling more than we can know: Exposure effects without learning. *Journal of Personality and Social Psychology, 37,* 811-821.

Zajonc, R.B. (1968). Attitudinal effects of mere exposures. *Journal of Personality and Social Psychology, 9* (2, Pt. 2),1-27.

Zajonc, R.B. (1980). Feeling and thinking: Preferences need no inferences. *American Psychologist, 35,* 151-175.

Zajonc, R.B. (2000). Feeling and thinking: Closing the debate over the independence of affect. In J.P. Forgas (Ed.), *Feeling and thinking: The role of affect in social cognition* (pp. 31-58). Cambridge, England: Cambridge University Press.

Zola-Morgan, S., Squire, L.R., Alvarez-Royo, P., & Clower, R.P. (1991). Independence of memory functions and emotional behavior. *Hippocampus, 1,* 207-220.

Critical Thinking Questions

1. The author calls the mere-repeated-exposure phenomenon an "absurdly simple" way to acquire a preference. Explain why he might have said this in relation to other ways in which preferences are acquired.

2. In this article, the author presents research on nonhuman animals (e.g.,Rajecki, 1974). Summarize the findings of this research and explain how it is used to support the mere-repeated-exposure phenomenon. How does the research with nonhuman animals help support his evolutionary argument?

3. The author presents research that demonstrates that repeated exposure actually led to better moods in participants (i.e., Monahan, Murphy, & Zajonc, 2000). Summarize this study. What are some of the implications of these findings for stimuli to which we often are exposed repeatedly (e.g., television commercials, songs on the radio, news about a player on your favorite football team)?

4. Review what you learned about classical conditioning from your introductory psychology course. In this article, the author makes the claim that "the very absence of a noxious consequence could well act as a US." Evaluate this claim given your knowledge of classical conditioning. Do you buy into it?

Automaticity and the Amygdala: Nonconscious Responses to Emotional Faces

Arne Öhman[1]

Department of Clinical Neuroscience, Karolinska Institute, Stockholm, Sweden

Abstract

The human face is an evolved adaptation for social communication. This implies that humans are genetically prepared to produce facial gestures that are automatically decoded by observers. Psychophysiological data demonstrate that humans respond automatically with their facial muscles, with autonomic responses, and with specific regional brain activation of the amygdala when exposed to emotionally expressive faces. Attention is preferentially and automatically oriented toward facial threat. Neuropsychological data, as well as a rapidly expanding brain-imaging literature, implicate the amygdala as a central structure for responding to negative emotional faces, and particularly to fearful ones. However, the amygdala may not be specialized for processing emotional faces, but may instead respond to faces because they provide important information for the defense appraisal that is its primary responsibility.

Keywords

faces; amygdala; automaticity

To say that the eye is the mirror of the soul is a misattribution. What can be gleaned about the movements of the soul by looking someone in the eyes derives less from the eyes themselves than from their surroundings. The pupils may provide information about emotional activation, but to visually differentiate, say, the wide pupil of fright from that of erotic excitement, the muscular context is more informative than the eyes themselves. The muscles of the face are amazingly complex. There are about 20 mimetic muscles that have nothing better to do than to produce diverse patterns of psychologically meaningful facial movements (Fridlund,1994).

THE FACE AS AN EVOLVED BIOLOGICAL STRUCTURE

The facial muscles are unique in their function because they primarily move skin rather than body limbs. It is precisely the ability of the facial muscles to change the visual appearance of the face that makes the face a better candidate than the eyes for serving as the mind's mirror. As Darwin recognized, the design of the face suggests that it has evolved to communicate social signals. Indeed, many human facial displays are similar to those of other primates, and quite convincing evolutionary histories can be constructed for some expressions. Nevertheless, the human face has a more complex musculature than that of other primates, with a more versatile neural innervation.

From an evolutionary perspective, it appears that the proliferation and diversification of facial muscles coincided in time with the rapid enlargement of hominid brain volume during the past million years. This is consistent with one of the major hypotheses about which evolutionary contingencies promoted the recent enhancement of human intelligence. When hominids exchanged the rain forests for a life on the savanna, living in extended groups provided an important advantage in securing food through scavenging and hunting, and gaining protection against predators. Successful survival and procreation in large groups required social or "Machiavellian" intelligence to recognize, remember, relate to, exploit, and predict the behavior of other group members. A related factor promoting fine-tuned control of facial muscles was the emergence of language, with the associated need to use the muscles around the mouth to articulate sounds. As a consequence, exquisite voluntary control of the lower face emerged (Fridlund, 1994). This development not only benefited sound articulation, but also allowed voluntarily controlled facial gestures that could override more primitive systems of facial muscle control by brain systems concerned with reflexive facial movements. Thus, the evolution of improved neural control of facial muscles may have been intimately related to the expansion of the anterior part of the brain known as the prefrontal cortex, and to the emergence of Machiavellian intelligence in the social arena.

AUTOMATICALLY ELICITED RESPONSES TO FACIAL STIMULI

Facial Responses

If facial signals are important components of an evolutionarily shaped social intelligence, vigilance for the signals is likely to have coevolved with their evolution. From this perspective, therefore, humans should be able not only to produce communicative facial signals but also to efficiently and automatically decode facial gestures. Dimberg, Thunberg, and Elmehed (2000) tested this hypothesis using electromyography (EMG) to assess the responses of facial muscles to facial stimuli. To ensure that the facial responses of participants were under automatic, rather than conscious, control, they employed a backward-masking procedure that prevented participants from consciously recognizing the emotions portrayed in the faces. Different groups of participants were exposed to briefly (30 ms) presented angry, neutral, and happy faces, respectively, which were immediately followed by a much longer (5 s) presentation of a neutral face as a masking stimulus. Even though the masking procedure effectively prevented conscious recognition of the target stimulus, participants exposed to masked happy faces showed larger responses in the *zygomaticus major* muscle (which pulls the corner of the mouth toward the ear to produce a smile) than participants exposed to masked neutral and angry faces. Furthermore, participants exposed to masked angry faces showed larger responses in the *corrugator supercilii* muscle (which pulls the eyebrows together to produce the deep furrow of anger in the forehead) than participants exposed to masked neutral and happy faces. Thus, the participants' facial muscles appeared to mimic the facial expression of the emotional target face even though they consciously saw only the neutral masking face.

Autonomic Responses

Further support for the notion of automatic decoding of facial signals comes from experiments focusing on the emotional potential of threatening angry faces as assessed through recordings of autonomic nervous system activity. (The autonomic nervous system, the part of the peripheral nervous system that controls involuntary visceral responses, mobilizes bodily resources for coping with emotional stimuli such as threats.) The first phase in these experiments involved conditioning participants to associate a mildly aversive electric shock to the fingers with critical facial stimuli presented in full view. In the second phase, the stimuli were presented in a backward-masking arrangement that prevented their conscious recognition. Nevertheless, participants continued to show elevated skin-conductance responses (SCRs; i.e., responses of palmar sweat glands controlled by the autonomic nervous system) to conditioned angry faces (e.g., Esteves, Dimberg, & Ohman, 1994). Furthermore, although SCRs were conditioned when masked, nonrecognizable angry faces were paired with an aversive electric shock, this response could not be conditioned when the critical stimuli were masked happy faces (Esteves, Parra, Dimberg, & Öhman, 1994). Thus, not only can responses be elicited by emotionally provocative facial stimuli (with or without previous conditioning), but new responses can also be associated to masked, nonconsciously presented stimuli. This implies that people may be influenced by subtle (automatically perceivable) facial gestures in face-to-face interaction, and that they may learn to associate such gestures with fear without being aware of it.

Attentional Biases to Threatening Facial Stimuli

The observation that automatic, nonconscious perception of faces is sufficient to elicit emotional responses suggests that emotionally provocative stimuli may be effective in capturing attention. For example, to assess the mood of a crowd of people, it is important to attend to the facial signals of its members. In particular, it is important to quickly locate potentially hostile individuals in the crowd. To test this hypothesis, my colleagues and I (Ohman, Lundqvist, & Esteves, 2001) asked research participants to indicate whether all faces presented in a matrix of faces had the same emotional expression or whether a discrepant facial emotion was present in the crowd. To control the physical characteristics of the stimuli, we used a stimulus set of schematic faces in which a threatening angry face was physically as discrepant from a neutral face as were friendly happy faces. The results were consistent with an evolutionary analysis in that angry faces were more quickly and accurately detected than happy faces in crowds of neutral or emotional faces. This advantage was obvious for both upright and inverted faces, and it was specific to threatening rather than negatively evaluated faces in general (a sad expression was not detected more quickly than a friendly face). In a study supporting automatic control of the attentional bias for threat, Mogg and Bradley (1999) demonstrated that threatening real faces recruited attention even if masked by scrambled faces.

ROLE OF THE AMYGDALA IN EMOTIONAL RESPONSES TO FACIAL STIMULI

The Amygdala in Face-to-Face Social Interaction

The amygdala, a collection of neural nuclei located in the temporal lobe, is a central structure for the integration of emotion in face-to-face primate interaction

(Emery & Amaral, 2000). The amygdala receives input from all sensory modalities and controls various kinds of emotional responses, including stress-hormone output, autonomic responses, movement of facial muscles, and production of defensive reflexes. The basolateral complex of the amygdala is thought to be involved in the interpretation of facial signals in a social context (Emery & Amaral, 2000). The amygdala became larger during primate evolution, and across species its size correlates with volume of the cerebral cortex and with social-group size, suggesting that it has been evolutionarily shaped for social information processing (Baron & Aggleton, 2000).

An indication of the importance of the amygdala in social information processing is the fact that primate individuals with bilateral amygdala lesions slide downward in social rank, eventually to become social isolates. As a consequence, they do not survive for long in wild or semi-wild settings (Emery & Amaral, 2000). This type of finding is echoed in neuropsychological data on the effect of lesions in the human amygdala. Adolphs, Tranel, and Damasio (1998) reported that three individuals with rare bilateral amygdala lesions were unique in judging as quite approachable and trustworthy the very faces that were deemed the least approachable and trustworthy by a normative sample. Furthermore, Baron-Cohen et al. (1999) used functional magnetic resonance imaging (fMRI) to delineate the activation of a left-frontotemporal network of brain structures that included the amygdala in individuals requested to interpret the emotional meaning of expressive eyes. They interpreted this network as controlling shifts in social perspective and demonstrated that, consistent with this interpretation, the network was not activated by this task in autistic individuals, who have difficulties in understanding social information.

Responses of the Human Amygdala to Facial Emotion

Several brain-imaging studies (using fMRI or positron emission tomography, PET) have demonstrated that regional blood flow in the amygdala increases when research participants view pictures expressing facial emotion, and particularly fear (see the review by Whalen, 1998). Whalen et al. (1998) used backward-masking techniques to present fearful and happy faces outside of awareness in an fMRI study. The masked fearful faces had a robust effect on activation of the amygdala, supporting the hypothesis that it is automatically activated by facial emotion.

My colleagues and I (Morris, Öhman, & Dolan, 1998) enhanced the emotional impact of a specific angry face by pairing it with an aversive noise in a conditioning procedure. Using PET scans to assess regional blood flow changes in the brain, we found that masked presentations of these faces produced reliable and specific activation of the right amygdala. Subsequently (Morris, Öhman, & Dolan, 1999), we reported that two structures related to visual processing in the brain, the superior colliculus of the midbrain and the right pulvinar of the thalamus, provided a pathway that could activate the amygdala without passing through the cortex, thus resulting in automatic activation of the amygdala. The superior colliculus and the pulvinar are closely linked to attentional systems that control eye movements and the selection of salient visual objects. These results are consistent with the view that information reaches the amygdala through two distinct routes, one slow cortical pathway that conveys fully analyzed perceptual information and one rapid subcortical route that activates the amygdala after only a superficial analysis of the stimulus (e.g., LeDoux, 1996). Backward masking disrupts the former but not the latter route, thus allowing activation of emotional responses via the amygdala. In addition to explaining the lack of effect of masking on emotional responses, these data offer an explanation for the quicker detection of threatening than friendly faces (Öhman et al., 2001), because the subcortical route picking up facial threat engages brain structures involved with rapid shifts of attention.

Neuropsychological data suggest that bilateral amygdala lesions result in impaired recognition of negative facial emotion, particularly of fear but also to some extent of anger, sadness, and perhaps disgust (Adolphs et al., 1999). However, recognition of happy faces is intact in individuals with such lesions. Similarly, brain-imaging studies show consistent activation of the amygdala in response to fearful faces (e.g., Whalen et al., 1998). For angry faces, however, the situation is less clear, because there are data showing larger activation in response to fearful faces than angry faces, particularly in the central-medial part of the amygdala (Whalen, 1998). Thus, both imaging and brain lesion studies concur in consistently tying fearful faces to activation of the amygdala.

KEY QUESTIONS FOR FURTHER RESEARCH

A key question raised by this literature is whether the amygdala is part of a network specialized to recognize emotional facial expression. An alternative possibility is that it has a more general role in assessing the emotional significance of stimuli (e.g., Whalen, 1998). Behind this question there is another more fundamental one, which concerns how emotional facial expressions should be understood. Traditionally, the movements of facial muscles associated with particular emotions have been interpreted as *expressing* these emotions. From such a perspective, a primary priority for affective neuroscience is to delineate the neural machinery behind the basic emotions as they are revealed in the face.

Alternatively, however, facial movements can be seen as facial gestures that provide information about the state and response readiness of the bearer of the face. More than disclosing hidden ongoing emotion, facial gestures thus may signal the motivation and intentions that are likely to govern the unfolding social interaction (Fridlund,1994). To the extent that these gestures are relevant in a defensive context, the amygdala would be activated to assess the threat.

A related question concerns an apparent inconsistency between the threat value of facial expressions and their potency in activating the amygdala, because angry faces should be more threatening than fearful ones. However, Whalen (1998) argued that a facial expression of fear is more informative than one of anger when it comes to assessing threat. Facial gestures of fear in conspecifics imply that they are exposed to danger, and the source of danger may provide a threat that needs immediate attention. Furthermore, if the observer is the source of danger, it is safest to continue assessing the fear-displaying individual, because the desired behavioral outcome, the opponent's flight, can easily be turned into its closely allied defensive posture, that of attack. Thus, gestures of fear may require more continued vigilance than those of anger, whose behavioral consequences are more straightforward (be submissive or flee). On the other hand, angry faces, whose threat value can be enhanced through conditioning, may activate the amygdala via conditioned fear (Morris et al., 1998). Similarly, when an angry face is hidden in a crowd of faces, it is more informative than a happy face, and consequently it is likely to recruit attention (Öhman et al., 2001).

From this perspective, to the extent that facial gestures of emotion are effective in activating the amygdala, they do so because they belong to a stimulus category of pervasive importance to primate behavior. Thus, if a central role of the amygdala is to look out for any early signs of threat, the inherent significance and characteristics of faces make them primary targets for rapidly alerting the defense network that is controlled by the amygdala. Furthermore, because facial gestures are composed of salient, easily isolated, and relatively invariant individual features, they have the potential for rapidly accessing the amygdala through a "quick and dirty" analysis by a simple subcortical network rather than via complete analysis in the slower cortical routes. In this way, emotional facial expression may have an edge compared with other stimuli in preferentially activating the amygdala network. Thus, isolating the facial features and actions that may directly access the amygdala remains an important research priority that may shed light on emotional activation in a broader perspective.

Recommended Reading

Aggleton, J.P. (Ed.). (2000). *The amygdala: A functional analysis* (2nd ed.). New York: Oxford University Press.
Dimberg, U., and Öhman, A. (1996). Behold the wrath: Psychophysiological responses to facial stimuli. *Motivation and Emotion, 20,* 149-182.
Fridlund, A.J. (1994). (See References)
Öhman, A., & Mineka, S. (2001). Fears, phobias, and preparedness: Toward an evolved module of fear and fear learning. *Psychological Review, 108,* 483-522.
Whiten, A., & Byrne, R.W. (Eds.). (1997). *Machiavellian intelligence 11: Extensions and evaluations* Cambridge, England: Cambridge University Press.

Note

1. Address correspondence to Arne Öhman, Psychology Section, Department of Clinical Neuroscience, Karolinska Institute and Hospital, Z6, S-171 76 Stockholm, Sweden; e-mail: arne.ohman@ks.se.

References

Adolphs, R., Tranel, D., & Damasio, A.R. (1998). The human amygdala in social judgment. *Nature, 393,* 470-474.
Adolphs, R., Tranel, D., Hamann, S., Young, A.W., Calder, A.J., Phelps, E.A., Anderson, A., Lee, G.P., & Damasio, A.R. (1999). Recognition of facial emotion in nine individuals with bilateral amygdala damage. *Neuropsychologia, 37,* 1111-1117.
Baron-Cohen, S., Ring, H.A., Wheelwright, S., Bullmore, E.T., Brammer, M.J., Simmons, A., & Williams, S.C.R. (1999). Social intelligence in the normal and autistic brain: An fMRI study. *European Journal of Neuroscience,11,*1891-1898.
Barton, R.A., & Aggleton, J.P. (2000). Primate evolution and the amygdala. In J.P. Aggleton (Ed.), *The amygdala: A functional analysis* (2nd ed., pp. 479-508). New York: Oxford University Press.

Dimberg, U., Thunberg, M., & Elmehed, K. (2000). Unconscious facial reactions to emotional facial expressions. *Psychological Science, 11,* 86-89.

Emery, NJ., & Amaral, D.G. (2000). The role of the amygdala in primate social cognition. In R. Lane & L. Nadel (Eds.), *The cognitive neuroscience of emotion* (pp. 156-191). New York: Oxford University Press.

Esteves, F., Dimberg, U., & Öhman, A. (1994). Automatically elicited fear: Conditioned skin conductance responses to masked facial expressions. *Cognition and Emotion, 8,* 393-413.

Esteves, F., Parra, C., Dimberg, U., & Öhman, A. (1994). Nonconscious associative learning: Pavlovian conditioning of skin conductance responses to masked fear-relevant facial stimuli. *Psychophysiology, 31,* 375-385.

Fridlund, A.J. (1994). *Human facial expression: An evolutionary view.* San Diego: Academic Press.

LeDoux, J.E.(1996). *The emotional brain: The mysterious underpinnings of emotional life.* New York: Simon & Schuster.

Mogg, K., & Bradley, B.P. (1999). Orienting of attention to threatening facial expressions presented under conditions of restricted awareness. *Cognition and Emotion, 13,* 713-740.

Morris, J.S., Öhman, A., & Dolan, R.J. (1998). Conscious and unconscious emotional learning in the human amygdala. *Nature, 393,*467-470.

Morris, J.S., Öhman, A., & Dolan, R.J. (1999). A subcortical pathway to the right amygdala mediating "unseen" fear. *Proceedings of the National Academy of Sciences, USA, 96,*1680-1685.

Öhman, A., Lundqvist, D., & Esteves, F. (2001). The face in the crowd revisited: A threat advantage with schematic stimuli. *Journal of Personality and Social Psychology, 80,* 381-396.

Whalen, P.J. (1998). Fear, vigilance and ambiguity: Initial neuroimaging studies of the human amygdala. *Current Directions in Psychological Science, 7,* 177-188.

Whalen, P.J., Ranch, S.L., Etcoff, N.L., McInerney, S.C., Lee, M.B., & Jenike, M.A. (1998). Masked presentations of emotional facial expression modulate amygdala activity without explicit knowledge. *Journal of Neuroscience,18,* 411-418.

Critical Thinking Questions

1. Summarize the research that indicates that facial gestures are effective in activating the amygdala. Explain why this might be advantageous from an evolutionary standpoint.

2. Describe what is meant by *backward-masking*. What has this technique shown us about our ability to automatically decode facial signals?

3. Describe how the authors tested the hypothesis that "emotionally provocative stimuli may be effective in capturing attention" using a matrix of faces. Again, explain why this might be advantageous from an evolutionary standpoint.

Universals and Cultural Differences in Recognizing Emotions

Hillary Anger Elfenbein[1] and Nalini Ambady
*Department of Organizational Behavior and Industrial Relations,
University of California, Berkeley, California (H.A.E.), and
Department of Psychology, Harvard University, Cambridge,
Massachusetts (N.A.)*

Abstract

Moving beyond the earlier nature-versus-nurture debate, modern work on the communication of emotion has incorporated both universals and cultural differences. Classic research demonstrated that the intended emotions in posed expressions were recognized by members of many different cultural groups at rates better than predicted by random guessing. However, recent research has also documented evidence for an in-group advantage, meaning that people are generally more accurate at judging emotions when the emotions are expressed by members of their own cultural group rather than by members of a different cultural group. These new findings provide initial support for a dialect theory of emotion that has the potential to integrate both classic and recent findings. Further research in this area has the potential to improve cross-cultural communication.

Keywords

emotion; universality; cross-cultural differences

The scientific study of how people express emotion has been intertwined with the question of whether or not emotions are universal across cultures and species. Many psychology textbooks describe classic research from the 1960s demonstrating that participants around the world could judge the intended basic emotional states portrayed in posed photographs at rates better than would be expected from random guessing (Ekman, 1972; Izard, 1971). On the basis of these and related studies, many psychologists concluded that the recognition of emotion is largely universal, with the implication that this skill is not learned, but rather has an evolutionary and thus biological basis.

More recently, researchers have attempted to move beyond an either-or approach to the nature-versus-nurture debate, in order to explore how differences across cultures may affect the universal processes involved in expressing and understanding emotions. In this article, we contrast the ability of two theories to account for recent research findings.

EVIDENCE FOR BOTH UNIVERSALS AND CULTURAL DIFFERENCES IN COMMUNICATING EMOTION

The communication of emotion has a strong universal component. For example, people of different cultures can watch foreign films and understand much of their original feeling. Likewise, people can develop strong bonds with pets while

48

communicating largely through nonverbal displays of emotion. Thus, messages on an emotional level can cross the barrier of a cultural or species difference.

Still, although much of an emotional message is retained across these barriers, some of the message gets lost along the way. For example, when traveling or living abroad, or when working in multinational environments, many people develop an intuition that their basic communication signals tend to be misinterpreted more frequently when they interact with individuals from cultures foreign to them than when they interact with compatriots. Therefore, it is not a contradiction to say that the expression of emotion is largely universal but there are subtle differences across cultures that can create a challenge for effective communication.

New Interpretations of Classic Research

The early researchers who studied how people communicate emotion across cultures focused their efforts on establishing universality, and therefore did not pay as much attention to the cultural differences as to the cross-cultural similarities in their data (Matsumoto & Assar, 1992). For example, Table 1 lists the results from Ekman's (1972) five-culture study. Participants viewed photographs and for each one selected an emotion label from six possible choices, so that guessing entirely at random would yield one correct answer out of six, or 16.7% accuracy. Because all cultural groups' performance for all six emotional expressions was much higher than 16.7%, Ekman and his colleagues concluded that there is a *universal affect program*, a biologically programmed guide that governs the communication of emotion.

However, other researchers have noticed different patterns in these same data. For example, Matsumoto (1989) noted that U.S. participants outperformed the Japanese in the study. He argued that some cultures, such as Japanese culture, encourage the use of decoding rules (Buck, 1984), social norms that inhibit the understanding of emotion in cases when understanding may be disruptive to social harmony. Further, he argued that some languages, such as English, are superior to others in their emotion vocabulary (Matsumoto & Assar, 1992). Thus, he argued that Americans are generally more effective than most other cultural groups at understanding emotion.

We noticed yet a different pattern in the data in Table 1: The group with the highest performance is also the same group from which the experimental stimuli originated (Elfenbein & Ambady, 2002b). All participants in the study viewed photographs of American facial expressions, so Americans were the only participants to view members of their own cultural group, or in-group. Everyone else in the study judged expressions from a foreign group, or out-group. We found it interesting that the South American participants were only slightly less accurate than U.S. participants, whereas the difference in performance was larger for the Japanese, who were the most culturally distant.

New Findings on In-Group Advantage

In explaining these cultural differences, earlier researchers tended to focus either on the attributes of the group expressing the emotions or on the attributes of the group perceiving the emotions. In contrast, we tried to think about both groups at the same time, in terms of the match between them. In other words, we considered whether observers were judging emotional expressions made by members of their own cultural in-group or made by members of a cultural out-group. In a meta-analysis (a statistical analysis that combines the results of multiple studies), we assembled the results of 97 studies, which involved 182 different samples representing more than 22,000 total participants (Elfenbein & Ambady, 2002a). These studies included the classic research of Ekman (1972) and Izard (1971), more recent work on the understanding of emotions across cultures, and unintentionally cross-cultural studies in which researchers borrowed testing materials that portrayed people who were not from the geographic location where they were conducting their research.

Our results strongly replicated the earlier finding that people can understand the intended emotional state in posed expressions from other cultures with accuracy greater than predicted by chance guessing. However, this observation alone does not necessarily mean that emotion recognition is governed entirely by universals (Russell, 1994). We also found evidence for an *in-group advantage* in the understanding of emotion: Participants were generally more accurate in recognizing emotions expressed by members of their own culture than in recognizing emotions expressed by members of a different cultural group. The in-group advantage was replicated across a range of experimental methods, positive and negative emotions, and different nonverbal channels of communicating emotion, such as facial expressions, tone of voice, and body language.

Even when the cultural differences in understanding emotion are small, they can still have important real-world consequences. If cross-cultural interactions are slightly less smooth than same-culture interactions, then misunderstandings can accumulate over time and make interpersonal relationships less satisfying. However, the findings of this and our other studies also provide a hopeful message regarding cross-cultural communication: The in-group advantage is lower when groups are nearer geographically or have greater cross-cultural contact with each other, and over time participants appeared to learn how to understand the emotions of people from foreign cultures (Elfenbein & Ambady, 2002b, 2003a, 2003b).

The idea of an in-group advantage has been controversial (Elfenbein & Ambady, 2002a, Matsumoto, 2002), largely because of a theoretical disagreement about whether it is necessary to force members of different cultures to express their emotions using exactly the same style. Researchers are divided as to whether the studies that have not done this are a valid test of the in-group advantage. Understanding this controversy requires first understanding some theoretical perspectives on the communication of emotion.

A PRELIMINARY DIALECT THEORY

Researchers have attempted to weave together diverse strands of evidence to develop theory about how biology and culture influence the communication of emotion.

Ekman's Neurocultural Theory

The neurocultural theory of emotion (Ekman, 1972), based on Tomkins's earlier work (Tomkins & McCarter, 1964), posits the existence of a universal *facial affect program* that provides a one-to-one map between the emotion a person feels and the facial expression the person displays. According to this theory, the facial affect program is the same for all people in all cultures, and therefore everyone expresses emotion in the same manner in nonsocial settings. However, in social settings, people use conscious "management techniques" (Ekman, 1972, p. 225) called *display rules* to control and override the operation of the universal facial affect program. These display rules can vary across cultures, and they are norms that serve to intensify, diminish, neutralize, or mask emotional displays that would otherwise be produced automatically. Extending neurocultural theory from the expression to the perception of emotion, Matsumoto (1989) argued that all people in all cultures perceive emotional expressions in the same manner, but that there are culturally specific norms (i.e., decoding rules) about whether or not to acknowledge that one has understood.

Developing a Dialect Theory

Tomkins and McCarter (1964) articulated the metaphor that cultural differences in emotional expression are like "dialects" of the "more universal grammar of emotion" (p. 127): Just as dialects of a language (e.g., American vs. British English) can differ in accent, grammar, and vocabulary, the universal language of emotion may also have dialects that differ subtly from each other.

Expanding on these ideas, we developed the new dialect theory of emotion to account for the empirical evidence of an in-group advantage in understanding emotion. Earlier researchers who had noticed this effect referred to it as *bias* and argued that participants were more motivated and perhaps paid closer attention when judging in-group members than when judging out-group members. However, our evidence did not support this interpretation, because in many of the studies reviewed in our meta-analysis, participants could not have known that the emotional expressions were from a foreign culture (this was the case, e.g., in studies in which Caucasians judged facial expressions of Caucasians from other cultures and in studies in which filtered vocal tones served as stimuli). Translation difficulties (i.e., mismatches between the emotion words participants used to judge stimuli and experimenters used to instruct the posers who generated the stimuli) could have contributed to the in-group effect but could not fully explain it, given that the in-group advantage also existed across cultural groups speaking the same language. Thus, we had to find another explanation for the in-group advantage.

Two central observations inspired the dialect theory. The first observation was that any explanation of the in-group advantage must consider the cultural match between the expresser and the perceiver of an emotional display, rather than considering either group independently. This was a logical point because the definition of the in-group advantage is that perceivers' emotion judgments are more accurate with culturally matched than culturally mismatched materials. The second observation was that the cultural differences that cause the in-group advantage must be contained within the appearance of the emotional expressions themselves, because the in-group advantage was found when participants did not have any other cues about the cultural identity of the expresser. For example, Americans could have outperformed other Caucasian cultural groups when judging American facial expressions only if there was something particularly American about the expressions.

The dialect theory arose from these two observations. It begins with a universal affect program, [2] a guide for expressing emotions that is the same for all cultural groups. Because a person can express any single emotion in multiple ways, this program is not necessarily the one-to-one map of neurocultural theory.[3] Additionally, each cultural group has a *specific affect program* that incorporates some adjustments to the universal program. Acquired through social learning, these adjustments create subtle differences in the appearance of emotional expression across cultures. These stylistic differences do not necessarily have a specific purpose or meaning; thus, they differ from display and decoding rules, which are conscious management techniques for the benefit of social harmony. Figure 1 illustrates the relation between the universal affect program and specific affect programs from different cultures.

Figure 2 illustrates the dialect theory of how emotion is communicated and perceived. A key distinction between dialect theory and neurocultural theory is that dialect theory suggests that cultural differences in emotional expression can arise from two sources—the specific affect program and display rules—rather than from display rules alone. Similarly, dialect theory posits two different sources of cultural differences in perceiving emotion—the specific affect program and decoding rules—rather than decoding rules alone.

A second key distinction from neurocultural theory is that dialect theory suggests there is a direct link between the cultural differences that arise in the expression and perception of emotion. This link is the specific affect program, which governs the two complementary processes. After all, people tend to interpret another person's behavior in terms of what they would have intended if they had used the same expression. In contrast, neurocultural theory posits that cultural differences in emotional expression and perception emerge from two separate processes: display rules and decoding rules. Because these two sets of rules are not explicitly linked to each other, neurocultural theory does not account for the empirical evidence of the in-group advantage. This is because, as we have noted, any explanation of the in-group advantage must consider the cultural match between the expresser and the perceiver of an emotional display, rather than either group independently.

Evidence for the In-Group Advantage

This background assists in clarifying the disagreement regarding whether the evidence supports the existence of an in-group advantage in emotion. Matsumoto (2002) argued that an in-group advantage in perceiving emotion should result only from differences across perceivers. This is because his theoretical perspective treats cultural differences in expressing and perceiving emotion as two unlinked processes, and he argued that they should be examined separately. Thus, he argued that a valid test of the in-group advantage in emotion recognition should remove all cultural differences in the appearance of emotional expressions in order to achieve "stimulus equivalence" (Matsumoto, 2002, p. 236). However, according to dialect theory, there are cultural differences in the appearance of emotional expressions resulting from the specific affect program. Therefore, forcibly eliminating all cultural differences in the appearance of facial expressions also would eliminate one of the two matched processes responsible for the in-group advantage, cultural differences in expression and perception that arise from the specific affect program. Thus, failures to demonstrate an in-group advantage under stimulus equivalence fit rather than disconfirm the predictions of dialect theory. Further, not only is eliminating cultural differences in the appearance of emotional expression an undesirable step for researchers according to dialect theory, but recent empirical evidence demonstrates that in practice it can be nearly impossible to do so—such differences are so robust that they can leak through processes designed specifically to neutralize them (Marsh, Elfenbein, & Ambady, 2003).

FUTURE DIRECTIONS

Universals and cultural differences in the communication of emotion have been hotly debated and will likely continue to be. Research studies that can help to tease apart the competing perspectives—while acknowledging the complex roles of both nature and nurture—would greatly benefit the field.

The dialect theory of emotion is still speculative and being developed primarily on the basis of recent empirical data. The theory requires direct testing. The most authoritative studies would uncover the particular aspects of emotional expression that vary across cultures—such as specific facial muscle movements, features of vocal tones, or body movements—and would map the use of these cues directly to cross-cultural differences in perceiving emotion. It is important to do this research in a context that limits alternative explanations for the in-group advantage, such as language differences and bias. Further research could determine how these cues are learned.

Although differences in emotion across cultures can create a barrier to effective communication, it is heartening to know that people can overcome these barriers. Further work in this field has the potential to help bridge intergroup differences by contributing to training and intervention programs that can help to improve cross-cultural communication.

Recommended Reading

Darwin, C. (1998) *The expression of the emotions in man and animals* (3rd ed.). New York: Oxford University Press. (Original work published 1872)
Ekman, P. (1993) Facial expression and emotion. *American Psychologist, 48,* 384-392.
Elfenbein, H.A., & Ambady, N. (2002b). (See References)
Russell, J.A. (1994). (See References)

Acknowledgements—We thank James Russell, Anita Williams Woolley, and Kevyn Yong for their helpful comments on the manuscript.

Notes

1. Address correspondence to Hillary Anger Elfenbein, Department of Organizational Behavior and Industrial Relations, Haas School of Business, University of California, Berkeley, CA 94720-1900; e-mail:hillary@post.Harvard.edu.

2. We do not refer to the universal affect program as a facial affect program in order to emphasize that it includes additional nonverbal channels of communication, such as vocal tone and body movements.

3. We thank James Russell for this observation.

References

Brunswick, E. (1955). Representative design and probabilistic theory in a functional psychology. *Psychology Review, 62,* 193-217

Buck, R. (1984). *The communication of emotion.* New York: Guilford Press

Ekman, P. (1972). Universals and cultural differences in facial expressions of emotion. In J. Cole (Ed.), *Nebraska Symposium on Motivation, 1971* (Vol. 19, pp. 207-282). Lincoln: University of Nebraska Press.

Elfenbein, H.A., & Ambady, N. (2002a). Is there an in-group advantage in emotion? *Psychological Bulletin, 128,* 243-239.

Elfenbein, H.A., & Ambady, N. (2002b). On the universality and cultural specificity of emotion recognition: A meta-analysis. *Psychological Bulletin, 128,* 203-235.

Elfenbein, H.A., & Ambady, N. (2003a). Cultural similarity's consequences: A distance perspective on cross-cultural differences in emotion recognition. *Journal of Cross-Cultural Psychology, 34,* 92-110.

Elfenbein, H.A., & Ambady, N. (2003b). *When familiarity breeds accuracy: Cultural exposure and facial emotion recognition.* Manuscript submitted for publication .

Izard, C.E. (1971). *The face of emotion.* New York: Appleton-Century-Crofts.

Marsh, A., Elfenbein, H.A., & Ambady, N. (2003). Nonverbal "accents": Cultural differences in facial expressions of emotion. *Psychological Science, 14,* 373-376.

Matsumoto, D. (1989). Cultural influences on the perception of emotion. *Journal of Cross-Cultural Psychology, 20,* 92-105.

Matsumoto, D. (2002). Methodological requirements to test a possible in-group advantage in judging emotions across cultures: Comments on Elfenbein and Ambady and evidence. *Psychological Bulletin, 128,* 236-242.

Matsumoto, D., & Assar, M. (1992). The effects of language on judgments of universal facial expressions of emotion. *Journal of Nonverbal Behavior, 16,* 85-99.

Russell, J.A. (1994). Is there universal recognition of emotion from facial expression? A review of the cross-cultural studies. *Psychological Bulletin, 115,* 102-141.

Tomkins, S.S., & McCarter, R. (1964). What and where are the primary affects: Some evidence for a theory. *Perceptual and Motor Skills, 18,* 119-158.

Critical Thinking Questions

1. The authors refer to the nature-versus-nurture debate at the beginning and the conclusion of their article. How does their theory of emotion recognition fit into the nature-versus-nurture debate? On which side does it stand?

2. Describe the concept of in-group advantage. How does Elfenbein and Ambady's meta-analysis support this concept?

3. Describe the dialect theory and relate it to language dialects. How can this theory be reconciled with Ekman's classic neurocultural theory?

Culture and Causal Cognition

Ara Norenzayan and Richard E. Nisbett[1]
*Centre de Récherche en Epistemologie Appliquée, Ecole
Polytechnique, Paris, France (A.N.), and Department of Psychology,
University of Michigan, Ann Arbor, Michigan (R.E.N.)*

Abstract

East Asian and American causal reasoning differs significantly. East Asians understand behavior in terms of complex interactions between dispositions of the person
or other object and contextual factors, whereas Americans often view social behavior primarily as the direct unfolding of dispositions. These culturally differing causal
theories seem to be rooted in more pervasive, culture-specific mentalities in East
Asia and the West. The Western mentality is analytic, focusing attention on the
object, categorizing it by reference to its attributes, and ascribing causality based on
rules about it. The East Asian mentality is holistic, focusing attention on the field
in which the object is located and ascribing causality by reference to the relationship between the object and the field.

Keywords

causal attribution; culture; attention; reasoning

Psychologists within the cognitive science tradition have long believed that fundamental reasoning processes such as causal attribution are the same in all cultures (Gardner, 1985). Although recognizing that the content of causal beliefs
can differ widely across cultures, psychologists have assumed that the ways in
which people come to make their causal judgments are essentially the same, and
therefore that they tend to make the same sorts of inferential errors. A case in
point is the fundamental attribution error, or FAE (Ross, 1977), a phenomenon
that is of central importance to social psychology and until recently was held to
be invariable across cultures.

The FAE refers to people's inclination to see behavior as the result of dispositions corresponding to the apparent nature of the behavior. This tendency often
results in error when there are obvious situational constraints that leave little or
no role for dispositions in producing the behavior. The classic example of the FAE
was demonstrated in a study by Jones and Harris (1967) in which participants read
a speech or essay that a target person had allegedly been required to produce by
a debate coach or psychology experimenter. The speech or essay favored a particular position on an issue, for example, the legalization of marijuana. Participants'
estimates of the target's actual views on the issue reflected to a substantial extent
the views expressed in the speech or essay, even when they knew that the target
had been explicitly instructed to defend a particular position. Thus, participants
inferred an attitude that corresponded to the target person's apparent behavior,
without taking into account the situational constraints operating on the behavior.
Since that classic study, the FAE has been found in myriad studies in innumer-
able experimental and naturalistic contexts, and it has been a major focus of theorizing and a continuing source of instructive pedagogy for psychology students.

CULTURE AND THE FAE

It turns out, however, that the FAE is much harder to demonstrate with Asian populations than with European-American populations (Choi, Nisbett, & Norenzayan, 1999). Miller (1984) showed that Hindu Indians preferred to explain ordinary life events in terms of the situational context in which they occurred, whereas Americans were much more inclined to explain similar events in terms of presumed dispositions. Morris and Peng (1994) found that Chinese newspapers and Chinese students living in the United States tended to explain murders (by both Chinese and American perpetrators) in terms of the situation and even the societal context confronting the murderers, whereas American newspapers and American students were more likely to explain the murders in terms of presumed dispositions of the perpetrators.

Recently Jones and Harris's (1967) experiment was repeated with Korean and American participants (Choi et al., 1999). Like Americans, the Koreans tended to assume that the target person held the position he was advocating. But the two groups responded quite differently if they were placed in the same situation themselves before they made judgments about the target. When observers were required to write an essay, using four arguments specified by the experimenter, the Americans were unaffected, but the Koreans were greatly affected. That is, the Americans' judgments about the target's attitudes were just as much influenced by the target's essay as if they themselves had never experienced the constraints inherent in the situation, whereas the Koreans almost never inferred that the target person had the attitude expressed in the essay.

This is not to say that Asians do not use dispositions in causal analysis or are not occasionally susceptible to the FAE. Growing evidence indicates that when situational cues are not salient, Asians rely on dispositions or manifest the FAE to the same extent as Westerners (Choi et al., 1999; Norenzayan, Choi, & Nisbett,1999). The cultural difference seems to originate primarily from a stronger East Asian tendency to recognize the causal power of situations.

The cultural differences in the FAE seem to be supported by different folk theories about the causes of human behavior. In one study (Norenzayan et al., 1999), we asked participants how much they agreed with paragraph descriptions of three different philosophies about why people behave as they do: (a) a strongly dispositionist philosophy holding that "how people behave is mostly determined by their personality," (b) a strongly situationist view holding that behavior "is mostly determined by the situation" in which people find themselves, and (c) an interactionist view holding that behavior "is always jointly determined by personality and the situation." Korean and American participants endorsed the first position to the same degree, but Koreans endorsed the situationist and interactionist views more strongly than did Americans.

These causal theories are consistent with cultural conceptions of personality as well. In the same study (Norenzayan et al., 1999), we administered a scale designed to measure agreement with two different theories of personality: entity theory, or the belief that behavior is due to relatively fixed dispositions such as traits, intelligence, and moral character, and incremental theory, or the belief that behavior is conditioned on the situation and that any relevant dispositions are subject to change (Dweck, Hong, & Chiu, 1993). Koreans for the most part rejected entity theory, whereas Americans were equally likely to endorse entity theory and incremental theory.

ANALYTIC VERSUS HOLISTIC COGNITION

The cultural differences in causal cognition go beyond interpretations of human behavior. Morris and Peng (1994) showed cartoons of an individual fish moving in a variety of configurations in relation to a group of fish and asked participants why they thought the actions had occurred. Chinese participants were inclined to attribute the behavior of the individual fish to factors external to the fish (i.e., the group), whereas American participants were more inclined to attribute the behavior of the fish to internal factors. In studies by Peng and Nisbett (reported in Nisbett, Peng, Choi, & Norenzayan, in press), Chinese participants were shown to interpret even the behavior of schematically drawn, ambiguous physical events—such as a round object dropping through a surface and returning to the surface—as being due to the relation between the object and the presumed medium (e.g., water), whereas Americans tended to interpret the behavior as being due to the properties of the object alone.

The Intellectual Histories of East Asia and Europe

Why should Asians and Americans perceive causality so differently? Scholars in many fields, including ethnography, history, and philosophy of science, hold that, at least since the 6th century B.C., there has been a very different intellectual tradition in the West than in the East (especially China and those cultures, like the Korean and Japanese, that were heavily influenced by China; Nisbett et al., in press). The ancient Greeks had an *analytic* stance: The focus was on categorizing the object with reference to its attributes and explaining its behavior using rules about its category memberships. The ancient Chinese had a *holistic* stance, meaning that there was an orientation toward the field in which the object was found and a tendency to explain the behavior of the object in terms of its relations with the field.

In support of these propositions, there is substantial evidence that early Greek and Chinese science and mathematics were quite different in their strengths and weaknesses. Greek science looked for universal rules to explain events and was concerned with categorizing objects with respect to their essences. Chinese science (some people would say it was a technology only, though a technology vastly superior to that of the Greeks) was more pragmatic and concrete and was not concerned with foundations or universal laws. The difference between the Greek and Chinese orientations is well captured by Aristotle's physics, which explained the behavior of an object without reference to the field in which it occurs. Thus, a stone sinks into water because it has the property of gravity, and a piece of wood floats because it has the property of levity. In contrast, the principle that events always occur in some context or field of forces was understood early on in China.

Some writers have suggested that the mentality of East Asians remains more holistic than that of Westerners (e.g., Nakamura, 1960/1988). Thus, modern East Asian laypeople, like the ancient Chinese intelligentsia, are attuned to the field and the overall context in determining events. Western civilization was profoundly shaped by ancient Greece, so one would expect the Greek intellectual stance of object focus to be widespread in the West.

Attention to the Field Versus the Object

If East Asians tend to believe that causality lies in the field, they would be expected to attend to the field. If Westerners are more inclined to believe that causality inheres in the object, they might be expected to pay relatively more attention to the object than to the field. There is substantial evidence that this is the case.

Attention to the field as a whole on the part of East Asians suggests that they might find it relatively difficult to separate the object from the field. This notion rests on the concept of *field dependence* (Witkin, Dyk, Faterson, Goodenough, & Karp, 1974). Field dependence refers to a relative difficulty in separating objects from the context in which they are located. One way of measuring field dependence is by means of the rod-and-frame test. In this test, participants look into a long rectangular box at the end of which is a rod. The rod and the box frame can be rotated independently of one another, and participants are asked to state when the rod is vertical. Field dependence is indicated by the extent to which the orientation of the frame influences judgments of the verticality of the rod. The judgments of East Asian (mostly Chinese) participants have been shown to be more field dependent than those of American participants (Ji, Peng, & Nisbett, in press).

In a direct test of whether East Asians pay more attention to the field than Westerners do (Masuda & Nisbett, 1999), Japanese and American participants saw underwater scenes that included one or more *focal* fish (i.e., fish that were larger and faster moving than other objects in the scene) among many other objects, including smaller fish, small animals, plants, rocks, and coral. When asked to recall what they had just viewed, the Japanese and American participants reported equivalent amounts of detail about the focal fish, but the Japanese reported far more detail about almost everything else in the background and made many more references to interactions between focal fish and background objects. After watching the scenes, the participants were shown a focal fish either on the original background or on a new one. The ability of the Japanese to recognize a particular focal fish was impaired if the fish was shown on the "wrong" background. Americans' recognition was uninfluenced by this manipulation.

ORIGINS OF THE CULTURAL DIFFERENCE IN CAUSAL COGNITION

Most of the cross-cultural comparisons we have reviewed compared participants who were highly similar with respect to key demographic variables, namely, age, gender, socioeconomic status, and educational level. Differences in cognitive abilities were controlled for or ruled out as potential explanations for the data in studies involving a task (e.g., the rod-and-frame test) that might be affected by such abilities. Moreover, the predicted differences emerged regardless of whether the East Asians were tested in their native languages in East Asian countries or tested in English in the United States. Thus, the lack of obvious alternative explanations, combined with positive evidence from intellectual history and the convergence of the data across a diverse set of studies (conducted in laboratory as well as naturalistic contexts), points to culturally shared causal theories as the most likely explanation for the group differences.

But why might ancient societies have differed in the causal theories they produced and passed down to their contemporary successor cultures? Attempts to answer such questions must, of course, be highly speculative because they involve complex historical and sociological issues. Elsewhere, we have summarized the views of scholars who have suggested that fundamental differences between societies may result from ecological and economic factors (Nisbett et al., in press). In China, people engaged in intensive farming many centuries before Europeans did. Farmers need to be cooperative with one another, and their societies tend to be collectivist in nature. A focus on the social field may generalize to a holistic understanding of the world. Greece is a land where the mountains descend to the sea and large-scale agriculture is not possible. People earned a living by keeping animals, fishing, and trading. These occupations do not require so much intensive cooperation, and the Greeks were in fact highly individualistic. Individualism in turn encourages attending only to the object and one's goals with regard to it. The social field can be ignored with relative impunity, and causal perception can focus, often mistakenly, solely on the object. We speculate that contemporary societies continue to display these mentalities because the social psychological factors that gave rise to them persist to this day.

Several findings by Witkin and his colleagues (e.g., Witkin et al., 1974), at different levels of analysis, support this historical argument that holistic and analytic cognition originated in collectivist and individualist orientations, respectively. Contemporary farmers are more field dependent than hunters and industrialized peoples; American ethnic groups that operate under tighter social constraints are more field dependent than other groups; and individuals who are attuned to social relationships are more field dependent than those who are less focused on social relationships.

FUTURE DIRECTIONS

A number of questions seem particularly interesting for further inquiry. Should educational practices take into account the differing attentional foci and causal theories of members of different cultural groups? Can the cognitive skills characteristic of one cultural group be transferred to another group? To what extent can economic changes transform the sort of cultural-cognitive system we have described? These and other questions about causal cognition will provide fertile ground for research in the years to come.

Recommended Reading

Choi, I., Nisbett, R.E., & Norenzayan, A. (1999). (See References)
Fiske, A., Kitayama, S., Markus, H.R., & Nisbett, R.E. (1998). The cultural matrix of social psychology. In D.T. Gilbert, S.T. Fiske, & G. Lindzey (Eds.), *The handbook of social psychology* (4th ed., Vol. 2, pp. 915-981). Boston: McGraw-Hill.

Lloyd, G.E.R. (1996). Science in antiquity: The Greek and Chinese cases and their relevance to problems of culture and cognition. In D.R. Olson & N. Torrance (Eds.), *Modes of thought: Explorations in culture and cognition* (pp. 15-33). Cambridge, England: Cambridge University Press.

Nisbett, R.E., Peng, K., Choi, I., & Norenzayan, A. (in press). (See References)

Sperber, D., Premack, D., & Premack, A.J. (Eds.). (1995). *Causal cognition: A multidisciplinary debate*. Oxford, England: Oxford University Press.

Note

1. Address correspondence to Richard E. Nisbett, Department of Psychology, University of Michigan, Ann Arbor, MI 48109; e-mail: nisbett@umich.edu.

References

Choi, I., Nisbett, R.E., & Norenzayan, A. (1999). Causal attribution across cultures: Variation and universality. *Psychological Bulletin, 125,* 47-63.

Dweck, C.S., Hong, Y.-Y., & Chiu, C.-Y. (1993). Implicit theories: Individual differences in the likelihood and meaning of dispositional inference. *Personality and Social Psychology Bulletin, 19,* 644-656.

Gardner, H. (1985). *The mind's new science.* New York: Basic Books.

Ji, L., Peng, K., & Nisbett, R.E. (in press). Culture, control, and perception of relationships in the environment. *Journal of Personality and Social Psychology.*

Jones, E.E., & Harris, V.A. (1967). The attribution of attitudes. *Journal of Experimental Social Psychology, 3,* 1-24.

Masuda, T., & Nisbett, R.E. (1999). *Culture and attention to object vs. field.* Unpublished manuscript, University of Michigan, Ann Arbor.

Miller, J.G. (1984). Culture and the development of everyday social explanation. *Journal of Personality and Social Psychology, 46,* 961-978.

Morris, M.W., & Peng, K. (1994). Culture and cause: American and Chinese attributions for social and physical events. *Journal of Personality and Social Psychology, 67,* 949-971.

Nakamura, H. (1988). *The ways of thinking of eastern peoples.* New York: Greenwood Press. (Original work published 1960)

Nisbett, R.E., Peng, K., Choi, I., & Norenzayan, A. (in press). Culture and systems of thought: Holistic vs. analytic cognition. *Psychological Review.*

Norenzayan, A., Choi, I., & Nisbett, R.E. (1999). *Eastern and Western folk psychology and the prediction of behavior.* Unpublished manuscript, University of Michigan, Ann Arbor.

Ross, L. (1977). The intuitive psychologist and his shortcomings. In L. Berkowitz (Ed.), *Advances in experimental social psychology* (Vol. 10, pp. 173-220). New York: Academic Press.

Witkin, H.A., Dyk, R.B., Faterson, H.F., Goodenough, D.R., & Karp, S.A. (1974). *Psychological differentiation.* Potomac, MD: Erlbaum.

Critical Thinking Question

1. Describe the difference between analytic versus holistic cognition. How do the authors use the ancient history of each culture to explain these types of cognition?

2. The authors state that for Eastern cultures "causality lies in the field" whereas for Western cultures "causality inheres in the object." Explain what they mean by this and how this relates to the Fundamental Attribution Error.

3. In the article, the authors present a fascinating study using focal fish as stimuli (Masuda & Nisbett, 1999). Briefly summarize the results of this study and explain how they inform the idea of cultural differences in the Fundamental Attribution Error.

Close Relationships:
Love, Sex, and Marriage

Literature, film, music, and art provide insight into what people value. A casual glance reveals that, throughout the ages and cultures, in various forms and media, close relationships are important to people. In its early years, the scientific study of relationships met with ridicule and disdain, hailed as common sense and scorned as the domain of poets. Fortunately, relationships researchers ignored their critics, and turned their attention to issues such as relationship development and dissolution, the advantages of close relationships for physical health and psychological well-being, and the evolutionary underpinnings of sexual jealousy. As Fincham (2003) notes, not every finding in the arena of close relationships has supported common sense. And, although researchers like poets record their insights on paper, those insights are complementary not redundant.

Poets and writers recognize that different individuals can have very different conceptions of the ideal relationship or partner. The insights uniquely provided by relationship researchers are specifications of the origins of these different conceptions, and models of how these different conceptions may predict variations in satisfaction, views of the relationship, or propensities to leave or go. For example, both Furman (2002) and Fincham (2003) note that some theorists have speculated that the type of attachment a child develops with a caregiver creates a general model of how relationships operate. A child whose needs are consistently met without being smothered learns to trust the caregiver enough to explore; as adults, people who developed this secure model tend to trust their romantic partners and explore through work and leisure. The recognition of similarities between parent-child relationships and adult romantic relationships is not an effort to equate the two, of course: Compared to healthy adult relationships, healthy parent-child relationships do not include a sexual relationship. The latter usually also involve unidirectional (rather than bidirectional) care-giving.

Whether currently in a relationship or seeking a relationship, people often possess ideas about the kind of relationship and partner that they would prefer to have. Some people care primarily about popularity and money; some care primarily about having an attractive sexual partner; some care primarily about having someone with whom to share thoughts and feelings. Fletcher and Simpson (2000) suggest that discrepancies between romantic ideals and actual relationships predict conflict and relationship quality. If dating someone from another ethnic group compromises valued social standing, there will be conflict. If a romantic partner is not as amorous as one would like, one might be tempted to look elsewhere. Whether a person actually terminates the close relationship, of course, depends upon more than just discrepancies between ideals and actuality. People may remain together because the alternative (e.g., being alone) is unacceptable, because familiarity feels safe and predictable, or because they are able to explain away the negative behaviors of their partners.

Resolving relationship conflict requires work on the part of the partners. During disagreements or when one's feelings are hurt, one may be tempted to bring up the other's past failings, attribute a current slight to the other's negative qualities, throw stinky sneakers in the partner's direction, or storm out of the room. Most couples have disagreements, but there is considerable variation in how disagreements are resolved. Social psychologists who are interested in relationship conflict and resolution obviously cannot invade people's apartments and homes as new conflicts arise, but they can observe how couples attempt to resolve minor existing conflicts in laboratory settings. Relying in part on laboratory observations, Fincham (2003) demonstrates that patterns can be observed that differentiate distressed and nondistressed couples: the former express negative thoughts and feelings, show patterns of demands that are unresolved, and fail to find ways to attribute negative behaviors to situational factors. Consistent conflict in long-term formal relationships such as marriage are associated with poorer health outcomes and depression. Depending on the criterion, remaining in a bad romantic relationship can be worse than simply terminating it.

Given the importance of the decision regarding the selection of a long-term partner, "trying on" different kinds of relationships certainly has its value. [Indeed, some scholars have suggested that romantic relationships that terminate before marriage ultimately undercut the divorce rate!!] Relationship ideals are put to their initial tests through dating, usually beginning during adolescence. In contemporary Western cultures at least, early romantic relationships may look a good deal like cross-sex friendships, with a sexuality component. During this critical time of transition, parents and peers may provide care-giving and support, respectively. Furman (2002) indicates that romantic relationships during the college years (i.e., young adulthood) are especially important for social and emotional support. Thus, relationships in young adulthood seem to include the mutual care-giving found in adult romantic relationships. It bears mention, of course, that some findings about adolescent romantic relationships are bounded by culture and era. In Shakespeare's day, Juliet was of a marriageable age at 12, and she probably had very few (if any) male friends! But the story tells us one thing quite plainly: Sexual interest increases along with the physical changes that occur during adolescence.

The poets and artists also appear to have hit the mark with respect to sexual interest: As a general rule, men exhibit greater interest in sex, think about it more, and express a desire for more partners than do women. Some theorists suggest that these gender differences derive from the human system of reproduction, and are rooted in evolution. Women only have one opportunity each month to reproduce and pass along their own genes; as the individual who carries the fetus and initially provides for the infant, women may tend to be more finicky about their mating choices than are men. Where the poets and artists have been relatively silent, though, is in thinking about differences in sexual interest over the lifespan. As Peplau (2003) indicates, women exhibit more variability than do men: women's receptivity to experimenting with different kinds of sexual activity and frequency of engaging in sexual activity varies considerably across time. These gender differences are manifested in both heterosexual and homosexual individuals and, according to Peplau, may derive from women's valuing of psychological intimacy (and viewing sexual activity as a way of developing and maintaining psychological intimacy).

Most people view close relationships with their family, friends, lovers, or spouses as the most important part of their lives. What exactly people want from relationships varies across time (e.g., adolescence versus adulthood) and gender, and also varies along individual differences in ideals or attachment styles. Although they can be the source of conflict, relationships also can provide social support and intimacy, sexual gratification, social status and resources. Relationships are as important to study as they are interesting to study. Certainly, there remains ample grist for the mills of relationships researchers, with plenty to spare for the novelists, artists, and poets.

Ideal Standards in Close Relationships: Their Structure and Functions

Garth J.O. Fletcher and Jeffry A. Simpson[1]

Department of Psychology, University of Canterbury, Christchurch, New Zealand (G.J.O.F.), and Department of Psychology, Texas A&M University, College Station, Texas (J.A.S.)

Abstract

This article describes the Ideals Standards Model, which deals with the content and functions of partner and relationship ideals in intimate relationships. This model proposes that there are three distinct categories of partner ideals (warmth-loyalty, vitality-attractiveness, and status-resources), and that ideals have three distinct functions (evaluation, explanation, and regulation). The model also explains how perceived discrepancies between ideals and perceptions of one's current partner or relationship can have different consequences, depending on which of two motivating forces is active (the need to see the partner or relationship positively or the need to be accurate). Recent empirical studies that support some of the main features of the model are described.

Keywords

ideals; functions; discrepancies; relationships

How do people know whether they are in a good or a bad intimate relationship? On what basis do people decide whether to become more involved, live together, get married, or look for another mate? One answer to such questions is that judgments about a particular relationship might be based on the consistency between ideal standards, on the one hand, and perceptions of the current partner or relationship, on the other. This idea is in common currency in folk wisdom but has received relatively little attention in the scientific literature. Our research and theoretical program over the past few years has confirmed that ideal standards do serve as pivotal knowledge structures in close relationships. However, it has also suggested that the psychological processes through which ideal standards operate are complex.

THE IDEALS STANDARDS MODEL

Relationship and partner ideals are central components of the social mind that people use to guide and regulate their interpersonal worlds. According to our Ideals Standards Model (Simpson, Fletcher, & Campbell, in press), partner and relationship ideals may predate—and causally influence—important judgments and decisions in relationships. These ideals comprise three interlocking components: perceptions of the self, the partner, and the relationship. For example, a person's partner ideal of "handsome and warm" represents a personally held ideal that specifies what the individual hopes and desires (the self), describes a hypothetical other (the partner), and specifies what the ideal would be like in an intimate relationship with the self (the relationship).

According to our model, partner and relationship ideals should be based around three evaluative dimensions: (a) warmth, commitment, and intimacy; (b) health, passion, and attractiveness; and (c) status and resources. We derived these predictions from recent evolutionary models which suggest that each of these dimensions represents a different "route" to obtaining a mate and promoting one's own reproductive fitness (see Gangestad & Simpson, in press). For example, by being attentive to a partner's capacity for intimacy and commitment, an individual should increase his or her chances of finding a cooperative, committed partner who is likely to be a devoted parent. By focusing on attractiveness and health, an individual is likely to acquire a mate who is younger, healthier, and perhaps more fertile (especially in the case of men choosing women). And by considering a partner's resources and status, an individual should be more likely to obtain a mate who can ascend social hierarchies and form coalitions with other people who have—or can acquire—valued social status or other resources.

Why do people not "want it all" in terms of their ideals, seeking out mates who are incredibly attractive, rich, and warm? First, relatively few people fit such a stellar description. Second, most people could not attract such a person, even if one were available. Third, even if someone succeeded in attracting such a paragon, it might be difficult to keep him or her. In short, people must normally make trade-offs between these attributes when deciding whom to date or marry.

Our Ideals Standards Model proposes that partner and relationship ideals serve three functions: evaluation, explanation, and regulation. More specifically, the size of discrepancies between ideal standards and perceptions of the current partner or relationship should be used by individuals to (a) estimate and evaluate the quality of their partners and relationships (e.g., assess the appropriateness of potential or current partners or relationships), (b) explain or provide an understanding of relationship events (e.g., give causal accounts explaining relationship satisfaction, problems, or conflicts), and (c) regulate and make adjustments in their relationships (e.g., predict and possibly control current partners or relationships).

Many relationship theorists have proposed that people need to idealize and enhance their romantic partners and relationships. Indeed, there is good evidence that individuals often do perceive their partners and relationships in an excessively positive, Pollyanna-ish light, and that the tendency to idealize one's partner is associated with greater relationship satisfaction and lower rates of dissolution (see Murray & Holmes, 1996).

It is not difficult to understand why people are motivated to idealize their partners and relationships. To begin with, the costs of relationship conflict and dissolution should motivate most individuals to perceive their partners and relationships in the best possible light. From a rational standpoint, most people know that approximately 50% of marriages end in divorce, at least in Western countries. Despite this realization, the vast majority of people get married and have children at some point in their lives. Committing to a long-term relationship, therefore, requires a leap of faith and a level of confidence that may well be difficult to justify on purely rational grounds. As a result, psychological pressures to make charitable and benevolent judgments about one's partner and relationship must be strong to counteract these forces. This might explain the potency of the enhancement motive in most relationships.

Thomas Huxley (1884) once lamented that "the great tragedy of Science [is] the slaying of a beautiful hypothesis by an ugly fact" (p. 244). In this case, the beautiful hypothesis is the presumed pervasiveness and dominance of the relationship-enhancement motive. The ugly fact is that the vast majority of romantic relationships eventually break up. This latter fact suggests that the relationship-enhancement motive is often either inoperative or displaced by other basic motives in certain contexts.

Our model proposes that partner and relationship idealization will sometimes conflict with the goal of being accurate, especially when the effective prediction, explanation, and control of partners and relationships become important. Attempting to accurately understand and attribute motives and beliefs to others should be highly adaptive in certain situations (such as when deciding whether or not to start or remain in a relationship, or when deciding how best to predict or control the behavior of others).

Indeed, evolutionary pressures should have selected humans to ascertain and face the truth—no matter how bleak and depressing—in situations in which it was dangerous or extremely costly to do otherwise.

How can the coexistence of these two contrasting motives be reconciled? We believe that both enhancement and accuracy motives operate, but under different conditions. Relationship interactions that are highly threatening ought to increase the power of esteem-maintenance goals, subverting accurate attributions about the partner or the relationship. However, when the need to make accurate, unbiased judgments becomes critical in relationships (such as when individuals must decide whether or not to date someone, get married, or have a child), the accuracy motive should take precedence. When couples settle into a comfortable relationship phase of maintenance, the enhancement motive should once again become ascendant.

These contrasting motives have important implications for understanding the consequences of discrepancies between ideals and perceptions of the current partner or relationship. For example, when enhancement motives predominate, people should try to reduce ideal-perception discrepancies (and, thus, improve the evaluations that stem from them) by using cognitive strategies that involve rationalizing inconsistencies, altering attributions, or changing what they value in their partner or relationship. We suspect that such processes often occur automatically and largely outside of conscious awareness. However, in situations that demand greater accuracy (e.g., when important relationship decisions must be made, when attractive alternative partners become available, or when difficult relationship problems arise), moderate to large ideal-perception discrepancies should motivate individuals to engage in more in-depth analysis and information processing. To reduce discrepancies, accuracy-motivated individuals are likely to use behavioral strategies, perhaps attempting to change their own or their partners' behavior. If individuals eventually come to the conclusion that the discrepancies are important but simply cannot be reduced, they may leave the relationship, look for new partners, or seek solace in other activities.

EMPIRICAL EVIDENCE FOR THE MODEL

We currently are testing some of our model's basic postulates. We initially set out to identify the structure and content of partner and relationship ideals (Fletcher, Simpson, Thomas, & Giles, 1999). Adopting an inductive approach to identifying the ideals dimensions that people spontaneously use, in a first study we asked men and women to list all the traits or characteristics that described their ideal romantic partners and their ideal romantic relationships.

In a second study, another sample of men and women then rated the 78 items gathered in the first study in terms of perceived importance for their own standards concerning ideal partners and ideal relationships (using 7-point scales where 1 = *very unimportant* and 7 = *very important*). In order to determine the underlying structure of the perceived-importance ratings of the ideals, we carried out two exploratory factor analyses. A factor analysis of the ideal-partner items revealed the three factors we expected: (a) partner characteristics relevant to intimacy, warmth, trust, and loyalty; (b) personality and appearance characteristics concerning how attractive, energetic, and healthy the partner is; and (c) characteristics relevant to the partner's social status and resources. The ideal-relationship items produced two factors that resembled two of the partner-based ideals: (a) the importance of intimacy, loyalty, and stability in a relationship and (b) the importance of excitement and passion in a relationship. The results of the factor analyses (the correlation, or loading, of each item on each factor) were used to assess which items belonged to which factors. We then summed the scores for items belonging to each factor, separately for each participant, to produce five separate scores representing the perceived importance of each general ideal category. Additional analyses and studies have confirmed the reliability and validity of these derived measures of the five factors.

The final study we reported (Fletcher, Simpson, Thomas, & Giles,1999) tested a basic postulate of our model—that individuals evaluate their current partners and relationships by comparing them against their ideal standards. To test this hypothesis, we asked a new sample of men and women to rank the importance of various ideal attributes and also to report their perceptions of their current partner or relationship on items taken from the ideal-partner and ideal-relationship scales. In addition, we asked subjects to rate how satisfied they were with their relationships. As predicted, individuals who reported smaller discrepancies between their ideal standards and their perceptions of the current partner and relationship rated their relationships more favorably.

Although these studies provided initial support for our model, they were cross-sectional in design and, therefore, could not test for possible causal relationships. To address this issue, we conducted a longitudinal study (Fletcher, Simpson, & Thomas, 1999). A large sample of individuals in newly formed dating relationships completed a battery of measures assessing perceptions of their current partner or relationship, the quality of their relationship, and their ideal standards once a month for 3 months, and then at 12 months after the beginning of the relationship. The first measurement typically occurred 3 weeks after individuals had started dating someone.

As predicted, greater consistency between ideals and perceptions of the current partner or relationship (assessed at earlier times in the relationship) predicted increases in relationship satisfaction over time. Indeed, how closely partners matched individuals' ideals during the first month of dating strongly predicted how individuals felt about their relationships a full 12 months after the dating started. However, also as expected, higher initial levels of relationship satisfaction did not predict changes in levels of consistency between ideals and perceptions. These results suggest that cognitive comparisons between ideal standards and perceptions of the current partner or relationship are firmly in the cognitive driving seat in the initial stages of dating relationships.

We are currently investigating how self-perceptions, along with the flexibility of ideal standards, are related to how individuals set their ideal standards (Campbell, Simpson, Kashy, & Fletcher, in press). The higher that individuals set their ideal standards, the more demanding they are in terms of how closely they expect their partners to match their ideal standards. Although this may seem paradoxical, it is understandable in terms of other results showing that individuals with more positive self-views (e.g., on the vitality-attractiveness dimension) also possess both higher ideal standards and less flexible ideal standards. For example, if a man perceives himself as very fit and highly attractive, he can set high expectations for obtaining a partner who is also highly fit and attractive. Moreover, if the chosen partner subsequently turns into a "couch potato" and gains weight, and this change is monitored by the man, then he is in a strong position to look for—and possibly find—an alternative partner who meets his exacting standards.

Many intriguing and important questions remain to be investigated. First, our theorizing concerning the different functions of relationship-enhancement and accuracy motives remains speculative. Second, we still know relatively little about how individuals establish and adjust their ideal standards over time. Third, and perhaps most important, there is a need to understand and research how ideals function and change within their natural home—the dyadic relationship. We know very little, for instance, about how ideal standards are communicated to the partner, or what happens when one partner is motivated to be accurate when the other partner is motivated to enhance the relationship. We also know almost nothing about whether possessing ideal standards that are similar to those held by one's partner facilitates a relationship's functioning and quality, or how partners might influence one another concerning the perceived importance of particular ideals.

CONCLUSION

It is hard to think of another domain in social life in which the needs for prediction, control, and explanation are more pressing than in intimate relationships. The research and theory we have reported here are part of a burgeoning area within social psychology that is examining social cognition in close relationships. For years, it has been assumed that judgments and perceptions of relationships depend mainly on the nature of the individuals and interactions involved. Our research shows that there exist hidden "third parties"—mental images of ideal partners and ideal relationships—that also play a critical role in influencing judgments about relationships.

Recommended Reading

Fletcher, G.J.O., Simpson, J.A., Thomas, G., & Giles, L. (1999). (See References)
Fletcher, G.J.O., & Thomas, G. (1996). Lay theories in close relationships: Their structure and function. In G.J.O. Fletcher & J. Fitness (Eds.), *Knowledge structures in close relationships: A social psychological approach*(pp. 3-24). Mahwah, NJ: Erlbaum.
Murray, S.L., & Holmes, J.G. (1996). (See References)
Simpson, J.A., Fletcher, G.J.O., & Campbell, L.J. (in press). (See References)

Note

1. Address correspondence to either Garth Fletcher, Department of Psychology, University of Canterbury, Christchurch, New Zealand, e-mail: g.fletcher@psyc.canterbury.ac.nz, or to Jeffry A. Simpson, Department of Psychology, Texas A&M University, College Station, TX 77843-4235, e-mail: jas@psyc.tamu.edu.

References

Campbell, L.J., Simpson, J.A., Kashy, D.A., & Fletcher, G.J.O. (in press). Ideal standards, the self, and flexibility of ideals in close relationships. *Personality and Social Psychology Bulletin.*
Fletcher, G.J.O., Simpson, J.A., & Thomas, G. (1999). *The role of ideals in early relationship development.* Unpublished manuscript, University of Canterbury, Christchurch, New Zealand.
Fletcher, G.J.O., Simpson, J.A., Thomas, G., & Giles, L. (1999). Ideals in intimate relationships. *Journal of Personality and Social Psychology, 76,* 72-89.
Gangestad, S.W., & Simpson, J.A. (in press). The evolution of human mating: Trade-offs and strategic pluralism. *Behavioral and Brain Sciences.*
Huxley, T.H. (1884). *Biogenesis and abiogenesis; collected essays, Vol. 8.* London: Macmillan.
Murray, S.L., & Holmes, J.G. (1996). The construction of relationship realities. In G.J.O. Fletcher & J. Fitness (Eds.), *Knowledge structures in close relationships: A social psychological approach* (pp. 91-120). Mahwah, NJ: Erlbaum.
Simpson, J.A., Fletcher, G.J.O., & Campbell, L.J. (in press). The structure and functions of ideal standards in close relationships. In G.J.O. Fletcher & M.S. Clark (Eds.), *Blackwell handbook of social psychology: Interpersonal processes.* London: Blackwell.

Critical Thinking Questions

1. Many social psychology textbooks describe two basic social motives; 1) the need to feel good about oneself and 2) the need to view the world accurately. Explain how these two basic social motives underlie the Ideals Standard Model.

2. The authors propose that partner ideals are based around three evaluative dimensions. Explain the evolutionary advantage that might have led to these three dimensions.

3. The authors suggest several questions that need further research. One of these involves how people adjust their ideal standards over time. Speculate on this idea. How might one's ideal standards change over the course of a relationship?

4. The authors state that their research demonstrates a hidden "third party" in relationships. Explain why they would use this terminology and indicate how their research supports this idea.

The Emerging Field of Adolescent Romantic Relationships

Wyndol Furman[1]
Department of Psychology, University of Denver, Denver, Colorado

Abstract

Romantic relationships are central in adolescents' lives. They have the potential to affect development positively, but also place adolescents at risk for problems. Romantic experiences change substantially over the course of adolescence; the peer context plays a critical role as heterosexual adolescents initially interact with the other sex in a group context, then begin group dating, and finally have dyadic romantic relationships. Adolescents' expectations and experiences in romantic relationships are related to their relationships with their peers as well as their parents. Although research on adolescents' romantic relationships has blossomed in the past decade, further work is needed to identify the causes and consequences of romantic experiences, examine the diversity of romantic experiences, and integrate the field with work on sexuality and adult romantic relationships.

Keywords

romantic relationships; attachment; love; friendships; adolescent adjustment

A review of the literature on adolescent romantic relationships a decade ago would have uncovered very little empirical research. The work that had been conducted consisted primarily of descriptive studies on the frequency of dating or other romantic behaviors. A substantial amount of work on sexual behavior had been conducted, but much of that was descriptive as well, and did not say much about the relational context in which the sexual behavior occurred. In other words, the literature contained a lot of information about the proportions of adolescents of different ages or backgrounds who were sexually active, but much less about who their partners were and what their relationships with them were like.

Happily, the field has changed substantially in the past decade. A cadre of social scientists have been studying adolescents' romantic relationships, and the number of articles and conference presentations seems to increase each year. The fields of adolescent romantic relationships and sexual behavior are still not well integrated, but the connections between them are increasing. Most of the work has been done on heterosexual relationships, but research on lesbian, gay, and bisexual relationships is beginning as well.

The increasing interest in adolescents' romantic relationships may partially stem from a recognition that these relationships are not simply trivial flings. As young people move from preadolescence through late adolescence, their romantic relationships become increasingly central in their social world. Preadolescents spend an hour or less a week interacting with the other sex. By the 12th grade, boys spend an average of 5 hr a week with the other sex, and girls spend an average of 10 hr a week. Furthermore, 12th-grade boys and girls spend an additional 5 to 8 hr a week thinking about members of the other sex when not with them (Richards, Crowe, Larson, & Swarr,1998). Romantic partners are also a major source of support for many adolescents. Among 10th graders, only close friends provide more support. During the college years, romantic relationships are the most supportive relationships for males, and among the most supportive relationships for females (Furman & Buhrmester, 1992).

Romantic relationships may also affect other aspects of adolescents' development. For example, they have been hypothesized to contribute to the development of an identity, the transformation of family relationships, the development of close relationships with peers, the development of sexuality, and scholastic achievement and career planning (Furman & Shaffer, in press). One particularly interesting question is whether adolescent romantic experiences influence subsequent romantic relationships, including marriages. Unfortunately, there is limited empirical data on these possible impacts.

Adolescent romantic relationships are not, however, simple "beds of roses." One fifth of adolescent women are victims of physical or sexual abuse by a dating partner (Silverman, Raj, Mucci, & Hathaway, 2001). Breakups are one of the strongest predictors of depression (Monroe, Rhode, Seeley, & Lewinsohn, 1999). Sexually transmitted diseases and teenage pregnancy are also major risks.

Of course, the benefits and risks of particular romantic experiences vary. Having romantic experiences at an early age and having a high number of partners are associated with problems in adjustment (see Zimmer-Gembeck, Siebenbruner, & Collins, 2001), although researchers do not know yet the direction of the influence. That is, the romantic experiences may lead to the difficulties, but it is also possible that adolescents who are not well adjusted are more likely than their better adjusted peers to become prematurely or overly involved in romantic relationships. Moreover, little is known about how the length or qualities of romantic relationships may be linked to adjustment.

DEVELOPMENTAL COURSE

Adolescents vary widely in when they become interested in romantic relationships, and the experiences they have once they begin dating. Accordingly, there is not one normative pattern of development. Some commonalities in the nature and sequence of heterosexual experiences can be seen, however. Prior to adolescence, boys and girls primarily interact with same-sex peers. In early adolescence, they begin to think more about members of the other sex, and then eventually to interact more with them (Richards et al., 1998). Initial interactions typically occur in mixed boy-girl groups; then group dating begins, with several pairs engaging in some activity together; finally, dyadic romantic relationships begin to form (Connolly, Goldberg, & Pepler, 2002). Having a large network of other-sex friends increases the likelihood of developing a romantic relationship with someone (Connolly, Furman, & Konarski, 2000).

The developmental course of romantic experiences for gay, lesbian, and bisexual youths is less charted, but is likely to be somewhat different. Most have some same-sex sexual experience, but relatively few have same-sex romantic relationships because of both the limited opportunities to do so and the social disapproval such relationships may generate from families or heterosexual peers (Diamond, Savin-Williams, & Dubé, 1999). Many sexual-minority youths date

71

other-sex peers; such experiences can help them clarify their sexual orientation or disguise it from others.

The nature of heterosexual or homosexual romantic relationships changes developmentally. Early relationships do not fulfill many of the functions that adult romantic relationships often do. Early adolescents do not commonly turn to a partner for support or provide such care-giving for a partner. In fact, what may be important is simply having such a relationship, especially if the partner is a popular or desired one.

Eventually, adolescents develop some comfort in these interactions and begin to turn to their partners for specific social and emotional needs. Wehner and I proposed that romantic relationships become important in the functioning of four behavioral systems—affiliation, sex-reproduction, attachment, and caregiving (Furman & Wehner, 1994). The affiliative and sexual-reproductive systems are the first to become salient, as young adolescents spend time with their partners and explore their sexual feelings. The attachment and caretaking systems become more important during late adolescence and early adulthood, as relationships become more long term. Several findings are consistent with our proposal. When asked to describe their romantic relationships, adolescents mention affiliative features more often than attachment or caregiving features (Feiring, 1996). Similarly, in another study, young adults retrospectively described their romances in adolescence in terms of companionship and affiliation, and described their relationships in young adulthood in terms of trust and support (Shulman & Kipnis, 2001).

The work on the developmental course of romantic experiences illustrates several important points. First, these relationships do not occur in isolation. Relationships with peers typically serve as a social context for the emergence of heterosexual relationships, and often are a deterrent for gay and lesbian relationships. Second, adolescents' romantic relationships are more than simple sexual encounters; at the same time, one could not characterize most of them as the fullblown attachment relationships that committed adult relationships become (Shaver & Hazan, 1988). Affiliation, companionship, and friendship seem to be particularly important aspects of most of these relationships. Finally, the developmental changes in these relationships are striking. Although at first they are based on simple interest, in the course of a decade, adolescents go from simply being interested in boys or girls to having significant relationships that are beginning to be characterized by attachment and caregiving. Because the changes are qualitative as well as quantitative, they present challenges for investigators trying to describe them or to compare the experiences of different adolescents. Wehner and I (Furman & Wehner, 1994) have tried to provide a common framework for research by examining adolescents' expectations for and beliefs about these relationships, a point I discuss more extensively in the next section.

LINKS WITH OTHER RELATIONSHIPS

Much of the current research on adult romantic relationships has been guided by attachment theory. More than a decade ago, Shaver and Hazan (1988) proposed that committed romantic relationships could be characterized as attachments, just as relationships between parent and child were. Moreover, they suggested that experiences with parents affect individuals' expectations of romantic relationships. Individuals who had secure relationships with parents would be likely to have secure expectations of romantic relationships and, in fact, would be likely to develop secure romantic attachments, whereas those who had adverse experiences with parents would be expected to develop insecure expectations of romantic relationships.

Although researchers generally emphasized the links between relationships with parents and romantic relationships, Wehner and I suggested that friendships would be related to romantic relationships as well (Furman & Wehner, 1994). Friendships and romantic relationships are both egalitarian relationships characterized by features of affiliation, such as companionship and mutual intimacy. Accordingly, we proposed that adolescents' experiences with friends and expectations concerning these relationships influence their expectations of romantic relationships. Subsequently, several studies using multiple methods of assessment demonstrated links between adolescents' expectations of friendships and romantic relationships (see Furman, Simon, Shaffer, & Bouchey, 2002). In fact, these links were more consistent than those between parent-child relationships and romantic relationships. Interestingly, the latter links were found to strengthen over the course of adolescence. Such a developmental shift may occur as the attachment and caregiving features of romantic relationships become increasingly salient.

These studies were cross-sectional, and thus cannot support inferences about causality. However, the findings again underscore the importance of recognizing that romantic relationships are peer relationships and thus, links with friendships are likely as well.

At the same time, various types of relationships have only moderate effects on one another. Experiences in other relationships may influence romantic relationships, but romantic relationships also present new challenges, and thus past experiences are not likely to be simply replicated. What influence do past romantic relationships have on future romantic relationships? Individuals' perceptions of support and negative interaction in their romantic relationships have been found to be stable over the span of a year, even across different relationships (Connolly et al., 2000), but otherwise researchers know little about what does and does not carry over from one romantic relationship to the next.

CURRENT AND FUTURE DIRECTIONS

The existing literature on romantic relationships has many of the characteristics of initial research on a topic. One such characteristic is the methodologies used to date: Investigators have principally relied on questionnaires, administered at one point in time. Interview and observational studies are now beginning to appear, though, and investigators conducting longitudinal studies have begun to report their results concerning adolescent romantic relationships. For example, Capaldi and Clark (1998) found that having a parent whose behavior is antisocial and who is unskilled in parenting is predictive of antisocial behavior in mid-adolescence, which in turn is predictive of aggression toward dating partners in late adolescence. Reports from other ongoing longitudinal studies of the childhood precursors of adolescent romantic relationships and the consequences of these relationships for subsequent development should appear shortly.

In this article, I have described some of the common developmental changes characteristic of adolescent romantic relationships and how these relationships may be influenced by relationships with friends and parents. At the same time, the diversity of romantic experiences should be underscored. The links between romantic experiences and adjustment vary as a function of the timing and degree of romantic involvement (Zimmer-Gembeck et al., 2001). Investigators are beginning to examine how romantic experiences may be associated with characteristics of the adolescent, such as antisocial or bullying behavior, health status, or sensitivity to being rejected. To date, most of the work has focused on heterosexual youths from middle-class Euro-American backgrounds, and further work with other groups is certainly needed. Additionally, almost all of the research has been conducted in Western societies, yet romantic development is likely to be quite different in other societies where contacts with the other sex are more constrained, and marriages are arranged.

Efforts to integrate the field with related ones are needed. Just as research on sexual behavior could profit from examining the nature of the relationships between sexual partners, investigators studying romantic relationships need to examine the role of sexual behavior in romantic relationships. Ironically, few investigators have done so, and instead these relationships have been treated as if they were platonic. Similarly, research on adolescent relationships could benefit from the insights of the work on adult romantic relationships, which has a rich empirical and theoretical history. At the same time, investigators studying adult relationships may want to give greater consideration to the developmental changes that occur in these relationships and to their peer context—themes that have been highlighted by adolescence researchers. In sum, research on adolescent romantic relationships has blossomed in the past decade, but a broad, integrative perspective will be needed to fully illuminate their nature.

Recommended Reading

Bouchey, H.A., & Furman, W. (in press). Dating and romantic experiences in adolescence. In G.R. Adams & M. Berzonsky (Eds.), *The Blackwell handbook of adolescence*. Oxford, England: Blackwell.

Florsheim, P. (Ed.). (in press). *Adolescent romantic relations and sexual behavior: Theory, research, and practical implications*. Mahwah, NJ: Erlbaum.

Furman, W., Brown, B.B., & Feiring, C. (Eds.). (1999). *The development of romantic relationships in adolescence*. New York: Cambridge University Press.

Shulman, S., & Collins, W. (Eds.). (1997). *Romantic relationships in adolescence: Developmental perspective.* San Francisco: Jossey-Bass.

Shulman, S., & Seiffge-Krenke, I. (Eds.). (2001). Adolescent romance: From experiences to relationships [Special issue]. *Journal of Adolescence, 24* (3).

Acknowledgments—Preparation of this manuscript was supported by Grant 50106 from the National Institute of Mental Health.

Note

1. Address correspondence to Wyndol Furman, Department of Psychology, University of Denver, Denver, CO 80208; e-mail: wfurman@nova.psy.du.edu.

References

Capaldi, D.M., & Clark, S. (1998). Prospective family predictors of aggression toward female partners for at-risk young men. *Developmental Psychology, 34,* 1175-1188.

Connolly, J., Furman, W., & Konarski, R. (2000). The role of peers in the emergence of romantic relationships in adolescence. *Child Development, 71,* 1395-1408.

Connolly, J., Goldberg, A., & Pepler, D. (2002). *Romantic development in the peer group in early adolescence.* Manuscript submitted for publication.

Diamond, L.M., Savin-Williams, R.C., & Dubé, E.M. (1999). Sex, dating, passionate friendships, and romance: Intimate peer relations among lesbian, gay, and bisexual adolescents. In W. Furman, B.B. Brown, & C. Feiring (Eds.), *The development of romantic relationships in adolescence* (pp. 175-210). New York: Cambridge University Press.

Feiring, C. (1996). Concepts of romance in 15-year-old adolescents. *Journal of Research on Adolescence, 6,* 181-200.

Furman, W., & Buhrmester, D. (1992). Age and sex differences in perceptions of networks of personal relationships. *Child Development, 63,*103-115.

Furman, W., & Shaffer, L. (in press). The role of romantic relationships in adolescent development. In P. Florsheim (Ed.), *Adolescent romantic relations and sexual behavior: Theory, research, and practical implications.* Mahwah, NJ: Erlbaum.

Furman, W., Simon, V.A., Shaffer, L., & Bouchey, H.A. (2002). Adolescents' working models and styles for relationships with parents, friends, and romantic partners. *Child Development, 73,* 241-255.

Furman, W., & Wehner, E.A. (1994). Romantic views: Toward a theory of adolescent romantic relationships. In R. Montemayor, G.R. Adams, & G.P. Gullota (Eds.), *Advances in adolescent development: Vol. 6. Relationships during adolescence* (pp. 168-175). Thousand Oaks, CA: Sage.

Monroe, S.M., Rhode, P., Seeley, J.R., & Lewinsohn, P.M. (1999). Life events and depression in adolescence: Relationship loss as a prospective risk factor for first onset of major depressive disorder. *Journal of Abnormal Psychology, 108,* 606-614.

Richards, M.H., Crowe, P.A., Larson, R., & Swarr, A. (1998). Developmental patterns and gender differences in the experience of peer companionship during adolescence. *Child Development, 69,* 154-163.

Shaver, P., & Hazan, C. (1988). A biased overview of the study of love. *Journal of Social and Personal Relationships, 5,* 473-501.

Shulman, S., & Kipnis, O. (2001). Adolescent romantic relationships: A look from the future. *Journal of Adolescence, 24,* 337-351.

Silverman, J.G., Raj, A., Mucci, L.A., & Hathaway, J.E. (2001). Dating violence against adolescent girls and associated substance use, unhealthy weight control, sexual risk behavior, pregnancy, and suicidality. *Journal of the American Medical Association, 286,* 572-579.

Zimmer-Gembeck, M.J., Siebenbruner, J., & Collins, W.A. (2001). Diverse aspects of dating: Associations with psychosocial functioning from early to middle adolescence. *Journal of Adolescence, 24,* 313-336.

Critical Thinking Questions

1. Describe the typical developmental course of adolescent romantic relationships. Explain how research in this area supports the notion that these relationships develop in a social context.

2. The authors made the argument that peer friendships are related to adolescent romantic relationships. Explain how this statement might be consistent with Shaver and Hazan's attachment theory.

3. One criticism of this area of research is that it has relied primarily on questionnaires given at one point in time. Explain why this is such a problem. How can future researchers overcome this limitation?

Human Sexuality: How Do Men and Women Differ?

Letitia Anne Peplau[1]

Psychology Department, University of California, Los Angeles, Los Angeles, California

Abstract

A large body of scientific research documents four important gender differences in sexuality. First, on a wide variety of measures, men show greater sexual desire than do women. Second, compared with men, women place greater emphasis on committed relationships as a context for sexuality. Third, aggression is more strongly linked to sexuality for men than for women. Fourth, women's sexuality tends to be more malleable and capable of change over time. These male-female differences are pervasive, affecting thoughts and feelings as well as behavior, and they characterize not only heterosexuals but lesbians and gay men as well. Implications of these patterns are considered.

Keywords

human sexuality; sexual desire; sexual orientation; sexual plasticity

A century ago, sex experts confidently asserted that men and women have strikingly different sexual natures. The rise of scientific psychology brought skepticism about this popular but unproven view, and the pendulum swung toward an emphasis on similarities between men's and women's sexuality. For example, Masters and Johnson (1966) captured attention by proposing a human sexual response cycle applicable to both sexes. Feminist scholars cautioned against exaggerating male-female differences and argued for women's sexual equality with men. Recently, psychologists have taken stock of the available scientific evidence. Reviews of empirical research on diverse aspects of human sexuality have identified four important male-female differences. These gender differences are pervasive, affecting thoughts and feelings as well as behavior, and they characterize not only heterosexuals but lesbians and gay men as well.

SEXUAL DESIRE

Sexual desire is the subjective experience of being interested in sexual objects or activities or wishing to engage in sexual activities (Regan & Berscheid, 1999). Many lines of research demonstrate that men show more interest in sex than women (see review by Baumeister, Catanese, & Vohs, 2001). Compared with women, men think about sex more often. They report more frequent sex fantasies and more frequent feelings of sexual desire. Across the life span, men rate the strength of their own sex drive higher than do their female age-mates. Men are more interested in visual sexual stimuli and more likely to spend money on such sexual products and activities as X-rated videos and visits to prostitutes.

Men and women also differ in their preferred frequency of sex. When heterosexual dating and marriage partners disagree about sexual frequency, it is usually the man who wants to have sex more often than the woman does. In heterosexual couples, actual sexual frequency may reflect a compromise between the desires of the male and female partners. In gay and lesbian relationships, sexual frequency is decided by partners of the same gender, and lesbians report having sex less often than gay men or heterosexuals. Further, women appear to be more willing than men to forgo sex or adhere to religious vows of celibacy.

Masturbation provides a good index of sexual desire because it is not constrained by the availability of a partner. Men are more likely than women to masturbate, start masturbating at an earlier age, and do so more often. In a review of 177 studies, Oliver and Hyde (1993) found large male-female differences in the incidence of masturbation. In technical terms, the meta-analytic effect size[2] (d) for masturbation was 0.96, which is smaller than the physical sex difference in height (2.00) but larger than most psychological sex differences, such as the performance difference on standardized math tests (0.20). These and many other empirical findings provide evidence for men's greater sexual interest.

SEXUALITY AND RELATIONSHIPS

A second consistent difference is that women tend to emphasize committed relationships as a context for sexuality more than men do. When Regan and Berscheid (1999) asked young adults to define sexual desire, men were more likely than women to emphasize physical pleasure and sexual intercourse. In contrast, women were more likely to "romanticize" the experience of sexual desire, as seen in one young woman's definition of sexual desire as "longing to be emotionally intimate and to express love for another person" (p. 75). Compared with women, men have more permissive attitudes toward casual premarital sex and toward extramarital sex. The size of these gender differences is relatively large, particularly for casual premarital sex ($d = 0.81$; Oliver & Hyde, 1993). Similarly, women's sexual fantasies are more likely than men's to involve a familiar partner and to include affection and commitment. In contrast, men's fantasies are more likely to involve strangers, anonymous partners, or multiple partners and to focus on specific sex acts or sexual organs.

A gender difference in emphasizing relational aspects of sexuality is also found among lesbians and gay men (see review by Peplau, Fingerhut, & Beals, in press). Like heterosexual women, lesbians tend to have less permissive attitudes toward casual sex and sex outside a primary relationship than do gay or heterosexual men. Also like heterosexual women, lesbians have sex fantasies that are more likely to be personal and romantic than the fantasies of gay or heterosexual men. Lesbians are more likely than gay men to become sexually involved with partners who were first their friends, then lovers. Gay men in committed relationships are more likely than lesbians or heterosexuals to have sex with partners outside their primary relationship.

In summary, women's sexuality tends to be strongly linked to a close relationship. For women, an important goal of sex is intimacy; the best context for pleasurable sex is a committed relationship. This is less true for men.

SEXUALITY AND AGGRESSION

A third gendered pattern concerns the association between sexuality and aggression. This link has been demonstrated in many domains, including individuals' sexual self-concepts, the initiation of sex in heterosexual relationships, and coercive sex.

Andersen, Cyranowski, and Espindle (1999) investigated the dimensions that individuals use to characterize their own sexuality. Both sexes evaluated themselves along a dimension of being romantic, with some individuals seeing themselves as very passionate and others seeing themselves as not very passionate. However, men's sexual self-concepts were also characterized by a dimension of aggression, which concerned the extent to which they saw themselves as being aggressive, powerful, experienced, domineering, and individualistic. There was no equivalent aggression dimension for women's sexual self-concepts.

In heterosexual relationships, men are commonly more assertive than women and take the lead in sexual interactions (see review by Impett & Peplau, 2003). During the early stages of a dating relationship, men typically initiate touching and sexual intimacy. In ongoing relationships, men report initiating sex about twice as often as their female partners or age-mates. To be sure, many women do initiate sex, but they do so less frequently than their male partners. The same pattern is found in people's sexual fantasies. Men are more likely than women to imagine themselves doing something sexual to a partner or taking the active role in a sexual encounter.

Rape stands at the extreme end of the link between sex and aggression. Although women use many strategies to persuade men to have sex, physical force and violence are seldom part of their repertoire. Physically coercive sex is primarily a male activity (see review by Felson, 2002). There is growing recognition that stranger and acquaintance rape are not the whole story; some men use physical force in intimate heterosexual relationships. Many women who are battered by a boyfriend or husband also report sexual assaults as part of the abuse.

In summary, aggression is more closely linked to sexuality for men than for women. Currently, we know little about aggression and sexuality among lesbians and gay men; research on this topic would provide a valuable contribution to our understanding of gender and human sexuality.

SEXUAL PLASTICITY

Scholars from many disciplines have noted that, in comparison with men's sexuality, women's sexuality tends to have greater plasticity. That is, women's sexual beliefs and behaviors can be more easily shaped and altered by cultural, social, and situational factors. Baumeister (2000) systematically reviewed the scientific evidence on this point. In this section, I mention a few of the many supportive empirical findings.

One sign of plasticity concerns changes in aspects of a person's sexuality over time. Such changes are more common among women than among men. For example, the frequency of women's sexual activity is more variable than men's. If a woman is in an intimate relationship, she might have frequent sex with her partner. But following a breakup, she might have no sex at all, including masturbation, for several months. Men show less temporal variability: Following a romantic breakup, men may substitute masturbation for interpersonal sex and so maintain a more constant frequency of sex. There is also growing evidence that women are more likely than men to change their sexual orientation over time. In an illustrative longitudinal study (Diamond, 2003), more than 25% of 18- to 25-year-old women who initially identified as lesbian or bisexual changed their sexual identity during the next 5 years. Changes such as these are less common for men.

A further indication of malleability is that a person's sexual attitudes and behaviors are responsive to social and situational influences. Such factors as education, religion, and acculturation are more strongly linked to women's sexuality than to men's. For example, moving to a new culture may have more impact on women's sexuality than on men's. The experience of higher education provides another illustration. A college education is associated with more liberal sexual attitudes and behavior, but this effect is greater for women than for men. Even more striking is the association between college education and sexual orientation shown in a recent national survey (Laumann, Gagnon, Michael, & Michaels,1994). Completing college doubled the likelihood that a man identified as gay or bisexual (1.7% among high school graduates vs. 3.3% among college graduates). However, college was associated with a 900% increase in the percentage of women identifying as lesbian or bisexual (0.4% vs. 3.6%).

CONCLUSION AND IMPLICATIONS

Diverse lines of scientific research have identified consistent male-female differences in sexual interest, attitudes toward sex and relationships, the association between sex and aggression, and sexual plasticity. The size of these gender differences tends to be large, particularly in comparison to other male-female differences studied by psychologists. These differences are pervasive, encompassing thoughts, feelings, fantasies, and behavior.

Finally, these male-female differences apply not only to heterosexuals but also to lesbians and gay men.

Several limitations of the current research are noteworthy. First, much research is based on White, middle-class American samples. Studies of other populations and cultural groups would be valuable in assessing the generalizability of findings. Second, although research findings on lesbians and gay men are consistent with patterns of male-female difference among heterosexuals, the available empirical database on homosexuals is relatively small. Third, differences between women and men are not absolute but rather a matter of degree. There are many exceptions to the general patterns described. For instance, some women show high levels of sexual interest, and some men seek sex only in committed relationships. Research documenting male-female differences has advanced further than research systematically tracing the origins of these differences. We are only beginning to understand the complex ways in which biology, experience, and culture interact to shape men's and women's sexuality.

These four general differences between women's and men's sexuality can illuminate specific patterns of sexual interaction. For example, in heterosexual couples, it is fairly common for a partner to engage in sex when he or she is not really interested or "in the mood." Although both men and women sometimes consent to such unwanted sexual activity, women are more often the compliant sexual partner (see review by Impett & Peplau, 2003). Each of the gender differences I have described may contribute to this pattern. First, the stage is set by a situation in which partners have differing desires for sex, and the man is more often the partner desiring sex. Second, for compliant sex to occur, the more interested partner must communicate his or her desire. Men typically take the lead in expressing sexual interest. Third, the disinterested partner's reaction is pivotal: Does this partner comply or, instead, ignore or reject the request? If women view sex as a way to show love and caring for a partner, they may be more likely than men to resolve a dilemma about unwanted sex by taking their partner's welfare into account. In abusive relationships, women may fear physical or psychological harm from a male partner if they refuse. Finally, sexual compliance illustrates the potential plasticity of female sexuality. In this case, women are influenced by relationship concerns to engage in a sexual activity that goes against their personal preference at the time.

The existence of basic differences between men's and women's sexuality has implications for the scientific study of sexuality. Specifically, an adequate understanding of human sexuality may require separate analyses of sexuality in women and in men, based on the unique biology and life experiences of each sex. Currently, efforts to reconceptualize sexual issues have focused on women's sexuality. Three examples are illustrative.

Rethinking Women's Sexual Desire

How should we interpret the finding that women appear less interested in sex than men? One possibility is that researchers have inadvertently used male standards (e.g., penile penetration and orgasm) to evaluate women's sexual experiences and consequently ignored activities, such as intimate kissing, cuddling, and touching, that may be uniquely important to women's erotic lives. Researchers such as Wallen (1995) argue that it is necessary to distinguish between sexual desire (an intrinsic motivation to pursue sex) and arousability (the capacity to become sexually aroused in response to situational cues). Because women's sexual desire may vary across the menstrual cycle, it may be more appropriate to describe women's desire as periodic rather than weak or limited. In contrast, women's receptivity to sexual overtures and their capacity for sexual response may depend on situational rather than hormonal cues. Other researchers (e.g., Tolman & Diamond, 2001) argue that more attention must be paid to the impact of hormones that may have special relevance for women, such as the neuropeptide oxytocin, which is linked to both sexuality and affectional bonding.

Rethinking Women's Sexual Orientation

Some researchers have proposed new paradigms for understanding women's sexual orientation (e.g., Peplau & Garnets, 2000). Old models either assumed commonalities among homosexuals, regardless of gender, or hypothesized similarities between lesbians and heterosexual men, both of whom are attracted to women. In contrast, empirical research has documented many similarities in women's sexuality, regardless of their sexual orientation. A new model based on women's experiences might highlight the centrality of relationships to women's sexual orientation, the potential for at least some women to change their sexual orientation over time, and the importance of sociocultural factors in shaping women's sexual orientation.

Rethinking Women's Sexual Problems

Finally, research on women's sexuality has led some scientists to question current systems for classifying sexual dysfunction among women. The widely used *Diagnostic and Statistical Manual of Mental Disorders (DSM)* of the American Psychiatric Association categorizes sexual dysfunction on the basis of Masters and Johnson's (1966) model of presumed normal and universal sexual functioning. Critics (e.g., Kaschak & Tiefer, 2001) have challenged the validity of this model, its applicability to women, and its use as a basis for clinical assessment. They have also faulted the *DSM* for ignoring the relationship context of sexuality for women. Kaschak and Tiefer have proposed instead a new "woman-centered" view of women's sexual problems that gives prominence to partner and relationship factors that affect women's sexual experiences, and also to social, cultural, and economic factors that influence the quality of women's sexual lives.

Recommended Reading

Baumeister, R.F., & Tice, D.M. (2001). *The social dimension of sex.* Boston: Allyn and Bacon.
Kaschak, E., & Tiefer, L. (Eds.). (2001). (See References)
Peplau, L.A., & Garnets, L.D. (Eds.). (2000). (See References)
Regan, P.C., & Berscheid, E. (1999). (See References)

Notes

1. Address correspondence to Letitia Anne Peplau, Psychology Department, Franz 1285, University of California, Los Angeles, CA 90095-1563; e-mail: lapeplau@ucla.edu.
2. In a meta-analysis, the findings of multiple studies are analyzed quantitatively to arrive at an overall estimate of the size of a difference between two groups, in this case, between men and women. This effect size (known technically as d) is reported using a common unit of measurement. By convention in psychological research, 0.2 is considered a small effect size, 0.5 is a moderate effect size, and 0.8 is a large effect size.

References

Andersen, B.L., Cyranowski, J.M., & Espindle, D. (1999). Men's sexual self-schema. *Journal of Personality and Social Psychology, 76,* 645-661.
Baumeister, R.F. (2000). Gender differences in erotic plasticity. *Psychological Bulletin, 126,* 347-374.
Baumeister, R.F., Catanese, K.R., & Vohs, K.D. (2001). Is there a gender difference in strength of sex drive? *Personality and Social Psychology Review, 5,* 242-273.
Diamond, L.M. (2003). Was it a phase? Young women's relinquishment of lesbian /bisexual identities over a 5-year period. *Journal of Personality and Social Psychology, 84,*352-364.
Felson, R.B. (2002). *Violence and gender reexamined.* Washington, DC: American Psychological Association.
Impett, E., & Peplau, L.A. (2003). Sexual compliance: Gender, motivational, and relationship perspectives. *Journal of Sex Research, 40,* 87-100.

Kaschak, E., & Tiefer, L. (Eds.). (2001). *A new view of women's sexual problems.* New York: Haworth Press.

Laumann, E., Gagnon, J., Michael, R., & Michaels, S. (1994). *The social organization of sexuality.* Chicago: University of Chicago Press.

Masters, W.H., & Johnson, V.E. (1966). *Human sexual response.* Boston: Little, Brown, & Co. Oliver, M.B., & Hyde, J.S. (1993). Gender differences in sexuality: A meta-analysis. *Psychological Bulletin, 114,* 29-51.

Peplau, L.A., Fingerhut, A., & Beals, K. (in press). Sexuality in the relationships of lesbians and gay men. In J. Harvey, A. Wenzel, & S. Sprecher (Eds.), *Handbook of sexuality in close relationships.* Mahwah, NJ: Erlbaum.

Peplau, L.A., & Garnets, L.D. (Eds.). (2000). Women's sexualities: New perspectives on sexual orientation and gender [Special issue]. *Journal of Social Issues, 56* (2).

Regan, P.C., & Berscheid, E. (1999). *Lust: What we know about human sexual desire.* Thousand Oaks, CA: Sage.

Tolman, D.L., & Diamond, L.M. (2001). Desegregating sexuality research: Cultural and biological perspectives on gender and desire. *Annual Review of Sex Research, 12,* 33-74.

Wallen, K. (1995). The evolution of female sexual desire. In P. Abramson & S.D. Pinkerton (Eds.), *Sexual nature/sexual culture* (pp. 57-79). Chicago: University of Chicago Press.

Critical Thinking Questions

1. Research supports four important gender differences regarding sexuality. Summarize these four differences and speculate on how each might be both biologically and socially determined.

2. Indicate why feminist scholars might caution "against exaggerating male-female differences" with regard to sexuality.

3. The author uses research to demonstrate that each of the four gender differences in sexuality occur for both heterosexuals as well as lesbian women and gay men, with the exception of aggression. In the area of sexuality and aggression, she states that little is known about lesbian women and gay men. Speculate on why research in this area might be lagging behind the other three in light of these populations.

Marital Conflict: Correlates, Structure, and Context

Frank D. Fincham[1]

Psychology Department, University at Buffalo, Buffalo, New York

Abstract

Marital conflict has deleterious effects on mental, physical, and family health, and three decades of research have yielded a detailed picture of the behaviors that differentiate distressed from nondistressed couples. Review of this work shows that the singular emphasis on conflict in generating marital outcomes has yielded an incomplete picture of its role in marriage. Recently, researchers have tried to paint a more textured picture of marital conflict by studying spouses' backgrounds and characteristics, investigating conflict in the contexts of support giving and affectional expression, and considering the ecological niche of couples in their broader environment.

Keywords

conflict patterns; marital distress; support

Systematic psychological research on marriage emerged largely among clinical psychologists who wanted to better assist couples experiencing marital distress. In the 30 years since this development, marital conflict has assumed a special status in the literature on marriage, as evidenced by three indices. First, many of the most influential theories of marriage tend to reflect the view that "distress results from couples' aversive and ineffectual response to conflict" (Koerner & Jacobson, 1994, p. 208). Second, research on marriage has focused on what spouses do when they disagree with each other, and reviews of marital interaction are dominated by studies of conflict and problem solving (see Weiss & Heyman, 1997). Third, psychological interventions for distressed couples often target conflict-resolution skills (see Baucom, Shoham, Mueser, Daiuto, & Stickle,1998).

IS MARITAL CONFLICT IMPORTANT?

The attention given marital conflict is understandable when we consider its implications for mental, physical, and family health. Marital conflict has been linked to the onset of depressive symptoms, eating disorders, male alcoholism, episodic drinking, binge drinking, and out-of-home drinking. Although married individuals are healthier on average than the unmarried, marital conflict is associated with poorer health and with specific illnesses such as cancer, cardiac disease, and chronic pain, perhaps because hostile behaviors during conflict are related to alterations in immunological, endocrine, and cardiovascular functioning. Physical aggression occurs in about 30% of married couples in the United States, leading to significant physical injury in about 10% of couples. Marriage is also the most common interpersonal context for homicide, and more women are murdered by their partners than by anyone else. Finally, marital conflict is associated with important family outcomes, including poor parenting, poor adjustment of children, increased likelihood of parent-child conflict, and conflict between siblings. Marital conflicts that are frequent, intense, physical, unresolved, and child related have a particularly negative influence on children, as do marital conflicts that spouses attribute to their child's behavior (see Grych & Fincham, 2001).

WHAT ARE MARITAL CONFLICTS ABOUT?

Marital conflicts can be about virtually anything. Couples complain about sources of conflict ranging from verbal and physical abusiveness to personal characteristics and behaviors. Perceived inequity in a couple's division of labor is associated with marital conflict and with a tendency for the male to withdraw in response to conflict. Conflict over power is also strongly related to marital dissatisfaction. Spouses' reports of conflict over extramarital sex, problematic drinking, or drug use predict divorce, as do wives' reports of husbands being jealous and spending money foolishly. Greater problem severity increases the likelihood of divorce. Even though it is often not reported to be a problem by couples, violence among newlyweds is a predictor of divorce, as is psychological aggression (verbal aggression and nonverbal aggressive behaviors that are not directed at the partner's body).

HOW DO SPOUSES BEHAVE DURING CONFLICT?

Stimulated, in part, by the view that "studying what people say about themselves is no substitute for studying how they behave" (Raush, Barry, Hertel, & Swain, 1974, p. 5), psychologists have conducted observational studies, with the underlying hope of identifying dysfunctional behaviors that could be modified in couple therapy. This research has focused on problem-solving discussions in the laboratory and provides detailed information about how maritally distressed and nondistressed couples behave during conflict.

During conflict, distressed couples make more negative statements and fewer positive statements than nondistressed couples. They are also more likely to respond with negative behavior when their partner behaves negatively. Indeed, this negative reciprocity, as it is called, is more consistent across different types of situations than is the amount of negative behavior, making it the most reliable overt signature of marital distress. Negative behavior is both more frequent and more frequently reciprocated in couples that engage in physical aggression than in other couples. Nonverbal behavior, often used as an index of emotion, reflects marital satisfaction better than verbal behavior, and unlike verbal behavior does not change when spouses try to fake good and bad marriages.

Are There Typical Patterns of Conflict Behavior?

The sequences of behavior that occur during conflict are more predictable in distressed than in nondistressed marriages and are often dominated by chains of negative behavior that usually escalate and are difficult for the couple to stop. One of the greatest challenges for couples locked into negative exchanges is to find an adaptive way of exiting from such cycles. This is usually attempted through responses that are designed to repair the interaction (e.g., "You're not listening to me") but are delivered with negative affect (e.g., irritation, sadness). The partners tend to respond to the negative affect, thereby continuing the cycle. This makes their interactions structured and predictable. In contrast, nondistressed couples appear to be more responsive to attempts at repair and are thereby able to exit from negative exchanges early on. For example, a spouse may respond to "Wait, you're not letting me finish" with "Sorry ... please finish what you were saying." Their interaction therefore appears more random and less predictable.

A second important behavior pattern exhibited by maritally distressed couples is the demand-withdraw pattern, in which one spouse pressures the other with demands, complaints, and criticisms, while the partner withdraws with defensiveness and passive inaction. Specifically, behavior sequences in which the husband withdraws and the wife responds with hostility are more common in distressed than in satisfied couples. This finding is consistent with several studies showing that wives display more negative affect and behavior than husbands, who tend to not respond or to make statements suggestive of withdrawal, such as irrelevant comments. Disengagement or withdrawal is, in turn, related to later decreases in marital satisfaction. However, inferring reliable gender differences in demand-withdraw patterns would be premature, as recent research shows that the partner who withdraws varies according to which partner desires change. So, for example, when a man desires change, the woman is the one who withdraws. Finally, conflict patterns seem to be relatively stable over time (see Karney & Bradbury, 1995).

Is There a Simple Way to Summarize Research Findings on Marital Conflict?

The findings of the extensive literature on marital conflict can be summarized in terms of a simple ratio: The ratio of agreements to disagreements is greater than 1 for happy couples and less than 1 for unhappy couples. Gottman (1993) utilized this ratio to identify couple types. He observed husbands and wives during conversation, recording each spouse's positive and negative behaviors while speaking, and then calculated the cumulative difference between positive and negative behaviors over time for each spouse. Using the patterns in these difference scores, he distinguished regulated couples (increase in positive speaker behaviors relative to negative behaviors for both spouses over the course of conversation) from nonregulated couples (all other patterns). The regulated couples were more satisfied in their marriage than the nonregulated couples, and also less likely to divorce. Regulated couples displayed positive problem-solving behaviors and positive affect approximately 5 times as often as negative problem-solving behaviors and negative affect, whereas the corresponding ratio was approximately 1:1 for nonregulated couples.

Interestingly, Gottman's perspective corresponds with the findings of two early, often overlooked studies on the reported frequency of sexual intercourse and of marital arguments (Howard & Dawes, 1976; Thornton, 1977). Both showed that the ratio of sexual intercourse to arguments, rather than their base rates, predicted marital satisfaction.

Don't Research Findings on Marital Conflict Just Reflect Common Sense?

The findings described in this article may seem like common sense. However, what we have learned about marital interaction contradicts the long-standing belief that satisfied couples are characterized by a *quid pro quo* principle according to which they exchange positive behavior and instead show that it is dissatisfied spouses who reciprocate one another's (negative) behavior. The astute reader may also be wondering whether couples' behavior in the artificial setting of the laboratory is a good reflection of their behavior in the real world outside the lab. It is therefore important to note that couples who participate in such studies themselves report that their interactions in the lab are reminiscent of their typical interactions. Research also shows that conflict behavior in the lab is similar to conflict behavior in the home; however, laboratory conflicts tend to be less severe, suggesting that research findings underestimate differences between distressed and nondistressed couples.

THE SEEDS OF DISCONTENT

By the early 1980s, researchers were attempting to address the limits of a purely behavioral account of marital conflict. Thus, they began to pay attention to subjective factors, such as thoughts and feelings, which might influence behavioral interactions or the relation between behavior and marital satisfaction. For example, it is now well documented that the tendency to explain a partner's negative behavior (e.g., coming home late from work) in a way that promotes conflict (e.g., "he thinks only about himself and his needs"), rather than in less conflictual ways (e.g., "he was probably caught in traffic"), is related to less effective problem solving, more negative communication in problem-solving discussions, more displays of specific negative affects (e.g., anger) during problem solving, and steeper declines in marital satisfaction over time (Fincham, 2001). Explanations that promote conflict are also related to the tendency to reciprocate a partner's negative behavior, regardless of a couple's marital satisfaction. Research on such subjective factors, like observational research on conflict, has continued to the present time. However, it represents an acceptance and expansion of the behavioral approach that accords conflict a central role in understanding marriage.

In contrast, very recently, some investigators have argued that the role of conflict in marriage should be reconsidered. Longitudinal research shows that conflict accounts for a relatively small portion of the variability in later marital outcomes, suggesting that other factors need to be considered in predicting these outcomes (see Karney & Bradbury, 1995). In addition, studies have demonstrated a troubling number of "reversal effects" (showing that greater conflict is a predictor of improved marriage; see Fincham & Beach, 1999). It is difficult to account for such findings in a field that, for much of its existence, has focused on providing descriptive data at the expense of building theory.

Rethinking the role of conflict also reflects recognition of the fact that most of what we know about conflict behavior comes from observation of problem-solving discussions and that couples experience verbal problem-solving situations infrequently; about 80% of couples report having overt disagreements once a month or less. As a result, cross-sectional studies of distressed versus nondistressed marriages and longitudinal studies of conflict are being increasingly complemented by research designs that focus on how happy marriages become unhappy.

Finally, there is evidence that marital conflict varies according to contextual factors. For example, diary studies illustrate that couples have more stressful marital interactions at home on days of high general life stress than on other days, and at times and places where they are experiencing multiple competing demands; arguments at work are related to marital arguments, and the occurrence of stressful life events is associated with more conflictual problem-solving discussions.

NEW BEGINNINGS: CONFLICT IN CONTEXT

Although domains of interaction other than conflict (e.g., support, companionship) have long been discussed in the marital literature, they are only now emerging from the secondary status accorded to them. This is somewhat ironic given the simple summary of research findings on marital conflict offered earlier, which points to the importance of the context in which conflict occurs.

Conflict in the Context of Support Giving and Affectional Expression

Observational laboratory methods have recently been developed to assess supportive behaviors in interactions in which one spouse talks about a personal issue he or she would like to change and the other is asked to respond as she or he normally would. Behaviors exhibited during such support tasks are only weakly related to the conflict behaviors observed during the problem-solving discussions used to study marital conflict. Supportive spouse behavior is associated with greater marital satisfaction and is more important than negative behavior in determining how supportive the partners perceive an interaction to be. In addition, the amount of supportive behavior partners exhibit is a predictor of later marital stress (i.e., more supportive behavior correlates with less future marital stress), independently of conflict behavior, and when support is poor, there is an increased risk that poor skills in dealing with conflict will lead to later marital deterioration. There is also evidence that support obtained by spouses outside the marriage can influence positively how the spouse behaves within the marriage.

In the context of high levels of affectional expression between spouses, the association between spouses' negative behavior and marital satisfaction decreases significantly. High levels of positive behavior in problem-solving discussions also mitigate the effect of withdrawal or disengagement on later marital satisfaction. Finally, when there are high levels of affectional expression between spouses, the demand-withdraw pattern is unrelated to marital satisfaction, but when affectional expression is average or low, the demand-withdraw pattern is associated with marital dissatisfaction.

Conflict in the Context of Spouses' Backgrounds and Characteristics

Focus on interpersonal behavior as the cause of marital outcomes led to the assumption that the characteristics of individual spouses play no role in those

87

outcomes. However, increasing evidence that contradicts this assumption has generated recent interest in studying how spouses' backgrounds and characteristics might enrich our understanding of marital conflict.

The importance of spouses' characteristics is poignantly illustrated in the intergenerational transmission of divorce. Although there is a tendency for individuals whose parents divorced to get divorced themselves, this tendency varies depending on the offspring's behavior. Divorce rates are higher for offspring who behave in hostile, domineering, and critical ways, compared with offspring who do not behave in this manner.

An individual characteristic that is proving to be particularly informative for understanding marriage comes from recent research on attachment, which aims to address questions about how the experience of relationships early in life affects interpersonal functioning in adulthood. For example, spouses who tend to feel secure in relationships tend to compromise and to take into account both their own and their partner's interests during problem-solving interactions; those who tend to feel anxious or ambivalent in relationships show a greater tendency to oblige their partner, and focus on relationship maintenance, than do those who tend to avoid intimacy in relationships. And spouses who are preoccupied with being completely emotionally intimate in relationships show an elevated level of marital conflict after an involuntary, brief separation from the partner.

Of particular interest for understanding negative reciprocity are the findings that greater commitment is associated with more constructive, accommodative responses to a partner's negative behavior and that the dispositional tendency to forgive is a predictor of spouses' responses to their partners' transgressions; spouses having a greater tendency to forgive are less likely to avoid the partner or retaliate in kind following a transgression by the partner. Indeed, spouses themselves acknowledge that the capacity to seek and grant forgiveness is one of the most important factors contributing to marital longevity and satisfaction.

Conflict in the Context of the Broader Environment

The environments in which marriages are situated and the intersection between interior processes and external factors that impinge upon marriage are important to consider in painting a more textured picture of marital conflict. This is because problem-solving skills and conflict may have little impact on a marriage in the absence of external stressors. External stressors also may influence marriages directly. In particular, nonmarital stressors may lead to an increased number of negative interactions, as illustrated by the fact that economic stress is associated with marital conflict. There is a growing need to identify the stressors and life events that are and are not influential for different couples and for different stages of marriage, to investigate how these events influence conflict, and to clarify how individuals and marriages may inadvertently generate stressful events. In fact, Bradbury, Rogge, and Lawrence (2001), in considering the ecological niche of the couple (i.e., their life events, family constellation, socioeconomic standing, and stressful circumstances), have recently argued that it may be "at least as important to examine the struggle that exists between the couple . . . and the environment they inhabit as it is to examine the interpersonal struggles that are the focus of our work [observation of conflict]" (p. 76).

CONCLUSION

The assumption that conflict management is the key to successful marriage and that conflict skills can be modified in couple therapy has proved useful in propelling the study of marriage into the mainstream of psychology. However, it may have outlived its usefulness, and some researchers are now calling for greater attention to other mechanisms (e.g., spousal social support) that might be responsible for marital outcomes. Indeed, controversy over whether conflict has beneficial or detrimental effects on marriage over time is responsible, in part, for the recent upsurge in longitudinal research on marriage. Notwithstanding diverse opinions on just how central conflict is for understanding marriage, current efforts to study conflict in a broader marital context, which is itself seen as situated in a broader ecological niche, bode well for advancing understanding and leading to more powerful preventive and therapeutic interventions.

Recommended Reading

Bradbury, T.N., Fincham, F.D., & Beach, S.R.H. (2000). Research on the nature and determinants of marital satisfaction: A decade in review. *Journal of Marriage and the Family, 62,* 964-980.
Fincham, F.D., & Beach, S.R. (1999). (See References)
Grych, J.H., & Fincham, F.D. (Eds.). (2001). (See References)
Karney, B.R., & Bradbury, T.N. (1995). (See References)

Acknowledgments—This article was written while the author was supported by grants from the Templeton, Margaret L. Wendt, and J.M. McDonald Foundations.

Note

1. Address correspondence to Frank D. Fincham, Department of Psychology, University at Buffalo, Buffalo, NY 14260.

References

Baucom, D.H., Shoham, V., Mueser, K.T., Daiuto, A.D., & Stickle, T.R. (1998). Empirically supported couple and family interventions for marital distress and adult mental health problems. *Journal of Consulting and Clinical Psychology, 66,* 53-88.
Bradbury, T.N., Rogge, R., & Lawrence, E. (2001). Reconsidering the role of conflict in marriage. In A. Booth, A.C. Crouter, & M. Clements (Eds.), *Couples in conflict* (pp. 59-81). Mahwah, NJ: Erlbaum.
Fincham, F.D. (2001). Attributions and close relationships: From balkanization to integration. In G.J. Fletcher & M. Clark (Eds.), *Blackwell handbook of social psychology* (pp. 3-31). Oxford, England: Blackwell.
Fincham, F.D., & Beach, S.R. (1999). Marital conflict: Implications for working with couples. *Annual Review of Psychology, 50,* 47-77.
Gottman, J.M. (1993). The roles of conflict engagement, escalation, and avoidance in marital interaction: A longitudinal view of five types of couples. *Journal of Consulting and Clinical Psychology, 61,* 6-15.
Grych, J.H., & Fincham, F.D. (Eds.). (2001). *Interparental conflict and child development: Theory, research, and applications.* New York: Cambridge University Press.
Howard, J.W., & Dawes, R.M. (1976). Linear prediction of marital happiness. *Personality and Social Psychology Bulletin, 2,* 478-480.

89

Karney, B.R., & Bradbury, T.N. (1995). The longitudinal course of marital quality and stability: A review of theory, method, and research. *Psychological Bulletin, 118,* 3-34.

Koerner, K., & Jacobson, N.J. (1994). Emotion and behavior in couple therapy. In S.M. Johnson & L.S. Greenberg (Eds.), *The heart of the matter: Perspectives on emotion in marital therapy* (pp. 207-226). New York: Brunner/Mazel.

Raush, H.L., Barry, W.A., Hertel, R.K., & Swain, M.A. (1974). *Communication, conflict, and marriage.* San Francisco: Jossey-Bass.

Thornton, B. (1977). Toward a linear prediction of marital happiness. *Personality and Social Psychology Bulletin, 3,* 674-676.

Weiss, R.L., & Heyman, R.E. (1997). A clinical-research overview of couple interactions. In W.K. Halford & H. Markman (Eds.), *The clinical handbook of marriage and couples interventions* (pp. 13-41). Brisbane, Australia: Wiley.

Critical Thinking Questions

1. Are there typical patterns of conflict behavior? Use research evidence to support your answer. What are the implications of your answer for both marital counselors and researchers?

2. In this article, the author argues that research in martial conflict has "focused on descriptive data at the expense of building theory." Using your knowledge of research methods, explain what he means by this. Do you think that the research he describes supports his statement? Why or why not?

3. The author states that there is controversy about whether conflict has good or bad long-term effects on marriage. Cite some research that supports each side of this controversy. What might future researchers do to begin to resolve this controversy?

Interpersonal Extremes:

Prosocial Behavior and Aggression

Human behavior comprises ponderous contradictions, bizarre puzzles, and almost inconceivable extremes. A human being may sacrifice her own life to save a stranger, or throttle a romantic partner within inches of her life. A human being may suffer indignities at the hands of a stranger, and yet not wish ill upon that stranger. As a social species, humans behave in both prosocial and antisocial ways, helping and hurting, uplifting and undermining.

Besides representing the extremes of human behavior, what do prosocial behavior and aggression have in common? First, a sizable body of each literature historically has derived from biological or evolutionary explanations for human behavior; the trend in other areas of social psychology to recognize biological and evolutionary factors is fairly recent, and can trace the development of this reasoning back to prosocial and aggression research. For example, certain kinds of aggression (e.g., defending territory; obtaining access to mates and resources; maternal aggression) have survival value for a species; studies that focus upon hormones (e.g., testosterone) suggest a strong biological basis for aggression. Conversely, risking one's life for another person would seem, at first blush, to contradict survival instincts. Theorists point out, though, that risking one's life for another is most likely when the other person belongs to one's shared gene pool. From the logic of inclusive fitness, risking one's life for two siblings (who each share 50% of one's genes) is a fair trade, especially if those siblings are likely to reproduce in the future.

The purely biological explanations do not easily explain why some people risk their lives for strangers, or why individuals kill themselves, or fight when no apparent resources are at stake. Coping with this conundrum, the second common theme in these extreme behaviors is a long-standing focus on social learning. As Bushman and Phillips (2001) note, several decades of research has articulated the relation between aggression and viewing television violence. More contemporarily, researchers are considering the impact of playing violent videogames, in which the player takes an active role as an aggressor. Repeated exposure to violence, especially when it is rewarded, can increase aggressive behavior in subsequent encounters. Prosocial behavior, too, has a strong learned component. Donating to charity and volunteering one's time all are influenced by peers. Batson and Thompson (2001) note that one long-standing explanation of immoral behavior was the failure to learn the moral values and laws of one's society. Their research demonstrates quite keenly that people typically have learned to distinguish right from wrong. However, people do not always act in ways that demonstrate their understanding of the distinction. For instance, if the personal costs of behaving prosocially are too great (e.g., resources are lost, pain is experienced), people may act in ways that contradict their own moral understanding.

A third recurring theme in the research on prosocial behavior and aggression lies in the fact that many of the theories are motivational. The theorists focus on the desires, drives, or goals that encourage a person to behave in a particular way. With Batson and Thompson's (2001) approach to immoral behavior, these motivations are to appear moral and to avoid personal costs. Some other motivational theories of prosocial behavior have focused on motivations to reduce bad moods, to increase pleasant moods, or to obtain rewards and social accolades. Aggression theories similarly reveal a motivational twist, dating as far back as Freud's death instinct. People may behave aggressively in order to obtain revenge or retribution, to obtain resources otherwise unavailable to them, and to exert power and dominance over others. An interesting series of studies by Baumeister and his colleagues (Baumeister, Bushman, & Campbell, 2000) focuses on another motivation: the protection of fragile self-esteem. Baumeister and colleagues demonstrate that highly aggressive people tend to be narcissistic; narcissistic individuals possess high degrees of self-esteem, but that self-esteem is not stable. If the person's excessively high opinion of the self is threatened, the person becomes aggressive.

A final recurring theme in each literature is a recognition of personality factors and individual differences. In the area of aggression, personality characteristics such as authoritarianism, dispositional tendencies to interpret ambiguous events as provoking, and vengefulness have been associated with increased aggressive behavior. Baumeister and colleagues' (2000) recent focus on unstable self-esteem and narcissism are congruent with this theme. In the area of prosocial behavior, researchers have examined personality factors such as self-consciousness, which is a dispositional version of the objective self-awareness that can be created by mirrors (as noted by Batson & Thompson, 2001). Individuals high in self-consciousness (or who are objectively self-aware) are increasingly likely to behave according to moral norms and standards. Dispositional empathy or perspective-taking, both of which encourage identifying with the person who requires help, also are associated with increased levels of helping. McCullough's (2001) work on the prosocial behavior of forgiveness—setting aside desires for retribution or hoping that a transgressor later suffers—similarly relies upon personality differences.

Indeed, McCullough's (2001) work nicely ties the literatures of aggression and prosocial behavior together. Many transgressions against us are acts of aggression, whether those transgressions involved passive aggression (e.g., the person "forgot" one's birthday), covert verbal aggression (e.g., the person spread vile gossip behind one's back), or intentional physical violence (e.g., one is shoved or struck). In many cases, the victim desires for the aggressor to be punished, becomes less vengeful if the aggressor is punished indirectly, or experiences delight when the disliked aggressor experiences some unrelated negative event (which the German call *Schadenfreude*). McCullough's work on forgiveness provides a nice counterpoint for feelings and behaviors that potentially continue or escalate a cycle of aggression. In arenas such as intimate relationships or intergroup conflict, one party may need to forgive a transgression before rebuilding can begin in earnest.

Although we will witness countless acts of violent aggression on television and film, and also will watch our screen heroes risk their lives repeatedly to save strangers, most of us rarely will witness these actual behaviors in our daily lives. Thankfully, we also are unlikely to perform the most extreme levels of these extreme behaviors: we will not commit mass murder or throw ourselves onto a live grenade to save several dozen people. We will, however, regularly experience and perpetrate less dramatic acts of aggression and prosocial behavior. Social scientists show us that these acts are multiply-determined: a complex mixture of biology, learning, personality, and motivation. Human beings may manifest ponderous contradictions, bizarre puzzles, and nearly inconceivable extremes, but these increasingly can be understood through the lens of social psychology.

Why Don't Moral People Act Morally?
Motivational Considerations

C. Daniel Batson[1] and Elizabeth R. Thompson
Department of Psychology, University of Kansas, Lawrence, Kansas

Abstract

Failure of moral people to act morally is usually attributed to either learning deficits or situational pressures. We believe that it is also important to consider the nature of moral motivation. Is the goal actually to be moral (moral integrity) or only to appear moral while, if possible, avoiding the cost of being moral (moral hypocrisy)? Do people initially intend to be moral, only to surrender this goal when the costs of being moral become clear (overpowered integrity)? We have found evidence of both moral hypocrisy and overpowered integrity. Each can lead ostensibly moral people to act immorally. These findings raise important questions for future research on the role of moral principles as guides to behavior.

Keywords

morality; integrity; hypocrisy; motivational conflict

Moral people often fail to act morally. One of the most important lessons to be learned from the tragically common atrocities of the past century—the endless procession of religious wars, mass killings, ethnic cleansings, terrorist bombings, and corporate cover-ups of product dangers—is that horrendous deeds are not done only by monsters. People who sincerely value morality can act in ways that seem to show a blatant disregard for the moral principles held dear. How is this possible?

Answers by psychologists tend to be of two types. Those who approach the problem from a developmental perspective are likely to blame a learning deficit: The moral principles must not have been learned well enough or in the right way. Those who approach the problem from a social-influence perspective are likely to blame situational pressures: Orders from a higher authority (Milgram, 1974) and pressure to conform (Asch, 1956) can lead one to set aside or disengage moral standards (Bandura, 1999).

There is truth in each of these explanations of moral failure. Yet neither, nor the two combined, is the whole truth. Even people who have well-internalized moral principles, and who are in relatively low-pressure situations, can fail to act morally. To understand how, one needs to consider the nature of moral motivation.

MORAL HYPOCRISY

It is often assumed that moral individuals want to be moral, to display *moral integrity*. But our research suggests that at least some individuals want to appear moral while, if possible, avoiding the cost of actually being moral. We call this motive *moral hypocrisy*.

To examine the nature of moral motivation, we have used a simple—but real—moral dilemma. The dilemma involves having research participants assign themselves and another participant (actually fictitious) to different tasks. One task is clearly more desirable; it has positive consequences (the chance to earn raffle tickets). The other task has neutral consequences (no chance to earn raffle tickets) and is described as rather dull and boring. Participants are told that the other participant will not know that they were allowed to assign the tasks; the other participant will think the assignment was made by chance. Most research participants faced with this simple situation assign themselves the positive-consequences task (70% to 80%, depending on the specific study), even though in retrospect very few (less than 10%) say that this was the moral thing to do. Their actions fail to fit their moral principles (Batson, Kobrynowicz, Dinnerstein, Kampf, & Wilson, 1997).

Adding a Salient Moral Standard . . . and a Coin

Other participants have been confronted with a slightly more complex situation. The written instructions that inform them of the opportunity to assign the tasks include a sentence designed to make the moral standard of fairness salient: "Most participants feel that giving both people an equal chance—by, for example, flipping a coin—is the fairest way to assign themselves and the other participant to the tasks." A coin is provided for participants to flip if they wish. Under these conditions, virtually all participants say in retrospect that either assigning the other participant the positive-consequences task or using a fair method such as the coin flip is the most moral thing to do. Yet only about half choose to flip the coin.

Of those who choose not to flip, most (80% to 90%, depending on the specific study) assign themselves to the positive-consequences task. More interesting and revealing, the same is true of those who flip the coin; most (85% to 90%) assign themselves the positive consequences. In study after study, the proportion who assign themselves the positive-consequences task after flipping the coin has been significantly greater than the 50% that would be expected by chance. This was true even in a study in which the coin was labeled "SELF to POS" on one side and "OTHER to POS" on the other side. Clearly, some participants who flip the coin do not abide by the outcome. To appear fair by flipping the coin, yet still serve self-interest by ignoring the coin and assigning oneself the positive-consequences task, seems to be evidence of moral hypocrisy. Ironically, this hypocrisy pattern was especially strong among persons scoring high on a self-report measure of moral responsibility (Batson et al., 1997; Batson, Thompson, Seuferling, Whitney, & Strongman, 1999)

. . . And a Mirror

Other participants face an even more complex situation. After being provided the fairness standard and coin to flip, they assign the tasks while sitting in front of a mirror. The mirror is used to increase self-awareness and, thereby, pressure to reduce discrepancy between the moral standard of fairness and the task assignment (Wicklund, 1975). In a study that presented participants with this situation, exactly half of those who chose to flip the coin assigned themselves to the positive-consequences task. Apparently, having to face head-on the discrepancy between their avowed moral standard (be fair) and their standard-violating behavior (unfairly ignoring the result of the coin flip) was too much. In front of the mirror, those who wish to appear moral must be moral (Batson et al., 1999).

Taken together, the results of these studies seem to provide considerable evidence of moral hypocrisy. They conform precisely to the pattern we would expect if the goal of at least some research participants is to appear moral yet, if possible, avoid the cost of being moral. To the extent that moral hypocrisy is their motive, it is hardly surprising that ostensibly moral people fail to act morally. Any situational ambiguity that allows them to feign morality yet still serve self-interest—such as we provide by allowing participants to flip the coin—will undermine moral action if their motive is moral hypocrisy.

OVERPOWERED INTEGRITY

Before concluding that the world is full of moral hypocrites, it is important to consider a quite different motivational explanation for the failure of participants in our studies to act morally. Perhaps at least some of those who flip the coin do so with a genuine intent to assign the tasks fairly. Their initial motive is to be moral (moral integrity). But when they discover that the flip has gone against them and their intent to be moral will cost them the positive-consequences task, conflict arises. Self-interest overpowers integrity, with the result that they appear moral by flipping the coin, yet still serve self-interest. The general idea of overpowered integrity is, then, that a person's motivation to be truly moral may be overpowered by stronger self-interested motives when being moral entails personal cost (as it often does). In the words of the oft-quoted biblical phrase, "The spirit is willing, but the flesh is weak" (Matthew 26: 41).

Empirically Differentiating Moral Hypocrisy and Overpowered Integrity

How might one know which motivational process is operating, moral hypocrisy or overpowered integrity? The key difference between the two is the actor's intent when initially faced with a moral dilemma. In the former process, the initial motive is to appear moral yet avoid the cost of being moral; in the latter, the initial motive is to be moral. One factor that should clarify which of these motives is operating when people initially face a moral dilemma is whether they want to maintain control over the outcome of an apparently moral way to resolve the dilemma.

In our task-assignment paradigm, research participants motivated by moral hypocrisy, who intend to give themselves the positive consequences yet also appear moral, should be reluctant to let someone else flip the coin. If a coin is to be flipped, it is important that they be the ones to do so because only then can they rig the outcome. In contrast, participants initially motivated to be moral, who genuinely want to assign the tasks fairly, should have no need to maintain control of the flip. It should make no difference who flips the coin; any fair-minded person will do.

Following this logic, we gave participants an additional decision option: They could allow the task assignment to be determined by the experimenter flipping a coin. Of participants who were faced with this situation (no mirror present) and used a coin flip, 80% chose to have the assignment determined by the experimenter's flip rather than their own. This pattern suggested that many participants' initial motive was moral integrity, not moral hypocrisy (Batson, Tsang, & Thompson, 2000).

Two further studies provided evidence that this integrity could be overpowered. In these studies, we increased the cost of being moral. Instead of being neutral, consequences of the less desirable task were negative. Participants were told that every incorrect response on the negative-consequences task would be punished with a mild but uncomfortable electric shock. Faced with the prospect of receiving shocks, only one fourth of the participants were willing to let the experimenter's flip determine the task assignment. Another fourth flipped the coin themselves; of these, 91% assigned themselves the positive-consequences task, indicating once again a biased coin flip. Almost all of the remaining one half showed clear signs of overpowered integrity. They gave up any pretense of morality and assigned themselves the positive-consequences task without even feigning fairness. They were also quite ready, in retrospect, to admit that the way they assigned the tasks was not morally right.

Cost-Based Justification for Setting Morality Aside

How did these last participants deal with the clear discrepancy between their moral standards and their action? Comments made during debriefing suggest that many considered the relatively high personal cost introduced by the prospect of receiving electric shocks to be sufficient justification for not acting on their principles.

A cost-based justification for setting aside moral principles may seem quite understandable. After all, it is no surprise that participants do not want to receive electric shocks. But a cost-based justification carries ironic and chilling implications. just think: If personal cost is sufficient to justify setting aside moral principles, then one can set aside morality when deciding whether to stand by or intervene as the perpetrators of hate crimes pursue their victims. One can set aside morality when considering one's own position of wealth while others are in poverty. One can set aside morality when considering whether to recycle newspaper or plastic containers or whether to contribute one's fair share to public television. Yet is it not in precisely such situations that moral principles are supposed to do their most important work as guides to behavior?

If, as is often assumed, the social role of morality is to keep individuals from placing their own interests ahead of the parallel interests of others, then cost-based justification poses a serious problem. A principle that says, "Do not give your own interests priority ... unless there is personal cost," is tantamount to having no real principle at all. It turns morality into a luxury item—something one might love to have but, given the cost, is content to do without.

CONCLUSION

We have considered the interplay of three different motives: First is self-interest. If the self has no clear stake in a situation, then moral principles are not needed to restrain partiality. Second is moral integrity, motivation to be moral as an end in itself. Third is moral hypocrisy, motivation to appear moral while, if possible, avoiding the cost of actually being moral. We have suggested two motivational explanations for the failure of ostensibly moral people to act morally: moral hypocrisy and overpowered integrity. The latter is the product of a conflict between self-interest and moral integrity: A person sincerely intends to act morally, but once the costs of being moral become clear, this initial intent is overpowered by self-interest. Our research indicates that both moral hypocrisy and overpowered integrity exist, and that each can lead moral people to act immorally. Moreover, our research indicates that the problem is not simply one of inconsistency between attitude and behavior—between saying and doing—produced by failure to think about relevant behavioral standards. Making relevant moral standards salient (e.g., by suggesting that a coin toss would be the fairest way to assign tasks) did little to increase moral behavior. The moral lapses we have observed are, we believe, best understood motivationally.

We have only begun to understand the nature of moral motivation. There are persistent and perplexing questions still to be answered. For example, what socialization experiences stimulate moral integrity and hypocrisy, respectively? To what degree do parents preach the former but teach the latter? How might one structure social environments so that even those individuals motivated by moral hypocrisy or vulnerable to overpowered integrity might be led to act morally? Answers to such intriguing—and challenging—questions may help society avoid the atrocities of the past century in the next.

Recommended Reading

Bandura, A. (1999). (See References)
Batson, C.D., Kobrynowicz, D., Dinnerstein, J.L., Kampf, H.C., & Wilson, A.D. (1997). (See References)
Batson, C.D., Thompson, E.R., Seuferling, G., Whitney, H., & Strongman, J. (1999). (See References)
Bersoff, D.M. (1999). Why good people sometimes do bad things: Motivated reasoning and unethical behavior. *Personality and Social Psychology Bulletin, 25,*28-39.
Todorov, T. (1996). *Facing the extreme: Moral life in the concentration camps* (A. Denner & A. Pollak, Trans.). New York: Henry Holt.

Note

1. Address correspondence to C. Daniel Batson, Department of Psychology, University of Kansas, Lawrence, KS 66045.

References

Asch, S. (1956). Studies of independence and conformity: A minority of one against a unanimous majority. *Psychological Monographs, 70* (Whole No. 416).
Bandura, A. (1999). Moral disengagement in the perpetration of inhumanities. *Personality and Social Psychology Review, 3,* 193-209.
Batson, C.D., Kobrynowicz, D., Dinnerstein, J.L., Kampf, H.C., & Wilson, A.D. (1997). In a very different voice: Unmasking moral hypocrisy. Journal of Personality and Social Psychology, 72, 1335-1348.
Batson, C.D., Thompson, E.R., Seuferling, G., Whitney, H., & Strongman, J. (1999). Moral hypocrisy: Appearing moral to oneself without being so. *Journal of Personality and Social Psychology, 77,* 525-537.

Batson, C.D., Tsang, J., & Thompson, E.R. (2000). *Weakness of will: Counting the cost of being moral.* Unpublished manuscript, University of Kansas, Lawrence.

Milgram, S. (1974). *Obedience to authority: An experimental view.* New York: Harper & Row.

Wicklund, R.A. (1975). Objective self-awareness. In L. Berkowitz (Ed.), *Advances in experimental social psychology* (Vol. 8, pp. 233-275). New York: Academic Press.

Critical Thinking Questions

1. Immoral behavior typically has been addressed by either a developmental or a social influence perspective. Explain each perspective and describe how considering the motivation of immoral behavior goes beyond these two perspectives.

2. Distinguish between moral hypocrisy and overpowered integrity as motives for immoral behavior. Explain how each has been demonstrated experimentally.

3. Discuss the role of salience and self-awareness in moral hypocrisy. Describe the relevant research for each.

4. Describe the idea behind cost-based justification for acting immorally. What are some of the real-life implications for behaving this way?

Forgiveness: Who Does It and How Do They Do It?

Michael E. McCullough[1]
Department of Psychology, Southern Methodist University, Dallas, Texas

Abstract

Forgiveness is a suite of prosocial motivational changes that occurs after a person has incurred a transgression. People who are inclined to forgive their transgressors tend to be more agreeable, more emotionally stable, and, some research suggest, more spiritually or religiously inclined than people who do not tend to forgive their transgressors. Several psychological processes appear to foster or inhibit forgiveness. These processes include empathy for the transgressor, generous attributions and appraisals regarding the transgression and transgressor, and rumination about the transgression. Interpreting these findings in light of modern trait theory would help to create a more unified understanding of how personality might influence forgiveness.

Keywords

forgiveness; research; review; personality; theory

Relating to others—whether strangers, friends, or family—inevitably exposes people to the risk of being offended or harmed by those other people. Throughout history and across cultures, people have developed many strategies for responding to such transgressions. Two classic responses are avoidance and revenge—seeking distance from the transgressor or opportunities to harm the transgressor in kind. These responses are normal and common, but can have negative consequences for individuals, relationships, and perhaps society as a whole.

Psychologists have been investigating interpersonal transgressions and their aftermath for years. However, although many of the world's religions have advocated the concept of forgiveness as a productive response to such transgressions (McCullough & Worthington, 1999), scientists have begun only recently to devote sustained attention to forgiveness. Nevertheless, researchers have made substantial progress in illuminating forgiveness during this short amount of time.

WHAT IS FORGIVENESS?

Most psychologists concur with Enright, Gassin, and Wu (1992) that forgiveness is distinct from pardon (which is more apposite to the legal realm), condonation (which implies justifying the transgression), and excusing (which implies recognition that the transgressor had a good reason for committing the transgression). Most scholars also concur that forgiveness is distinct from reconciliation—a term implying restoration of a relationship. But what is forgiveness foundationally? The first definition for "forgive" in *Webster's New Universal Unabridged Dictionary* (1983) is "to give up resentment against or the desire to punish; to stop being angry with; to pardon" (p. 720). Although this definition conflates the concepts of forgiveness and pardon, it nearly suffices as an adequate psychological definition because it points to what is perhaps the essence of forgiveness: prosocial motivational change on the victim's part. By using the term "prosocial," I am suggesting that when people forgive, they become less motivated to harm their transgressor (or their relationship with the transgressor) and, simultaneously, become more motivated to act in ways that will benefit the transgressor (or their relationship with the transgressor).

My colleagues and I have assumed that most people are motivated (at least initially) to respond to transgressions with other forms of negative behavior—particularly, to avoid contact with the transgressor and to seek revenge. When people forgive, they counteract or modulate these motivations to avoid or seek revenge so that the probability of restoring benevolent and harmonious interpersonal relations with their transgressors is increased (McCullough, Bellah, Kilpatrick, & Johnson, 2001; McCullough et al., 1998; McCullough, Worthington, & Rachal, 1997). When people indicate that they have forgiven a transgressor, we believe they are indicating that their perceptions of the transgression and transgressor no longer stimulate motivations for avoidance and revenge. Instead, a forgiver experiences the return of benevolent, constructive motivations regarding the transgressor. In this conceptualization, forgiveness is not a motivation per se, but rather, a complex of prosocial changes in one's motivations.

Locating forgiveness at the motivational level, rather than at the level of overt behaviors, accommodates the fact that many people who would claim to have forgiven someone who has harmed them might not behave in any particularly new and benevolent way toward their transgressors. Forgiveness might not cause an employee who forgives her boss for an insult to behave any less negatively toward the boss: Avoidance and revenge in the workplace can put one's job at risk, so most people are probably careful to inhibit the expression of such negative motivations in the first place, regardless of how strong they might have been as a result of the transgression. The motivational definition does imply, however, that the employee would experience a reduced *potential* for avoidant and vengeful behavior (and an increased potential for benevolent behavior) toward the boss, which might or might not be expressed overtly. A motivational definition also accommodates the fact that someone can make public gestures of forgiveness toward his or her transgressor even in the absence of such prosocial motivational changes.

How would one describe the sorts of people who tend to engage in the motivational transformations collectively called forgiveness? What psychological processes appear to help people forgive? Several research teams have been investigating these questions in detail. In this article, I describe what psychological science has revealed about who tends to forgive and the psychological processes that may foster or hinder forgiveness for specific transgressions.

THE FORGIVING PERSONALITY

Researchers have found that the disposition to forgive is correlated (positively or negatively) with a broad array of variables, including several personality traits, psychological symptoms, moral emotions, hope, and self-esteem (e.g., see Berry,

Worthington, Parrott, O'Connor, & Wade, in press; Tangney, Fee, Reinsmith, Boone, & Lee, 1999). For simplicity, it is useful to reduce this potentially bewildering array of correlates to a smaller set of higher-order personality factors, such as those in the Five Factor (or Big Five) personality taxonomy (McCrae & Costa, 1999). Several recent research efforts suggest that the disposition to forgive may be related most strongly to two of these higher-order dimensions: agreeableness and emotional stability (Ashton, Paunonen, Helmes, & Jackson, 1998; Berry et al., in press; McCullough et al., 2001; McCullough & Hoyt, 1999). Some evidence also suggests that the disposition to forgive is related positively to religiousness and spirituality.

Agreeableness

Agreeableness is a personality dimension that incorporates traits such as altruism, empathy, care, and generosity. Highly agreeable people tend to thrive in the interpersonal realm and experience less conflict in relationships than less agreeable people do. Trait theorists and researchers have long been aware that agreeable people typically are rated highly on descriptors such as "forgiving" and low on descriptors such as "vengeful." Research specifically on the disposition to forgive has also confirmed the agreeableness-forgiveness association (Ashton et al., 1998; McCullough & Hoyt,1999).

People who appear dispositionally inclined to forgive also possess many of the lower-order traits that agreeableness subsumes. For instance, compared with people who are not inclined to forgive, they tend to be less exploitative of and more empathic toward others (Tangney et al., 1999). They also report higher levels of moral responsibility and demonstrate a greater tendency to share resources with people who have been rude and inconsiderate to them (Ashton et al., 1998).

Emotional Stability

Emotional stability is a personality dimension that involves low vulnerability to experiences of negative emotion. Emotionally stable people also tend not to be moody or overly sensitive. Several studies demonstrate that people who are high in emotional stability score higher on measures of the disposition to forgive than do their less emotionally stable counterparts (Ashton et al., 1998; Berry et al., in press; McCullough & Hoyt,1999).

Religiousness and Spirituality

A third personality trait that might be related to the disposition to forgive—and one that recent research suggests is empirically distinct from the Big Five personality factors—is religiousness or spirituality. A review of results from seven studies suggested that people who consider themselves to be highly religious or spiritual tend to value forgiveness more highly and see themselves as more forgiving than do people who consider themselves less religious or spiritual (McCullough & Worthington, 1999).

Despite the consistency of the existing evidence on this point, few studies have addressed whether religiousness and spirituality are associated with forgiving specific transgressors for specific, real-life transgressions. Indeed, studies addressing this issue hint that religiousness-spirituality and forgiveness of individual transgressions may be essentially unrelated (e.g., McCullough & Worthington, 1999). Therefore, it is possible that religious and spiritual people are no more forgiving than are less religious and spiritual people in real life, but only believe themselves (or aspire) to be highly forgiving. The connection of religiousness and spirituality to forgiveness of actual transgressions remains to be investigated more fully (McCullough & Worthington, 1999).

WHAT DO PEOPLE DO WHEN THEY FORGIVE?

Recent research has also helped to illuminate the psychological processes that people employ when they forgive. The processes that have been studied to date include empathy, attributions and appraisals, and rumination.

Empathy for the Transgressor

Empathy has been defined by some scholars as the vicarious experience of another person's emotional state, and by others as a specific emotion characterized by compassion, tenderness, and sympathy. Empathy (defined as a specific emotional state) for a particular transgressor correlates strongly with the extent to which a victim forgives the transgressor for a particular transgression. In several correlational studies (McCullough et al., 1997, 1998; Worthington et al., 2000), people's reports of the extent to which they had forgiven a specific transgressor were highly correlated with the extent to which they experienced empathy for the transgressor.

Empathy also helps explain why some social-psychological variables influence forgiveness. The well-known effect of transgressors' apologies on victims' likelihood of forgiving apparently is almost totally mediated by the effects of the apologies on victims' empathy for the transgressors (McCullough et al., 1997, 1998). When transgressors apologize, they implicitly express some degree of fallibility and vulnerability, which might cause victims to feel empathic, thereby motivating them to forgive the transgressors. Also, research on psychological interventions designed to help people forgive specific transgressors has revealed that empathy fosters forgiveness. Indeed, empathy for the transgressor is the only psychological variable that has, to date, been shown to facilitate forgiveness when induced experimentally (McCullough et al., 1997; Worthington et al., 2000), although experimental research on this issue is still in its infancy.

Generous Attributions and Appraisals

Another factor associated with the extent to which someone forgives a specific transgressor is the extent to which the victim makes generous attributions and appraisals about the transgression and transgressor. Compared with people who have not forgiven their transgressors, people who have forgiven their transgressors appraise the transgressors as more likable (Bradfield & Aquino, 1999), and the transgressors' explanations for the transgressions as more adequate and honest (Shapiro,1991). In such situations, forgiveness is also related to the victim's appraisal of the severity of the transgression (Shapiro, 1991). People who tend to forgive their spouses also tend to attribute less responsibility to their spouses for their negative behavior than do people who do not tend to forgive their spouses (Fincham, 2000). Thus, forgivers apparently are inclined to give their transgressors "the benefit of the doubt." Whether the correlations between appraisals-attributions and forgiveness reflect the causal effects of attributional and appraisal processes, or simply reflect victims' accurate perceptions of the actual qualities of transgressors and transgressions that cause them to be more or less forgivable, remains to be explored more fully in the future.

Rumination About the Transgression

A third factor associated with the extent to which someone forgives a specific transgressor is the extent to which the victim ruminates about the transgression. Rumination, or the tendency to experience intrusive thoughts, affects, and images about past events, appears to hinder forgiveness. The more people brood about a transgression, the higher are their levels of revenge and avoidance motivation (McCullough et al., 1998, 2001). In a recent longitudinal study, my colleagues and I also found that victims who continued to ruminate about a particular transgression made considerably less progress in forgiving the transgressor during an 8-week follow-up period (McCullough et al., 2001). This longitudinal evidence indicates that the degree to which people reduce their ruminations about a particular transgression over time is a good predictor of how much progress they will make in forgiving their transgressor.

FUTURE RESEARCH AND THEORY

So far, research has shown that people who are more agreeable, more emotionally stable, and (possibly) more spiritual or religious have a stronger disposition to forgive than do their less agreeable, less emotionally stable, and less spiritually and religiously inclined counterparts. Moreover, research has shown that empathizing with the transgressor, making generous attributions and appraisals regarding the transgressor and transgression, and refraining from rumination about the transgression are associated with the extent to which a victim forgives a specific transgressor.

An interesting step for future research on the personality factors and psychological mechanisms associated with forgiveness would be to explore the specific cognitive and emotional habits of agreeable, emotiorally stable, and (perhaps) religiously or spiritually inclined people that predispose them to forgive. For example, agreeableness reflects a tendency toward kindness and prosociality, so perhaps agreeable people are particularly inclined to experience empathy for their transgressors. They might also be inclined to perceive the transgressions they have incurred as less intentional and less severe, and their transgressors as more likable and contrite, than do less agreeable people.

Likewise, emotionally stable people might find forgiveness easier than people who are less emotionally stable because of perceptual processes: Emotionally stable people perceive many environmental factors—including physical pain and negative life events—less negatively than do less emotionally stable people. Emotionally stable people also ruminate less about negative life events. Research addressing such potential links between personality traits and psychological processes would enrich psychology's understanding of how personality might influence the extent to which people forgive particular transgressors.

Such empirical advances should be coupled with theoretical refinements. It might prove particularly useful to frame such investigations in the context of modern trait theory. Trait theorists such as McCrae and Costa (1999) have advocated for conceptualizing the empirical links between traits and real-life behavioral proclivities as causal connections that reflect how *basic tendencies* (i.e., traits) are "channelized" into *characteristic adaptations*, or approaches to negotiating life within one's own cultural and environmental context. Using McCrae and Costa's framework to theorize about forgiveness might explain how the basic, biologically based tendencies that are reflected in measures of higher-order personality dimensions lead people to use forgiveness to address certain problems encountered in daily life—namely, interpersonal transgressions.

Such a theoretical framework could lead to other interesting questions: Insofar as forgiveness can be viewed as a characteristic adaptation of agreeable and emotionally stable people, why might agreeable and emotionally stable people be predisposed to use forgiveness for navigating their social worlds? Is forgiveness a by-product of other characteristic adaptations resulting from agreeableness and emotional stability (such as a capacity for empathy, a tendency to make generous attributions regarding the negative behavior of other people, or an ability to refrain from rumination about negative events)? Or is it more accurate to view forgiveness as a goal to which agreeable and emotionally stable people actively strive, using the other characteristic psychological adaptations (e.g., capacity for empathy, tendency to form generous attributions, disinclination to ruminate) associated with agreeableness and emotional stability as footholds on the climb toward that goal? Answers to these questions would raise even more interesting questions. In any case, more sophisticated theorizing would transform this new area of research from simply a search for the correlates of forgiveness to a quest to truly understand forgiveness and its place in human personality and social functioning.

Recommended Reading

McCrae, R.R., & Costa, P.T., Jr. (1999). (See References)
McCullough, M.E., Bellah, C.G., Kilpatrick, S.D., & Johnson, J.L. (2001). (See References)
McCullough, M.E., Pargament, K.I., & Thoresen, C.T. (Eds.). (2000). *Forgiveness: Theory, research, and practice.* New York: Guilford.
McCullough, M.E., Rachal, K.C., Sandage, S.J., Worthington, E.L., Brown, S.W., & Hight, T.L. (1998). (See References)
McCullough, M.E., & Worthington, E.L. (1999). (See References)

Note

1. Address correspondence to Michael McCullough, Department of Psychology, Southern Methodist University, PO Box 750442, Dallas, TX 75275-0442; e-mail: mikem@mail.smu.edu.

References

Ashton, M.C., Paunonen, S.V., Helmes, E., & Jackson, D.N. (1998). Kin altruism, reciprocal altruism, and the Big Five personality factors. *Evolution and Human Behavior, 19,* 243-255.

Berry, J.W., Worthington, E.L., Parrott, L., O'Connor, L.E., & Wade, N.G. (in press). Dispositional forgivingness: Development and construct validity of the Transgression Narrative Test of Forgivingness (TNTF). *Personality and Social Psychology Bulletin.*

Bradfield, M., & Aquino, K. (1999). The effects of blame attributions and offender likeableness on forgiveness and revenge in the workplace. *Journal of Management, 25,* 607-631.

Enright, R.D., Gassin, E.A., & Wu, C. (1992). Forgiveness: A developmental view. *Journal of Moral Education, 21,* 99-114.

Fincham, F.D. (2000). The kiss of the porcupines: From attributing responsibility to forgiving. *Personal Relationships, 7,* 1-23.

McCrae, R.R., & Costa, P.T., Jr. (1999). A five-factor theory of personality. In L.A. Pervin & O.P. John (Eds.), *Handbook of personality: Theory and research* (pp. 139-153). New York: Guilford.

McCullough, M.E., Bellah, C.G., Kilpatrick, S.D., & Johnson, J.L. (2001). Vengefulness: Relationships with forgiveness, rumination, well-being, and the Big Five. *Personality and Social Psychology Bulletin, 27,* 601-610.

McCullough, M.E., & Hoyt, W.T. (1999, August). *Recovering the person from interpersonal forgiving.* Paper presented at the annual meeting of the American Psychological Association, Boston.

McCullough, M.E., Rachal, K.C., Sandage, S.J., Worthington, E.L., Brown, S.W., & Hight, T.L. (1998). Interpersonal forgiving in close relationships: II. Theoretical elaboration and measurement. *Journal of Personality and Social Psychology, 75,* 1586-1603.

McCullough, M.E., & Worthington, E.L. (1999). Religion and the forgiving personality. *Journal of Personality, 67,* 1141-1164.

McCullough, M.E., Worthington, E.L., & Rachal, K.C.(1997). Interpersonal forgiving in close relationships. *Journal of Personality and Social Psychology, 73,* 321-336.

Shapiro, D.L. (1991). The effects of explanations on negative reactions to deceit. *Administrative Science Quarterly, 36,* 614-630.

Tangney, J., Fee, R., Reinsmith, C., Boone, A.L., & Lee, N. (1999, August). *Assessing individual differences in the propensity to forgive.* Paper presented at the annual meeting of the American Psychological Association, Boston.

Webster's new universal unabridged dictionary. (1983). New York: Dorset and Baker.

Worthington, E.L., Kurusu, T.A., Collins, W., Berry, J.W., Ripley, J.S., & Baier, S.N. (2000). Forgiving usually takes time: A lesson learned by studying interventions to promote forgiveness. *Journal of Psychology and Theology, 28,* 3-20.

Critical Thinking Questions

1. Like the Batson and Thompson article in this section, the author emphasizes the role of motivation in social processes. Describe what he means by defining forgiveness as "a suite of prosocial motivational changes."

2. Describe the "forgiving personality." Use research in your description, and speculate on why certain personality traits might be associated with forgiveness.

3. Distinguish among empathy, attributions, and ruminations as psychological processes important in forgiving. Explain why examining processes, as well as personality traits, might lead to a more complete understanding of forgiveness.

Self-Esteem, Narcissism, and Aggression: Does Violence Result From Low Self-Esteem or From Threatened Egotism?

Roy F. Baumeister,[1] Brad J. Bushman, and W. Keith Campbell

Department of Psychology, Case Western Reserve University, Cleveland, Ohio (R.F.B., W.K.C.), and Department of Psychology, Iowa State University, Ames, Iowa (B.J.B.)

Abstract

A traditional view holds that low self-esteem causes aggression, but recent work has not confirmed this. Although aggressive people typically have high self-esteem, there are also many nonaggressive people with high self-esteem, and so newer constructs such as narcissism and unstable self-esteem are most effective at predicting aggression. The link between self-regard and aggression is best captured by the theory of threatened egotism, which depicts aggression as a means of defending a highly favorable view of self against someone who seeks to undermine or discredit that view.

Keywords

aggression; violence; self-esteem; narcissism

For decades, the prevailing wisdom has held that low self-esteem causes aggression. Many authors have cited or invoked this belief or used it as an implicit assumption to explain their findings regarding other variables (e.g., Gondolf,1985; Levin & McDevitt, 1993; Staub, 1989). The origins of this idea are difficult to establish. One can search the literature without finding any original theoretical statement of that view, nor is there any seminal investigation that provided strong empirical evidence that low self-esteem causes aggression. Ironically, the theory seemed to enter into conventional wisdom without ever being empirically established.

The view of low self-esteem that has emerged from many research studies does not, however, seem easily reconciled with the theory that low self-esteem causes aggression. A composite of research findings depicts people with low self-esteem as uncertain and confused about themselves, oriented toward avoiding risk and potential loss, shy, modest, emotionally labile (and having tendencies toward depression and anxiety), submitting readily to other people's influence, and lacking confidence in themselves (see compilation by Baumeister, 1993).

None of these patterns seems likely to increase aggression, and some of them seem likely to discourage it. People with low self-esteem are oriented toward avoiding risk and loss, whereas attacking someone is eminently risky. People with low self-esteem lack confidence of success, whereas aggression is usually undertaken in the expectation of defeating the other person. Low self-esteem involves submitting to influence, whereas aggression is often engaged in to resist and reject external influence. Perhaps most relevant, people with low self-esteem are confused and uncertain about who they are, whereas aggression is likely to be an attempt to defend and assert a strongly held opinion about oneself.

PAINTING THE PICTURE OF VIOLENT MEN

An alternative to the low-self-esteem theory emerges when one examines what is known about violent individuals. Most research has focused on violent men, although it seems reasonable to assume that violent women conform to similar patterns. Violent men seem to have a strong sense of personal superiority, and their violence often seems to stem from a sense of wounded pride. When someone else questions or disputes their favorable view of self, they lash out in response.

An interdisciplinary literature review (Baumeister, Smart, & Boden, 1996) found that favorable self-regard is linked to violence in one sphere after another. Murderers, rapists, wife beaters, violent youth gangs, aggressive nations, and other categories of violent people are all marked by strongly held views of their own superiority. When large groups of people differ in self-esteem, the group with the higher self-esteem is generally the more violent one.

When self-esteem rises or falls as a by-product of other events, aggressive tendencies likewise tend to covary, but again in a pattern precisely opposite to what the low-self-esteem theory predicts. People with manic depression, for example, tend to be more aggressive and violent during their manic stage (marked by highly favorable views of self) than during the depressed phase (when self-esteem is low). Alcohol intoxication has been shown to boost self-esteem temporarily, and it also boosts aggressive tendencies. Changes in the relative self-esteem levels of African-American and white American citizens have been accompanied by changes in relative violence between the groups, and again in the direction opposite to the predictions of the low-self-esteem view. Hence, it appears that aggressive, violent people hold highly favorable opinions of themselves. Moreover, the aggression ensues when these favorable opinions are disputed or questioned by other people. It therefore seems plausible that aggression results from threatened egotism.

AGGRESSION, HOSTILITY, AND SELF-REGARD

Thus, the low-self-esteem theory is not defensible. Should behavioral scientists leap to the opposite conclusion, namely, that high self-esteem causes violence? No. Although clearly many violent individuals have high self-esteem, it is also necessary to know whether many exceptionally nonviolent individuals also have high self-esteem.

Perhaps surprisingly, direct and controlled studies linking self-esteem to aggression are almost nonexistent. Perhaps no one has ever bothered to study the question, but this seems unlikely. Instead, it seems more plausible that such investigations have been done but have remained unpublished because they failed to find any clear or direct link. Such findings would be consistent with the view that the category of people with high self-esteem contains both aggressive and non-aggressive individuals.

One of the few studies to link self-esteem to hostile tendencies found that people with high self-esteem tended to cluster at both the hostile and the non-hostile extremes (Kernis, Grannemann, & Barclay, 1989). The difference lay in stability of self-esteem, which the researchers assessed by measuring self-esteem on several occasions and computing how much variability each individual showed over time. People whose self-esteem was high as well as stable—thus, people whose favorable view of self was largely impervious to daily events—were the least prone to hostility of any group. In contrast, people with high but unstable self-esteem scored highest on hostility. These findings suggest that violent individuals are one subset of people with high self-esteem. High self-esteem may well be a mixed category, containing several different kinds of people. One of those kinds is very non-aggressive, whereas another is quite aggressive.

The view that individuals with high self-esteem form a heterogeneous category is gaining ground among researchers today. Some researchers, like Kernis and his colleagues, have begun to focus on stability of self-esteem. Others are beginning to use related constructs, such as narcissism. Narcissism is defined by grandiose views of personal superiority, an inflated sense of entitlement, low empathy toward others, fantasies of personal greatness, a belief that ordinary people cannot understand one, and the like (American Psychiatric Association, 1994). These traits seem quite plausibly linked to aggression and violence, especially when the narcissist encounters someone who questions or disputes his or her highly favorable assessment of self. Narcissism has also been linked empirically to high but unstable self-esteem, so narcissism seems a very promising candidate for aggression researchers to study.

We have recently undertaken laboratory tests of links among self-esteem, narcissism, and aggression (Bushman & Baumeister, 1998). In two studies, participants were insulted (or praised) by a confederate posing as another participant, and later they were given an opportunity to aggress against that person (or another person) by means of sounding an aversive blast of loud noise. In both studies, the highest levels of aggression were exhibited by people who had scored high on narcissism and had been insulted. Self-esteem by itself had no effect on aggression, and neither did either high or low self-esteem in combination with receiving the insult. These results confirmed the link between threatened egotism and aggression and contradicted the theory that low self-esteem causes violence.

Narcissism has thus taken center stage as the form of self-regard most closely associated with violence. It is not, however, entirely fair to depict narcissists as generally or indiscriminately aggressive. In our studies (Bushman & Baumeister, 1998), narcissists' aggression did not differ from that of other people as long as there was no insulting provocation. Narcissism is thus not directly a cause of aggression and should instead be understood as a risk factor that can contribute to increasing a violent, aggressive response to provocation. The causal role of the provocation itself (in eliciting aggression by narcissists) is clearly established by the experimental findings.

Moreover, even when the narcissists were insulted, they were no more aggressive than anyone else toward an innocent third person. These patterns show that the aggression of narcissists is a specifically targeted, socially meaningful response. Narcissists are heavily invested in their high opinion of themselves, and they want others to share and confirm this opinion. When other people question or undermine the flattering self-portrait of the narcissist, the narcissist turns aggressive in response, but only toward those specific people. The aggression is thus a means of defending and asserting the grandiose self-view.

Do laboratory studies really capture what happens out in the real world, where violence often takes much more serious and deadly forms than pushing a button to deliver a blast of aversive noise? To answer this question, we conducted another study in which we obtained self-esteem and narcissism scores from incarcerated violent felons (Bushman, Baumeister, Phillips, & Gilligan, 1999). We assumed that the prisoners' responses to some items (e.g., "I certainly feel useless at times") would be affected by being in prison as well as by the salient failure experience of having been arrested, tried, convicted, and sentenced. These factors would be expected to push all scores toward low self-esteem and low narcissism.

Despite any such tendency, however, the prisoners' scores again pointed toward high narcissism as the major cause of aggression. The self-esteem scores of this group were comparable to the scores of published samples. The narcissism scores, meanwhile, were significantly higher than the published norms from all other studies. In particular, the prisoners outscored the baselines from other (non-incarcerated) groups to the largest degree on subscales measuring entitlement and superiority. (Again, though, the fact that the participants were in prison might have artificially lowered scores on some items, such as vanity, exhibitionism, and authority.) These findings suggest that the dangerous aspects of narcissism are not so much simple vanity and self-admiration as the inflated sense of being superior to others and being entitled to special privileges. It is apparently fine to love oneself quietly—instead, the interpersonal manifestations of narcissism are the ones associated with violence.

DEEP DOWN INSIDE

A common question raised about these findings is whether the apparent egotism of aggressive, violent people is simply a superficial form of bluster that is put on to conceal deep-rooted insecurities and self-doubts. This question is actually an effort to salvage the low-self-esteem theory, because it suggests that aggressive people really do have low self-esteem but simply act as if they do not. For example, perhaps murderers and wife beaters really perceive themselves as inferior beings, and their aggressive assertion of superiority is just a cover-up.

The question can be handled on either conceptual or empirical grounds. Empirically, some investigators have sought to find this inner core of self-doubt and reported that they could not do so. For example, Olweus (1994) specifically rejected the view that playground bullies secretly have low self-esteem, and Jankowski (1991) likewise concluded that members of violent gangs do not carry around a load of inner insecurities or self-doubts. Likewise, a number of experts who study narcissism have reported that they could not support the traditional clinical view of an egotistical outer shell concealing inner self-loathing. Virtually all studies that have measured self-esteem and narcissism have found positive correlations between the two, indicating that narcissists have high self-esteem.

Even if such evidence could be found, though, the view that low self-esteem causes aggression would still be wrong. It is by now clear that overt low self-esteem does not cause aggression. How can hidden low self-esteem cause aggression if non-hidden low self-esteem has no such effect? The only possible response is that the hidden quality of that low self-esteem would be decisive. Yet focusing the theory on the hidden quality of low self-esteem requires one to consider what it is that is hiding it—which brings the analysis back to the surface veneer of egotism. Thus, again, it would be the sense of superiority that is responsible for aggression, even if one could show that that sense of superiority is only on the surface and conceals an underlying low self-esteem. And no one has shown that, anyway.

CONCLUSION

It is time to abandon the quest for direct, simple links between self-esteem and aggression. The long-standing view that low self-esteem causes violence has been shown to be wrong, and the opposite view implicating high self-esteem is too simple. High self-esteem is a characteristic of both highly aggressive individuals and exceptionally non-aggressive ones, and so attempts at direct prediction tend to be inconclusive. Moreover, it is unwarranted to conclude that self-views directly cause aggression. At best, a highly favorable self-view constitutes a risk factor for turning violent in response to perceptions that one's favorable view of self has been disputed or undermined by others.

Researchers have started trying to look more closely at the people with high self-esteem in order to find the aggressive ones. Patterns of narcissism and instability of self-esteem have proven successful in recent investigations, although more research is needed. At present, the evidence best fits the view that aggression is most likely when people with a narcissistically inflated view of their own personal superiority encounter someone who explicitly disputes that opinion. Aggression is thus a means of defending a highly favorable view of self against someone who seeks (even unwittingly) to deflate it. Threatened egotism, rather than low self-esteem, is the most explosive recipe for violence.

Further research can benefit by discarding the obsolete view that low self-esteem causes violence and building on the findings about threatened egotism. It would be helpful to know whether a highly favorable view of self contributes to violent response by increasing the perception of insult (i.e., by making people oversensitive) or instead by simply producing a more aggressive response to the same perceived provocation. Further, research on whether narcissistic individuals would aggress against people who know bad information about them (but have not specifically asserted it themselves) would shed light on whether it is the critical view itself or the expression of it that is decisive. Another question is what exactly narcissistic people hope to accomplish by responding violently to an insult: After all, violence does not really refute criticism in any meaningful way, but it may discourage other people from voicing similar criticisms. The emotion processes involved in egotistical violence also need to be illuminated: How exactly do the shameful feelings of being criticized transform into aggressive outbursts, and does aggression genuinely make the aggressor feel better?

Recommended Reading

Baumeister, R. (1997). *Evil: Inside human violence and cruelty.* New York: W.H. Freeman.
Baumeister, R., Smart, L., & Boden, J. (1996). (See References)
Bushman, B., & Baumeister, R. (1998). (See References)
Kernis, M., Grannemann, B., & Barclay, L. (1989). (See References)

Note

1. Address correspondence to R. Baumeister, Department of Psychology, Case Western Reserve University, Cleveland, OH 44106-7123; e-mail: rfb2@po.cwru.edu.

References

American Psychiatric Association. (1994). *Diagnostic and statistical manual of mental disorders* (4th ed.). Washington, DC: Author.
Baumeister, R. (1993). *Self-esteem.* New York: Plenum Press.
Baumeister, R., Smart, L., & Boden, J. (1996). Relation of threatened egotism to violence and aggression: The dark side of high self-esteem. *Psychological Review, 103,* 5-33.
Bushman, B., & Baumeister, R. (1998). Threatened egotism, narcissism, self-esteem, and direct and displaced aggression: Does self-love or self-hate lead to violence? *Journal of Personality and Social Psychology, 75,* 219-229.
Bushman, B., Baumeister, R., Phillips, C., & Gilligan, J. (1999). *Narcissism and self-esteem among violent offenders in a prison population.* Manuscript submitted for publication.
Gondolf, E. (1985). *Men who batter.* Holmes Beach, FL: Learning Publications.
Jankowski, M.S. (1991). *Islands in the street: Gangs and American urban society.* Berkeley: University of California Press.
Kernis, M., Grannemann, B., & Barclay, L. (1989). Stability and level of self-esteem as predictors of anger arousal and hostility. *Journal of Personality and Social Psychology, 56,* 1013-1022.
Levin, J. & McDevitt, J. (1993). *Hate crimes.* New York: Plenum Press.
Olweus, D. (1994). Bullying at school: Long-term outcomes for the victims and an effective school-based intervention program. In R. Huesmann (Ed.), *Aggressive behavior: Current perspectives* (pp. 97-130). New York: Plenum Press.
Staub, E. (1989). *The roots of evil.* New York: Cambridge University Press.

Critical Thinking Questions

1. This article provides a perfect example of why social psychologists cannot rely on common sense and instead must conduct empirical research. Discuss the research evidence that challenges the common sense notion that low self-esteem causes aggression.

2. Explain what is meant by the notion that individuals with high self-esteem are heterogeneous. How do the traits of stability and narcissism support this notion?

3. This article, like the others in this section, emphasizes the importance of motivation in social processes. Explain how the link between narcissism and aggression might be motivational in nature.

If the Television Program Bleeds, Memory for the Advertisement Recedes

Brad J. Bushman[1] and Colleen M. Phillips
Department of Psychology, Iowa State University, Ames, Iowa

Abstract

In public surveys, the most common complaint about television is the amount of violence depicted on the screen. More than half the programs shown on television are violent, and hundreds of studies have shown that viewing TV violence causes an increase in societal violence. Nevertheless, advertisers continue to sponsor violent programs. For an advertisement to be effective, people should be able to remember the brand advertised and the message in the advertisement. This article reviews the effect of TV violence on memory for ads. A meta-analysis integrating the results from 12 studies involving more than 1,700 participants shows that TV violence impairs memory for ads. The impairment occurs for males and females, for children and adults, and for people who like and do not like to watch TV violence. These results suggest that sponsoring violent programs might not be a profitable venture for advertisers.

Keywords

televised violence; memory; commercials; meta-analysis

Since it was introduced at the 1939 World's Fair in New York, television has become an integral part of American society. The average number of American households with TV sets has increased from 9% in 1950 to over 98% in 1998. The ratio of television sets to people is higher in the United States than in any other country, about 776 per 1,000 people. There are more television sets in the United States today than there are toilets.

EXTENT OF VIOLENCE ON TELEVISION

Surveys indicate that most Americans believe there is too much violence on television. In one survey, for example, people were asked to say, in their own words, what made them angry about television programming. The most common complaint was "too much violence" (TV Guide, 1992). In the National Television Violence Study (1998), researchers videotaped more than 8,000 hr of programming on cable and broadcast television in the United States, sampling between the hours of 6:00 a.m. and 11:00 p.m., 7 days a week, for 3 consecutive years. A content analysis showed that about 60% of the programs contained violence. Less than 4% of the violent programs contained an antiviolence theme. In most programs, violence was depicted as trivial, glamorous, and sanitized.

Over time, the number of violent acts an individual sees on television can accumulate to a staggering amount. By the time the average American child graduates from elementary school, he or she will have seen more than 8,000 murders and more than 100,000 other assorted acts of violence (e.g., assaults, rapes) on network television (Huston et al., 1992). The numbers are even higher if the child has access to cable television or a videocassette player, as most children do.

EFFECT OF TELEVISED VIOLENCE ON SOCIETAL VIOLENCE

Scholars have been investigating television violence as a potential contributor to societal violence almost since television was introduced to society. One reason is that the trend of violence in the industrialized world has paralleled the increase in television usage during the second half of the 20th century. Research from hundreds of studies conducted over several decades has shown that viewing violence causes an increase in societal violence (see Bushman & Huesmann, 2001, for a review).

How Strong Is the Effect of TV Violence on Aggression?

The relation between televised violence and aggression is quite strong (see Fig. 1)—nearly as strong as the relation between smoking and lung cancer. The smoking analogy is a useful one (Bushman & Anderson, 2000). Not everyone who smokes gets lung cancer, and not everyone who gets lung cancer is a smoker. Although smoking is not the only factor that causes lung cancer, it is an important factor. Similarly, not everyone who watches violent television becomes aggressive, and not everyone who is aggressive watches violent television. Although televised violence is not the only factor that causes aggression, it is an important factor. Like a first cigarette, the first violent program seen can make a person nauseated. Later, however, the person craves more and more. Repeated exposure to both cigarettes and televised violence can also have harmful long-term effects. Smoking one cigarette has little impact on the likelihood that a person will get lung cancer, but repeated exposure to tobacco smoke dramatically increases the risk of lung cancer. Similarly, watching one violent TV pro-

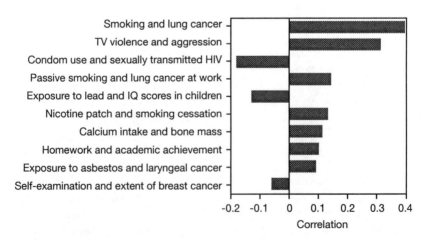

Fig. 1. Comparison of the effect of violent television programs on aggression with well-known effects from other domains. Based on meta-analytic data reported in Bushman and Anderson (2000). All of the correlations shown are significantly different from zero.

gram has little impact on the likelihood that a person will behave more aggressively, but repeated exposure to televised violence dramatically increases aggressive behavior (see Bushman & Huesmann, 2001, for a review).

I Watch TV Violence and It Doesn't Affect Me!

The fact that TV violence does not noticeably increase aggression in everybody does not mean that TV violence does not increase aggression in anybody. Medved (1995) pointed out that when an ad is shown on TV, no one expects that it will influence everybody. If the ad influences just 0.1% of viewers, it is considered highly successful. Suppose, for example, that a particular violent TV program increases aggression immediately in just 0.1% of viewers. Should society be concerned about a percentage so small? Yes! Suppose that 10 million people watch the program. If the program increases aggression in just 0.1% of viewers, then 10,000 people will behave more aggressively afterward. Because so many people are exposed to TV violence, the effect to society can be immense even if only a small percentage of people are immediately affected by what they see.

It might be that only 0.1% of viewers will behave more aggressively immediately after viewing a particular program, but the cumulative effects of watching violent TV are likely to increase the aggressiveness of most (if not all) of the viewers. Furthermore, laboratory experiments have shown that merely viewing 15 min of a relatively mild violent program increases the aggressiveness of a substantial proportion of the viewers, at least one fourth (Bushman,1995).

DOES TV VIOLENCE MIRROR VIOLENCE IN THE "REAL" WORLD?

Surveys indicate that most Americans consider "TV" to be an acronym for "too violent" (e.g., TV Guide, 1992). If most Americans say they do not like violent programs, then why do so many programs contain violence? Television industry leaders answer this question by claiming that their programs merely reflect the violence that already exists in society. For example, Leonard Goldenson of ABC said, "We are presently reaping the harvest of having laid it on the line at a time when many Americans are reluctant to accept the images reflected by the mirror we have held up to our society" ("The Industry: Fighting Violence," 1968, p. 59). However, few scholars of the subject accept this claim. As film critic Medved (1995) wrote:

If this were true, then why do so few people witness murders in real life but everybody sees them on TV and in the movies? The most violent ghetto isn't in South Central L.A. or Southeast Washington D.C.; it's on television. About 350 characters appear each night on prime-time TV, but studies show an average of seven of these people are murdered every night. If this rate applied in reality, then in just 50 days everyone in the United States would be killed and the last left could turn off the TV. (pp. 156-157)

If the television industry is a mirror that reflects the level of violence in society, then it is a funhouse mirror that provides a distorted, violent image of reality. There is far more violence in the "reel" world than in the "real" world. Even in reality-based TV programs, violence is grossly overemphasized.

WHY DO ADVERTISERS SPONSOR VIOLENT PROGRAMS?

Perhaps the most obvious reason that advertisers sponsor violent TV programs is because they believe that violent programs draw larger audiences than do nonviolent programs. A larger audience leads to a larger consumer population. Is there any truth to the belief that violent programs attract larger audiences? Historically, violent TV programs have actually attracted smaller audiences than have nonviolent programs (Hamilton, 1998). But even though violent programs do not attract larger audiences, they are valued by advertisers for at least two other reasons (see Hamilton, 1998). First, violent programs attract younger viewers. If the viewers of violent programs are categorized by age and gender, men aged 18 to 34 are the most common viewers, followed by women aged 18 to 34. Thus, although the primary audience of violent media is young men, young women have a good showing, too. This is important because women purchase many of the products that are used in households. Also, this age group of viewers is highly valuable to advertisers because younger consumers are more inexperienced than are older consumers. It takes a lot of money, time, and effort to persuade older consumers to switch brands or to try something new. It is much easier to persuade younger consumers. Second, violent programs are less expensive for advertisers to sponsor than are nonviolent programs, in terms of cost per thousand viewers in the 18- to 49-year age range.

EFFECT OF TELEVISED VIOLENCE ON MEMORY FOR COMMERCIAL MESSAGES

Advertisers especially want viewers to remember their ads. An ad may be interesting, enjoyable, and persuasive, but it may not be effective if the potential buyer cannot remember the brand advertised or the message contained in the ad. In this section, we review the scientific literature on the effect of violent programming on memory for commercial messages.

Scientific evidence from a collection of studies can be integrated and summarized in a narrative (qualitative) review or in a meta-analytic (quantitative) review. In a traditional narrative review, the reviewer uses "mental algebra" to combine the findings from a collection of studies, and describes the results verbally. In a meta-analytic review, the reviewer uses statistical procedures to integrate the findings from a collection of studies, and describes the results using a numerical effect-size estimate. An effect-size estimate provides a measure of how strongly two variables are related (e.g., smoking and lung cancer). Narrative reviews are more susceptible to the subjective judgments, preferences, and biases of a particular reviewer's perspective than are meta-analytic reviews. Therefore, we used meta-analytic procedures in our review of the effect of televised violence on memory for commercial messages.

To locate relevant studies, we searched *PsychINFO* (*PsychLIT and Psychological Abstracts*) from 1939 (the year TV was introduced to the American public) to 2000. We conducted a broad search to be sure that no relevant studies were excluded. The following terms were used: (*memory or remember* or recall* or recogni**) and (*violen* or aggress**). The asterisk allows terms to have all possible endings. For example, the term recogni* will retrieve studies that used the terms recognize, recognized, and recognition. The literature review yielded a total of 1,926 studies. We read the abstracts to determine which studies to include in the meta-analysis. A study was included if the researchers used at least one (a) violent TV program, (b) nonviolent TV program, (c) TV commercial, and (d) measure of memory for the commercial (e.g., recall, recognition). Twelve studies met the inclusion criteria. These 12 studies included a total of 1,772 participants. [2]

In the typical study on this topic, the researcher flips a coin to determine which participants watch a violent TV program and which participants watch a nonviolent TV program. The same ads are embedded in the two types of programs. After viewing the program, participants are given surprise memory tests (e.g., they are asked to recall the names of the brands advertised and the details in the commercial messages).

The average correlation between televised violence and memory for commercial messages for the 12 studies was -.19, with a 95% confidence interval ranging from -.23 to -.14. Because the confidence interval does not include the value zero, it can be concluded that televised violence significantly decreased memory for commercial messages in these studies. The average correlation is quite large. It is the same size as the correlation between wearing a condom and contracting HIV, the virus that causes AIDS (see Fig. 1).

No sex differences were found in any of the studies. That is, TV violence impaired memory for ads in both males and females. Also, no age differences were detected. TV violence impaired memory for ads in viewers of all ages. Habitual exposure to televised violence was measured in 4 of the 12 studies, but this variable did not affect the results. Television violence impaired memory for ads in people who preferred to watch violence and in people who preferred not to watch violence.

In 2 of the 12 studies, researchers included a delayed memory measure.[3] Memory was assessed 24 hr after exposure in one study and 1 month after exposure in the other study. In both studies, TV violence impaired delayed memory for ads ($r = -.22$ for 24 hr after exposure, $r = -.40$ for 1 month after exposure).

WHY DOES TV VIOLENCE IMPAIR MEMORY FOR COMMERCIAL MESSAGES?

The meta-analytic results clearly indicate that if the television program bleeds, then memory for the ad recedes. It is now time to move beyond the question of whether TV violence impairs memory for ads and ask why this impairment occurs. One possible reason is that televised violence puts people in a bad mood (e.g., it makes them angry). In a previous study (Bushman, 1998), we found that viewing violence made people angry, and the more angry people were the less they remembered about the ads. There are at least three reasons why anger might impair memory. First, negative moods interfere with the brain's encoding of information (e.g., Ellis, Thomas, & Rodriguez, 1984). Second, the angry mood induced by viewing violence might cause people to have aggressive thoughts that interfere with mental rehearsal of the ads (e.g., Berkowitz, 1984). Third, angry people might try to remedy or repair their bad mood, which takes a lot of effort (e.g., Morris & Reilly, 1987). During the time that advertisers hope viewers are absorbing the messages in ads, viewers might actually be focusing on themselves, trying to calm the anger brought on by what they have just seen on the screen. Other possible reasons for the impairment should be investigated in future research (e.g., physiological arousal, activation of aggressive thoughts).

IMPLICATIONS

It is unlikely that moral appeals from parents and other concerned citizens will influence the TV industry to reduce the amount of violent programming. The bottom line—profits—really determines what programs are shown on television. If advertisers refused to sponsor them, violent TV programs would become extinct. According to former CBS Programming Chief Jeff Sagansky, "The number one priority in television is not to transmit quality programming to viewers, but to deliver consumers to advertisers. We aren't going to get rid of violence until we get rid of advertisers" (Kim, 1994, p. 1434).

Several years ago, a spokesperson for the J. Walter Thompson Company stated: "The more we probe the issue, the more we are convinced that sponsorship of television violence is potentially bad business, as well as a social risk" ("Lousy Frames," 1977, p. 56). The scientific evidence reviewed in this article supports this conclusion. Advertisers might want to think twice about sponsoring violent programs.

The results reviewed in this article also have implications for people who are not advertisers. For example, many students study while watching television. This might be a bad idea if they are watching violent programs. If the violent programs put students in a bad mood, they might have a more difficult time recalling the material in the classroom during an exam and in the real world.

Recommended Reading

Bushman, B.J. (1998). (See References)
Hamilton, J.T. (1998). (See References)
Prasad, V.K., & Smith, L.J. (1994). Television commercials in violent programming: An experimental evaluation of their effects on children. *Journal of the Academy of Marketing Science, 22,* 340-351.

Acknowledgments—We would like to thank Craig Anderson, Veronica Dark, Len Eron, and Gary Wells for their helpful suggestions on an earlier draft of this article.

Notes

1. Address correspondence to Brad J. Bushman, Department of Psychology, Iowa State University, Ames, IA 500113180; e-mail: bushman@iastate.edu.
2. A list of the studies included in the meta-analysis can be obtained from the first author.
3. These two correlations were not included in the overall meta-analysis.

References

Berkowitz, L. (1984). Some effects of thoughts on anti-social and prosocial influences of media effects: A cognitive-neoassociation analysis. *Psychological Bulletin, 95,* 410-427.

Bushman, B.J. (1995). Moderating role of trait aggressiveness in the effects of violent media on aggression. *Journal of Personality and Social Psychology, 69,* 950-960.

Bushman, B.J. (1998). Effects of television violence on memory of commercial messages. *Journal of Experimental Psychology: Applied, 4,* 291-307.

Bushman, B.J., & Anderson, C.A. (2000). *Media violence and the American public: Scientific facts versus media misinformation.* Manuscript submitted for publication.

Bushman, B.J., & Huesmann, L.R. (2001). Effects of televised violence on aggression. In D.G. Singer & J.L. Singer (Eds.), *Handbook of children and the media* (pp. 223-254). Newbury Park, CA: Sage.

Ellis, H.C., Thomas, R.L., & Rodriguez, I.A. (1984). Emotional mood states and memory: Elaborative encoding, semantic processing, and cognitive effort. *Journal of Experimental Psychology: Learning, Memory, and Cognition, 10,* 470-482.

Hamilton, J.T. (1998). *Channeling violence: The economic market for violent television programming.* Princeton, NJ: Princeton University Press.

Huston, A.C., Donnerstein, E., Fairchild, H., Feshbach, N.D., Katz, P.A., Murray, J.P., Rubinstein, E.A., Wilcox, B.L., & Zuckerman, D. (1992). *Big world, small screen: The role of television in American society.* Lincoln: University of Nebraska Press.

The industry: Fighting violence. (1968, December 27). *Time, 92,* 58-59.

Kim, S.J. (1994). "Viewer discretion is advised": A structural approach to the issue of television violence. *University of Pennsylvania Law Review, 142,* 1383-1441.

Lousy frames for beautiful pictures: Are they changing? (1977, May 23). *Advertising Age, 48,* 56.

Medved, M. (1995, October). Hollywood's 3 big lies. *Reader's Digest, 147,* 155-158.

Morris, W.N., & Reilly, N.P. (1987). Toward the self-regulation of mood: Theory and research. *Motivation and Emotion, 11,* 215-249.

National Television Violence Study. (1998). *National television violence study* (Vol. 3). Santa Barbara, CA: The Center for Communication and Social Policy, University of California, Santa Barbara.

TV Guide. (1992, October 10-16). TV Guide poll: Would you give up TV for a million bucks? *TV Guide, 40,* 10-13, 15, 17.

Critical Thinking Questions

1. Using your knowledge of research methods, define meta-analysis, and describe its usefulness as a research technique. Explain how the authors use this technique in this article.

2. What does Figure 1 illustrate, and why would the authors include it in this article? From this figure, what can you conclude about television violence and aggression?

3. Summarize the research that indicates that advertisers should think twice about sponsoring violent programming. Describe some of the reasons that explain why they still do it.

Intergroup Conflict and Prejudice:
Effects and Resolutions

Humans form social groups with whom they interact regularly, relying upon their own group for necessities that groups especially can provide, such as protection, division of labor, and positive social regard. One's own social groups therefore are extremely important and, given the choice, people would prefer to allocate scarce resources to their own groups, protect their own groups, and evaluate their own groups favorably. In the course of ingroup favoritism, other social groups may fare less well by comparison. Prejudice, stereotyping, and discrimination can derive, at least in part, from the interplay between what people desire, value, and know about their own group relative to other groups.

Social psychologists typically construe prejudice as negative evaluations of and feelings about a group or person, simply because of group membership. Prejudice may take the form of subtle dislike, hatred, fear, or mild disquiet. Although stereotypes often include evaluative connotation, they typically are seen as a set of beliefs held about group members. Members of group X may be seen as likely to possess particular attributes and may be expected to possess those attributes. Finally, discrimination comprises negative behaviors expressed toward the outgroup. Discrimination can include institutional policies that withhold valued resources, behaviors perpetuated by groups such as ostracism from a popular clique, or behaviors perpetuated by individuals such as expressing ethnic slurs or gaze aversion.

When laypersons think about prejudice, stereotyping, and discrimination, they may call to mind blatant instances such as hate crimes, the prejudice likely to underlie ethnic slurs, and the stereotypic beliefs expressed by Archie Bunker-type television characters. A cursory look at the news indicates that, unfortunately, these instances of stereotyping, prejudice, and discrimination remain prevalent in society. As theorists have noted, however (see Fiske, 2001;), social scientists more recently have turned most of their attention to more subtle variations. In many countries, blatant discrimination and explicit expressions of prejudice and stereotyping carry legal and social sanctions. Although many individuals may avoid blatantly prejudiced behaviors because they have goals to be fair and unprejudiced in their dealings with others, other individuals simply recognize that such behaviors are socially and legally unacceptable. Prejudiced behavior may leak out when other plausible explanations are possible. For example, if an excellent outgroup member is rejected from an applicant pool, on-lookers may interpret the rejection as prejudice; if a mediocre outgroup member is rejected, on-lookers' attention may be directed toward the mediocrity (even if an equally mediocre ingroup member is not rejected).

Of course, not all outgroups are viewed identically or treated with the same level of disdain. Some laws, for example, extend protection against discrimination on the basis of ethnic group or gender, but may not extend explicitly to sexual orientation. Social norms may prohibit prejudiced statements about certain ethnic groups but not other groups (e.g., white heterosexual Americans are more reticent to express prejudiced opinions about black Americans than about people from the Middle East or about homosexual individuals). Fiske (2002) argues that perceptions of out-groups vary along two dimensions: respect and liking. For white Americans, for example, Asians may be viewed as competent (as reflected in stereotypic beliefs about savvy in math and computer science) and cold (as reflected in stereotypic beliefs about not being inclusive and behaving formally); white Americans therefore respect but dislike Asians, who are perceived as a threat to the availability of certain high-tech jobs. Conversely, women in traditionally "pink-collar" professions such as childcare workers or secretaries may be liked but not respected. Discriminatory behavior toward this group may be patronizing rather than aggressively protecting against threat.

Although concern about protecting limited resources is an important determinant of prejudice and discrimination, threats can be more broad and less tangible. Solomon, Greenberg and Pyszczynski (2000) point out that some outgroups are perceived as a threat to one's cultural worldview: Some ideas and values seem inherently correct to an ingroup, and threats to that worldview can elicit prejudiced responding. Beyond threatening cultural worldviews, research on terror management shows that anxiety about pain or death elicit prejudiced responding and ingroup favoritism. [The dramatic increase in the display of US patriotic symbols immediately after the 9/11 attack, which reaffirm cultural worldviews, easily could be interpreted in terms of terror management theory]. Herek's (2000) discussion of sexual prejudice against individuals who are not heterosexual also may derive in part from threat and anxiety. For some heterosexual individuals, the sexuality of gays and lesbians feels inconsistent with cultural values and morals. These perceived threats may, in turn, underlie discriminatory behavior and prejudiced attitudes.

People therefore discriminate against outgroups, stereotype them, view them with varying degrees of disrespect or dislike, and can experience outgroups as threatening. These phenomena are share the common thread of focusing on the perpetrator, that is, focusing on the person who expresses prejudice and stereotypic beliefs, or who enacts discriminatory behavior. The experience of the target of prejudice also merits attention but, until recently, has received relatively little attention from social psychologists. Recent work shows, for example, that targets experience stereotype threat, in which they worry so much about confirming a stereotype that their performance is impaired. Targets also may experience attributional ambiguity, in which they cannot always discern whether others' behavior toward them is based on their group membership or their personal aptitudes and efforts. Contrada and his colleagues (2000) further note that members of minority groups also may experience pressure from their fellow group members to conform to group norms. Belonging to a stereotyped group therefore carries subtle stresses and negative consequences beyond more tangible consequences such as job or housing discrimination, or hate crimes.

Given the negative consequences of prejudice—subtle or blatant—social psychological research in this area historically also has addressed an applied question: How is prejudice reduced, stereotypes disconfirmed, or discrimination undercut? One promising possibility lies in cooperative equal status interactions that create superordinate and inclusive group identities that can help reduce prejudice and discrimination. For example, a successful university marching band requires practice with one's fellow members, whose membership may cut across racial and ethnic lines, religious affiliations, and sexual orientations. When the group identity is 'our marching band,' prejudice can be undercut. Friendships with members of stereotyped groups (Dovidio & Gaertner, 1999; Fiske, 2002; Herek, 2000) similarly undercut prejudice and discrimination, presumably because the self is part of the friendship group. Thus, the positive regard that people have for their ingroups—which often underlies prejudice—also can be a powerful force in reducing prejudice.

What We Know Now About Bias and Intergroup Conflict, the Problem of the Century

Susan T. Fiske[1]

Department of Psychology, Princeton University, Princeton, New Jersey

Abstract

After nearly a century's study, what do psychologists now know about intergroup bias and conflict? Most people reveal unconscious, subtle biases, which are relatively automatic, cool, indirect, ambiguous, and ambivalent. Subtle biases underlie ordinary discrimination: comfort with one's own in-group, plus exclusion and avoidance of out-groups. Such biases result from internal conflict between cultural ideals and cultural biases. A small minority of people, extremists, do harbor blatant biases that are more conscious, hot, direct, and unambiguous. Blatant biases underlie aggression, including hate crimes. Such biases result from perceived intergroup conflict over economics and values, in a world perceived to be hierarchical and dangerous. Reduction of both subtle and blatant bias results from education, economic opportunity, and constructive intergroup contact.

Keywords

bias; stereotyping; prejudice; discrimination; intergroup conflict

People typically seek other people who are similar to themselves, being comfortable with others they perceive as members of their own in-group. From comfort follows, at best, neglect of people from out-groups and, at worst, murderous hostility toward out-groups perceived as threatening the in-group. Biases do vary by degree, and the psychologies of moderate and extreme biases differ considerably. Well-intentioned moderates reveal bias more subtle than the rants and rampages of extremists. By some counts, 80% of Western democratic populations intend benign intergroup relations but display subtle biases. In contrast, blatantly biased extremists are completely out-front. Although estimated to be a minority (perhaps 10%), they are salient, vocal, and dangerous.

After nearly a century's study, social psychology knows a lot about both forms of bias. Stereotyping, prejudice, and discrimination reflect, respectively, people's cognitive, affective, and behavioral reactions to people from other groups (Fiske, 1998). All constitute *bias*, reacting to a person on the basis of perceived membership in a single human category, ignoring other category memberships and other personal attributes. Bias is thus a narrow, potentially erroneous reaction, compared with individuated impressions formed from personal details.

SUBTLE BIAS AMONG WELL-INTENTIONED MODERATES

Automatic, Unconscious, and Unintentional

The big news from two recent decades of research: Bias is most often underground (Dovidio & Gaertner, 1986). First data showed that even among relatively unprejudiced people, racial category labels automatically prime (increase the accessibility of) stereotypes; scores of studies now support the essential automaticity of stereotypes (Fiske, 1998, 2000; Macrae & Bodenhausen, 2000). For example, even when out-group category labels are subliminally presented (i.e., presented too quickly to be consciously perceived), they activate stereotypic associations. In a more affective vein, out-group cues (such as faces or names) easily activate negative evaluative terms. Relatedly, brain imaging shows activation of the amygdala in response to out-group faces; because the amygdala is the center of fear and anxiety in the brain, its activation in response to out-groups is consistent with primitive emotional prejudices. Furthermore, automatic activation of out-group categories leads to behavior stereotypically associated with that group. For example, young people primed with the category "elderly" (vs. a neutral one) walk and respond more slowly; Whites primed with Black faces (vs. White ones) respond in a more hostile way than they normally do. Such responses create self-fulfilling prophecies in intergroup biases. Brain imaging and automatic behavior form the cutting edges of work on automatic biases.

Automatic reactions to out-group members matter in everyday behavior. Awkward social interactions, embarrassing slips of the tongue, unchecked assumptions, stereotypic judgments, and spontaneous neglect all exemplify the mundane automaticity of bias, which creates a subtly hostile environment for out-group members. The apparent automaticity of routine biases corroborates Allport's (1954) provocative early insights about the inevitability of categorization. Automaticity also shocks well-intentioned people who assume that both their own and other people's prejudice must be conscious and controllable.

All is not lost for the well-intentioned. Category activation is not *unconditionally* automatic. Although people can instantly identify another person's category membership (especially gender, race, and age), they may not always activate associated stereotypes. For example, sufficient mental overload blocks activation. People's long-term attitudes also have a moderating influence: Chronically low levels of prejudice can attenuate the activation of stereotypes. Temporary goals matter, too: Category activation depends on short-term motivations, including immediate threats to self-esteem and focused efforts toward accurate understanding.

Promising as they are, findings indicating that biases are automatic, unconscious, and unintentional remain controversial. For example, the ease of category activation differs depending on the nature of the stimuli: Activation is easy when people encounter verbal labels, harder when they encounter photographs, and hardest when they encounter real people. Some researchers believe that social categories inevitably activate associated biases, whereas others believe activation depends entirely on short-term goals and long-term individual differences (Devine, 2001).

Whether bias is conditionally or unconditionally automatic, less prejudiced perceivers still can compensate for their automatic associations with subsequent conscious effort. If category activation is conditionally automatic, then people may be able to inhibit it in the first place. In either case, motivation matters.

Moreover, even if people do activate biases associated with a category, they may not apply (or use) those biases. For example, once the category is activated, other information may be consistent or inconsistent with it, and perceivers have to decide what to do about the conflicting information. Inconsistency resolution and subsequent individuation of the other person require mental resources, which are allocated according to the perceiver's motivation and capacity. Overriding category use depends on metacognitive decisions (thinking about one's thinking) and higher-level executive functions (controlling one's thinking), not just brute attentional capacity. Other influences on whether activated categories are used go beyond the perceiver's motivation and capacity: For example, category use depends on the stimuli (general group-level abstractions encourage assimilation toward the stereotype, whereas individual exemplars encourage contrast away from it). Category use increases when the perceiver's personal theory holds that people's dispositions are fixed entities, rather than flexible states. Psychologists continue to debate the boundaries of automaticity.

Inhibition of both category activation and category application challenges even the most determined moderate. Direct suppression sometimes causes only a rebound of the forbidden biases. Depending on cognitive capacity, practice, age, and motivation, people can inhibit many effects of social categories on their thinking, feeling, and behaving. Indeed, when people adopt goals encouraging them to treat others as unique individuals or not at all as social objects, they no longer show even amygdala activation in response to faces from races other than their own (Wheeler & Fiske, 2001). The take-home message: Bias is more automatic than people think, but less automatic than psychologists thought.

Cool, Indirect, and Ambiguous

The biases of the moderate, well-intentioned majority not only live underground, they also wear camouflage. Consistent with people's biases reflecting in-group comfort at least as much as out-group discomfort, bias often consists of withholding positive emotions from out-groups. Moderates rarely express open hostility toward out-groups, but they may withhold basic liking and respect; hence, their responses represent cool neglect. People more rapidly assign positive attributes to the in-group than the out-group, but often show at best weak differences in assigning negative attributes. People withhold rewards from out-groups, relative to the in-group, reflecting favoritism (Brewer & Brown, 1998). But they rarely punish or derogate the out-group. The typical damage is relative.

Moderate biases are indirect, relying on norms for appropriate responses. If norms allow biases, they flourish. That is, biases most often appear when people have unprejudiced excuses. When contact or helping is discretionary, for example, if some people neglect out-group members, then most people do. If the out-group member behaves poorly, providing an excuse for prejudice, the resulting exclusion is more swift and sure than for a comparable in-group member. Biases also appear in political policy preferences for which one might have principled reasons (excuses), but regarding which one also just happens to have a series of opinions that all disadvantage the out-group relative to the in-group. Excuses for bias fulfill the social norm requiring rational, fair judgments, but empirically controlled comparisons reveal greater bias toward out-group members than toward comparable in-group members. Researchers continue to debate the meaning of these biases.

People also engage in attributional tricks that discourage sympathy by blaming the out-group for their own unfortunate outcomes: Members of the out-group should try harder, but at the same time they should not push themselves where they are not wanted (Catch 22). The blame goes further. Although the in-group might be excused for its failures (extenuating circumstances), the out-group brought it on themselves (unfortunate dispositions). People often attribute the out-group's perceived failings to their essence: Innate, inherent, enduring attributes, perhaps biological, especially genetic, define category distinctiveness.

In making sense of out-group members, people exaggerate cultural differences (in ability, language, religious beliefs, and sexual practices). The mere fact of categorizing into in-group "us" and out-group "them" exaggerates intercategory differences and diminishes intracategory differences: "Out-group members all are alike and different from us, besides." In short, moderates' bias is cool, indirect, and ambiguous.

Ambivalent and Mixed

Besides being underground and camouflaged, moderate biases are complex. Ambivalent racism entails, for moderate Whites, mixed "proBlack" pity and anti-Black resentment, which tips over to a predominantly positive or negative response, depending on circumstances. Ambivalent sexism is another example, demonstrating two correlated dimensions that differentiate hostile sexism (toward nontraditional women) and subjectively benevolent sexism (toward traditional women). In both cases, ambivalence indicates mixed forms of prejudice more subtle than unmitigated hostility.

Mixed biases turn out to be the rule, rather than the exception. Although various out-groups all are classified as "them," they form clusters (see Fig. 1). Some elicit less respect than others, and some elicit less liking than others. Not only is the bias of well-intentioned moderates of the cool variety (withholding the positive, rather than assigning the negative), but it is not even uniformly lacking in positive views. Specifically, some out-groups (Asians, Jews, career women, Black

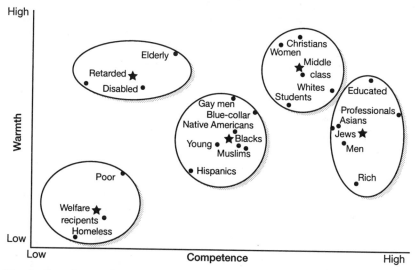

Fig. 1. Five-cluster solution showing the perceived distribution of American social groups, according to perceived competence and warmth (Fiske, Cuddy, Glick, & Xu, 2002, Study 2) Copyright by the American Psychological Association. Reprinted with permission.

professionals, rich people) are envied and respected for their perceived competence and high status, but they are resented and disliked as lacking in warmth because they compete with the in-group. Other out-groups (older people, disabled people, housewives) are pitied and disrespected for their perceived incompetence and low status, but they are nurtured and liked as warm because they do not threaten the in-group. Only a few out-groups (primarily homeless and poor people of any race) receive contempt, both dislike and disrespect, because they are seen as simultaneously low status and exploiting the in-group.

Ambivalent, mixed biases justify the status quo. Subordinated, pitied groups have an incentive to cooperate because they receive care, in return for not challenging the hierarchy. Conversely, dominant groups use subordinated groups to maintain their own relative advantage. Envied, competitive groups have an incentive to support the system because they are perceived to be succeeding, even if they are socially excluded by the culturally dominant group. For dominant groups, respecting envied groups acknowledges the ground rules for competition (which favor them also), but disliking those groups justifies social exclusion.

Moderate Biases Lead to Exclusion

Subtle biases motivate personal interactions that reek of discomfort and anxiety. Nonverbal indicators (distance, posture, voice tone) and people's own reports of their feelings all reveal intergroup interactions that are anything but smooth, mostly because of inexperience with the out-group.

Moreover, people mentally and behaviorally confirm their biased expectations, leading both groups to maintain their distance. *Self-fulfilling prophecy, expectancy effects,* and *behavioral confirmation* all name related phenomena whereby biased perceivers bring about the very behavior they anticipate, usually negative. These interpersonal processes result in subsequent avoidance, whenever people can choose the company they keep. Discretionary intergroup contact is minimized.

Furthermore, exclusion and avoidance extend to employment, housing, education, and justice that tend to favor the in-group and disadvantage the out-group. Ample evidence indicates that relatively automatic, cool, indirect, ambiguous, and ambivalent biases permit allocation of resources to maintain the in-group's advantage.

How Do Moderate Biases Originate?

Subtle prejudice comes from people's internal conflict between ideals and biases, both acquired from the culture. Direct, personal experience with out-group members may be limited. Given substantial de facto residential and occupational segregation, people lack experience in constructive intergroup interactions. Cultural media, then, supply most information about out-groups, so people easily develop unconscious associations and feelings that reinforce bias.

Simultaneously, contemporary Western ideals encourage tolerance of most out-groups. Complying with modern antiprejudice ideals requires conscious endorsement of egalitarian norms against prejudice. And moderates do endorse antiprejudice values. The upshot is a conflict between relatively implicit, unconscious biases and explicit, conscious ideals to be unprejudiced. The resulting prejudices are subtle, modern, and aversive to the people holding them.

BLATANT BIAS AMONG ILL-INTENTIONED EXTREMISTS

Hot, Direct, Unambiguous, and Conscious

In contrast to well-intentioned moderates, extremists openly resent out-groups and reject any possibility of intimacy with them (Pettigrew, 1998b). They resent out-groups—whether racial, cultural, gender, or sexual—as holding jobs that in-group members should have and (paradoxically) living on welfare unnecessarily. They believe that out-groups and the in-group can never be comfortable together. Extremists are particularly upset by intergroup intimacy. They report that they would be bothered by having a mixed grandchild, that they are unwilling to have sexual relations with out-group members, and that they are unwilling to have an out-group boss.

Extreme biases run in packs; people biased against one out-group tend to be biased against others. People's differing levels of ethnocentrism are reliably measured by old-fashioned prejudice scales that assess self-reported attitudes toward racial, ethnic, gender, and sexual out-groups.

Extreme Biases Underlie Aggression

The result is as simple as it is horrible. Because of hot, direct, unambiguous prejudices, extremists advocate segregation, containment, and even elimination of out-groups. Strong forms of bias correlate with approval of racist movements. Hate-crime perpetrators and participants in ethnic violence, not surprisingly, endorse attitudes (prejudices and stereotypes) that fit extreme forms of discrimination.

Aggression has two main goals: preserving hierarchies and preserving values perceived to be traditional. People with blatant prejudices often approve aggression to maintain the status quo, viewing current group hierarchies as inevitable and desirable. Highly prejudiced people gravitate toward jobs that enhance group hierarchy and defend the status quo (e.g., they tend to be police officers rather than social workers and businesspeople rather than educators). Blatant prejudice may also lead to self-righteous aggression against non-conformers and other people who threaten core values. If out-groups deviate and threaten traditional values, they become legitimate targets of aggression.

How Do Extreme Biases Originate?

Whether extremists are domestic or international, they endanger those they hate. People become biased extremists because they perceive threats to their in-group. Thus, extreme bias parallels the in-group favoritism of biased moderates, who also protect the in-group. Differences lie in the perceived nature and degree of threat.

Threat to economic standing has long been implicated in intergroup bias. Although still controversial, the most convincing but counterintuitive lesson here is that personal economic deprivation is not in fact the culprit. The state of people's own wallets does not motivate their degree of prejudice. Instead, the most reliable indicator is perceived threat to one's in-group. Group threat (e.g., high local unemployment) correlates with extreme biases against out-groups perceived to be responsible. The causal sequence seems to run from subjective social class to perceived group deprivation to prejudice.

Perceived threat to in-group economic status correlates with worldviews that reinforce a zero-sum, dog-eat-dog perspective. Tough-minded competition is perceived to reflect the state of intergroup relations. Economic conservatism results. Overall, blatant prejudice correlates with high social dominance orientation (Sidanius & Pratto, 1999), that is, endorsing views that superior groups should dominate inferior groups, that force may be necessary to maintain this dominance, and that group equality is neither desirable nor realistic.

Perceived threat to traditional values is the other prong of blatant bias. Extremists view the world as dangerous, with established authority and conventions in collapse. Social conservatism correlates with perceived threats to traditional values, and also with extreme bias (Altemeyer, 1996). Extremists move in tight ethnic circles and endorse right-wing authoritarian views: old-fashioned values, censorship, mighty leaders who fight evil, and suppression of troublemakers, freethinkers, women, and homosexuals.

The background of people who become extremists features limited intergroup contact—few out-group neighbors, acquaintances, and friends. Nor do extremists value such contact. They also tend to be less educated than moderates, for reasons not fully clear, although one might speculate that a liberal education broadens people's appreciation of different values.

WHAT REDUCES BIAS?

Given subtle biases that are unconscious and indirect, change is a challenge, resisting frontal assault. Similarly, given blatant biases rooted in perceived threat to group interests and core values, direct confrontation will likely fail again. Instead, more nuanced means do work.

Education does help. Economic opportunity does help. Moreover, for decades, social psychologists have studied the positive effects of constructive intergroup contact that increases mutual appreciation (Pettigrew, 1998a): When contact features (a) equal status within the immediate setting, (b) shared goals, (c) cooperation in pursuit of those goals, and (d) authorities' support, it provides a basis for intergroup friendship. Genuine intergroup friendships demonstrably do reduce stereotyping, prejudice, and discrimination of whatever sort.

WHERE NOW?

Much is known, but much remains to be learned. Promising lines of research range from imaging brain activity beyond the amygdala, to specifying intergroup emotions beyond mere antipathy, to explaining stereotype content beyond mere lists of negative traits, to predicting discrimination in all its guises, to assessing people's control over their own seemingly automatic reactions (Fiske, 2000). Bias researchers will not be unemployed any time soon.

Recommended Reading

Duckitt, J. (1992). *The social psychology of prejudice.* New York: Praeger. Eberhardt, J.L., & Fiske, S.T. (Eds.). (1998). *Confronting racism: The problem and the response.* Thousand Oaks, CA: Sage.
Oskamp, S. (Ed.), (2000). *Reducing prejudice and discrimination.* Mahwah, NJ: Erlbaum.

Note

1. Address correspondence to Susan T. Fiske, Department of Psychology, Green Hall, Princeton University, Princeton, NJ 08544-1010; e-mail: sfiske@princeton.edu.

References

Allport, G. (1954). *The nature of prejudice.* Reading, MA: Addison-Wesley.

Altemeyer, B. (1996). *The authoritarian specter.* Cambridge, MA: Harvard University Press.

Brewer, M.B., & Brown, R.J. (1998). Intergroup relations. In D.T. Gilbert, S.T. Fiske, & G. Lindzey (Eds.), *Handbook of social psychology* (4th ed., Vol. 2, pp. 554-594). New York: McGraw-Hill.

Devine, P.G. (2001). Implicit prejudice and stereotyping: How automatic are they? Introduction to the special section. *Journal of Personality and Social Psychology, 81,* 757-759.

Dovidio, J.F., & Gaertner, S.L. (Eds.). (1986). *Prejudice, discrimination, and racism.* San Diego, CA: Academic Press.

Fiske, S.T. (1998). Stereotyping, prejudice, and discrimination. In D.T. Gilbert, S.T. Fiske, & G. Lindzey (Eds.), *Handbook of social psychology* (4th ed., Vol. 2, pp. 357-411). New York: McGraw-Hill.

Fiske, S.T. (2000). Stereotyping, prejudice, and discrimination at the seam between the centuries: Evolution, culture, mind and brain. *European Journal of Social Psychology, 30,* 299-322.

Fiske, S.T., Cuddy, A.J., Glick, P., & Xu, J. (2002). A model of (often mixed) stereotype content: Competence and warmth respectively follow from perceived status and competition. *Journal of Personality and Social Psychology, 82,* 878-902.

Macrae, C.N., & Bodenhausen, G.V. (2000). Thinking categorically about others. *Annual Review of Psychology, 51,* 93-120.

Pettigrew, T.F. (1998a). Intergroup contact theory. *Annual Review of Psychology, 49,* 65-85.

Pettigrew, T.F. (1998b). Reactions toward the new minorities of western Europe. *Annual Review of Sociology, 24,* 77-103.

Sidanius, J., & Pratto, F. (1999). *Social dominance: An intergroup theory of social hierarchy and oppression.* New York: Cambridge University Press.

Wheeler, M.E., & Fiske, S.T. (2001, November). *fMRI study of three cognitive tasks that differentially modulate stereotype accessibility and human amygdala response to racial out-group faces.* Poster presented at the annual meeting of the Society for Neuroscience, San Diego, CA.

Critical Thinking Questions

1. Distinguish between the two types of biases presented in this article: subtle biases and blatant biases. How does each of these originate?

2. As brain imaging procedures become more advanced, researchers in social psychology are able to learn more about the role of the brain in social interaction. Describe the findings from brain imaging research with regard to subtle biases. Speculate on the implications of these findings.

3. The author states that bias is "more automatic than people think, but less automatic than psychologists thought." Describe the research that led to this conclusion.

4. Blatant bias against the outgroup can often have violent results, yet subtle bias can have harmful effects, too. Describe some of these effects and the societal problems these effects might cause.

Pride and Prejudice:
Fear of Death and Social Behavior

Sheldon Solomon,[1] Jeff Greenberg, and Tom Pyszczynski
*Department of Psychology, Brooklyn College, Brooklyn, New York
(S.S.); Department of Psychology, University of Arizona, Tucson,
Arizona (J.G.); and Department of Psychology, University of
Colorado at Colorado Springs, Colorado Springs, Colorado (T.P.)*

Abstract

Terror management theory posits that awareness of mortality engenders a potential for paralyzing terror, which is assuaged by cultural worldviews: humanly created, shared beliefs that provide individuals with the sense they are valuable members of an enduring, meaningful universe (self-esteem), and hence are qualified for safety and continuance beyond death. Thus, self-esteem serves the fundamental psychological function of buffering anxiety. In support of this view, studies have shown that bolstering self-esteem reduces anxiety and that reminders of mortality intensify striving for self-esteem; this research suggests that self-esteem is critical for psychological equanimity. Cultural worldviews serve the fundamental psychological function of providing the basis for death transcendence. To the extent this is true, reminders of mortality should stimulate bolstering of one's worldview. More than 80 studies have supported this idea, most commonly by demonstrating that making death momentarily salient increases liking for people who support one's worldview and hostility toward those with alternative worldviews. This work helps explain human beings' dreadful history of intergroup prejudice and violence: The mere existence of people with different beliefs threatens our primary basis of psychological security; we therefore respond by derogation, assimilation efforts, or annihilation.

Keywords

death; consciousness; anxiety; culture; self-esteem; prejudice; aggression

Why has history been plagued by a succession of appalling ethnic cleansings? Archaeologists have found bas-reliefs from 1100 B.C. depicting Assyrian invaders' practice of killing indigenous people by sticking them alive on stakes from groin to shoulder. These xenophobic propensities reached their zenith in the 20th century, when Hitler's Nazi regime perpetuated the most extensive effort at genocide in history, and have continued to resurface throughout the world in places such as Cambodia, Rwanda, Yugoslavia, and the United States—where in 1999 A.D. at Columbine High School in Littleton, Colorado, two Nazi-influenced teenagers massacred schoolmates, seemingly provoked by threats not to material well-being, but to the abstract entity known as self-esteem.

TERROR MANAGEMENT THEORY

Inspired by Ernest Becker's (e.g., 1975) interdisciplinary efforts to understand "man's inhumanity to man," terror management theory (TMT; Greenberg,

Pyszczynski, & Solomon, 1986) was developed to address two questions that had previously been neglected by academic psychologists, but are now recognized to be of fundamental importance for understanding human behavior: What are the psychological foundations of culture? What is the nature and function of self-esteem? The resulting theory is parsimonious and unique in its conceptual breadth and integrative potential (more than 80 studies have produced findings supporting hypotheses derived from TMT, investigating a wide range of topics, e.g., aggression, prejudice, in-group disidentification, sexuality, disgust, depression, self-esteem, self-awareness, defensive processes, risk taking, and creativity).

Grounded in evolutionary theory, TMT begins with two broad assumptions. First, humans share with all life forms a biological predisposition toward self-preservation and reproduction. Second, humans are unique in their use of linguistically mediated symbolic thought processes, rendering them conscious, and thus able to delay behavior in novel circumstances to ponder alternative responses and imagine that which does not yet exist, and transform the physical universe accordingly.

Consciousness is highly adaptive, but, as Kierkegaard said, brings with it the gift of awe and the burden of dread. It is awesome to be alive and know it, and dreadful to recognize that death is one's inevitable fate as an ambulatory assemblage of blood, tissue, and guts, inherently no more significant or enduring than a barnacle, a beetle, or a bell pepper. This awareness of death creates the potential for debilitating terror, managed through the development of cultural worldviews: humanly created belief systems that are shared by individuals in groups and function to minimize anxiety engendered by the awareness of death.

According to TMT, cultural worldviews lend meaning through accounts of the origin of the universe, prescriptions for behavior, and explanations of what happens after death. Cultures differ radically in their specific beliefs, but share claims that the universe is meaningful and orderly, and that immortality is attainable, be it literally, through concepts of soul and afterlife, or symbolically, through enduring accomplishments and identifications (e.g., pyramids and novels, nations and causes, wealth and fame, ancestors and offspring). Transcendence of death is based on meeting the cultural standards of value, which confers self-esteem, the belief that one is a valuable member of a meaningful universe and thereby elevated above mere material existence. TMT posits that a substantial proportion of human behavior is directed toward preserving faith in a cultural worldview and securing self-esteem in the service of death transcendence.

ISMS MAKE SCHISMS

If the cultural worldview and self-esteem serve a death-denying, anxiety-buffering function, other individuals who threaten self-esteem or espouse different cultural worldviews will typically be psychologically discombobulating because alternative conceptions of reality dispute the absolute validity of one's own. Consequently, exposure to people with different beliefs instigates a host of compensatory responses to restore psychological equanimity. These include derogating others to minimize the threat posed by their views, convincing them to abandon their beliefs in favor of one's own (e.g., missionary activity), or annihilating them entirely, thus proving the "truth" of one's own beliefs. From this perspective, the ongoing ethnic strife pervading human history is in large part the result of humans' inability to tolerate those with different death-denying visions of reality.

EMPIRICAL ASSESSMENT OF TMT

Self-Esteem as Anxiety Buffer

TMT research has been focused primarily on the anxiety-buffering capacity of self-esteem, and the death-denying function of cultural worldviews and self-esteem. In one study (Greenberg et al., 1992), we gave participants bogus personality feedback: Some received feedback intended to increase their self-esteem (increased self-esteem group), and the others received feedback that was not expected to affect their self-esteem (neutral self-esteem group). The participants then watched either video footage of an autopsy and electrocution or neutral footage. As predicted, although neutral self-esteem participants reported more anxiety after viewing the death video than did control subjects, increased self-esteem participants did not. In additional studies, we measured skin conductance (an indicator of physiological arousal associated with anxiety) of participants who received positive or neutral self-relevant feedback, and then expected to be exposed to painful electrical shocks (threat condition) or colored lights (control condition). Neutral self-esteem participants expecting shocks were more aroused than control subjects; however, increased self-esteem participants expecting shocks were significantly less aroused than their threatened neutral self-esteem counterparts. These findings support the hypothesis that self-esteem serves as an anxiety buffer.

Self-esteem has also been shown to reduce bias in reporting attributes associated with longevity. In one study, we manipulated self-esteem and told participants either that emotional people live longer than unemotional people or vice versa. In the neutral self-esteem condition, people subsequently claimed to be more or less emotional, depending on which quality predicted longevity. But this bias toward qualification for longevity was not obtained when self-esteem was temporarily elevated, or when it was dispositionally high (Greenberg, Solomon, & Pyszczynski, 1997). Research thus provides strong convergent evidence that self-esteem serves an anxiety-buffering function.

Mortality-Salience Paradigm

If cultural worldviews assuage anxiety associated with awareness of death, asking people to ponder their death (mortality salience) should increase their need for validation of the cultural worldview, resulting in affection for individuals who validate one's beliefs, and disdain for those who threaten them (worldview defense). The first mortality-salience study had American municipal court judges assign bail for an alleged prostitute after half of them completed a mortality-salience induction.[2] Because prostitution is generally considered a violation of American morals, we predicted the judges would be especially punitive after this induction. The findings confirmed this hypothesis: The average bail assigned was

$455 in the mortality-salience condition and $50 in the control condition. In a follow-up study with college students, a mortality-salience induction produced elevated bonds for the alleged prostitute, but only for participants who found prostitution immoral. Mortality salience was then shown to increase a monetary reward for heroic behavior in another scenario.[3]

Us and Them

Many studies have examined the effects of mortality salience on reactions to others who support or threaten participants' religious or political views. In one study, Christian participants evaluated Christian targets more positively and Jewish targets more negatively following a mortality-salience induction, although the targets were rated equally by control participants. In a variety of studies, American participants have evaluated pro- and anti-American essays attributed to foreign students following a mortality-salience induction or television control condition; the consistent finding is that the pro-American essay and its writer are rated more positively, and the anti-American essay and its writer are rated more negatively, after a mortality-salience induction than they are in control conditions (Greenberg et al., 1997).

Participants' preferences in these studies are a function not of in-group/out-group status, but rather of the validation or challenge to the participants' cultural worldview. In fact, when the cultural worldview includes strong stereotypes of an out-group, mortality salience should lead to increased liking for out-group members who conform to the stereotype and decreased liking for out-group members who deviate from it. In support of this reasoning, we found that mortality salience leads Euro-Americans to a strong preference for members of minority groups (African Americans and homosexual men) who conform to cultural stereotypes over members of these groups who deviate from cultural stereotypes (Schimel et al., 1999).

Coffins, Consensus, and Icons

One way to bolster one's cultural worldview is to convince oneself that others already agree with that worldview. To demonstrate this and obtain mortality-salience effects in a natural setting, we interviewed people in Germany directly in front of, or 100 m from, a funeral parlor. Participants reported their attitudes about German immigration policies and estimated the percentage of Germans who agreed with them. The funeral parlor served as a "natural" mortality-salience induction; the location 100 m away served as our control. We reasoned that because cultural worldviews are sustained primarily by social consensus, the funerary reminder of death should make people especially prone to exaggerate estimates of agreement with their position, and this is what we found (see Greenberg et al., 1997)[4]

Social consensus would not be sufficient to sustain cultural worldviews in the absence of cultural icons (e.g., monuments, flags, bibles), which provide a physical embodiment of the cultural drama; thus, as representations of the cultural worldview, these icons should also serve to assuage mortality concerns. Indeed, we have found that after a mortality-salience induction, Americans took longer, and felt more uncomfortable (relative to a control group), solving a problem that required them to use the American flag to sift sand out of black dye (damaging the flag) and bang a nail into a wall with a crucifix (Greenberg et al., 1997).

Inspired by an incident in which a cook spiked the breakfast of two policemen with Tabasco, McGregor et al. (1998) examined whether mortality salience would encourage actual physical aggression toward others with different worldviews. Following a mortality-salience or control induction, participants read an essay in which another participant supported or attacked their political views. In a second, supposedly unrelated study of personality and taste preferences, participants were asked to choose the quantity of an extremely spicy hot sauce for the essay writer to taste. As predicted, the allotment of hot sauce did not vary in the control condition, but following the mortality-salience induction, people prescribed a significantly higher dose of hot sauce to the writer who threatened the cultural worldview (26.31 g) than to the writer who supported the cultural worldview (11.86 g).

Mortality Salience, Striving for Self-Esteem, and Bases for Hope

Mortality salience should intensify striving for self-esteem, as well as defense of the worldview. Consistent with Otto Rank's proposition that a harmonious balance of competing motives for individuation and inclusion (i.e., the desire to simultaneously "stick out" and "fit in") functions to control anxiety by enhancing self-esteem, Simon et al. (1997) found that mortality salience led people told they were conformers to report low social consensus for their attitudes and people told they were very different from others to report high social consensus for their attitudes. These responses presumably enhanced individuality or similarity to others, respectively, in the service of restoring the optimum balance between individuation and inclusion. More direct evidence for the connection between mortality salience and striving for self-esteem comes from a recent series of studies by Taubman - Ben-Ari, Florian, and Mikulincer (1999; summarized by Taubman - Ben-Ari in the preceding article of this issue), in which mortality salience was shown to increase risky driving among individuals whose driving ability was relevant to their self-esteem. In a very different domain, we have found that whereas mortality salience leads individuals with high body self-esteem to increase identification with their bodies, it leads those who have low body self-esteem and who value appearance to reduce attention to their bodies (Goldenberg, McCoy, Pyszczynski, Greenberg, & Solomon, 2000). Recent work also suggests that mortality salience leads people to reduce identification with their own groups when these groups are portrayed in a negative light.

Bases for optimism regarding constructive responses to mortality concerns can be found in work on variables that moderate the effects of mortality salience. Because disparaging another person with different beliefs violates the cultural value of tolerance, we predicted and found that American participants who highly value tolerance or for whom the value of tolerance is made salient do not derogate a politically dissimilar target person following a mortality-salience induction (Greenberg et al., 1997). We also reasoned that high self-esteem should mitigate against defensive responses to mortality salience and found that both momentarily elevated and dispositionally high self-esteem eliminate the effect of mortality salience on worldview defense (Harmon-Jones et al., 1997). Current research is examining the possibility that coming to terms with death through workshops or therapy may also allow people to contemplate mortality without engaging worldview defense.

CONCLUSION

TMT posits that the awareness of mortality is a potentially terrifying by-product of human consciousness. People manage this potential for terror through the development of culture, which confers the sense that they are valuable members of a meaningful universe. Self-esteem serves to buffer anxiety, and reminders of mortality intensify striving for self-esteem and defense of the worldview. Mortality concerns contribute to prejudice because people who are different challenge the absolute validity of one's cultural worldview. Psychological equanimity is restored by bolstering self-worth and faith in the cultural worldview, typically by engaging in culturally valued behaviors and by venerating people who are similar to oneself, and berating, converting, or annihilating those who are different.

Recently, Serbian soldiers have been accused of raping Moslem women while fellow soldiers used heads of their decapitated children as soccer balls. Can our analysis of the fear of death and the elaborate cultural constructions designed to combat it fully account for egregious sadistic actions such as these? Of course not: No single perspective can accomplish this. But there is good reason to believe that the uniquely human fear of death and the cultural worldviews humans use to quell it contribute substantially to these phenomena.

A recent theory and ongoing body of research on conscious and unconscious death defenses (Pyszczynski, Greenberg, & Solomon, 1999) has clarified the processes underlying the effects of mortality salience. Continued study is needed to further explain individual and cultural differences in forms of terror management and to develop measures of cultural worldviews and their components. Additionally, the implications of TMT for matters pertaining to urban violence, international relations, medical practice, and law and public policy require exploration. We hope, with Becker (1975), that such efforts might eventually help to "introduce just that minute measure of reason to balance destruction" (p. 170).

Recommended Reading

Becker, E. (1973). *The denial of death.* New York: Free Press.
Greenberg, J., Solomon, S., & Pyszczynski, T. (1997). (See References)
Pyszczynski, T., Greenberg, J., & Solomon, S. (1999). (See References)
Solomon, S., Greenberg, J., & Pyszczynski, T. (1991). A terror management theory of social behavior: The psychological functions of self-esteem and cultural worldviews. In M.P. Zanna (Ed.), *Advances in experimental social psychology* (Vol. 24, pp. 91-159). San Diego: Academic Press.

Acknowledgments—This work was supported by grants from the National Science Foundation (SBR-9731626 and SBR-9729946), the Ernest Becker Foundation, and Skidmore College.

Notes

1. Responsibility for this article is shared equally among the authors. Address correspondence to Sheldon Solomon, Department of Psychology, Brooklyn College, 2900 Bedford Ave., Brooklyn, NY 11210; e-mail: ssolomon@brooklyn.cuny.edu.

2. In a typical mortality-salience induction, participants complete open-ended questions embedded in questionnaires: for example, "Please briefly describe the emotions that the thought of your own death arouse in you" and "Jot down, as specifically as you can, what you think will happen to you as you physically die." Control conditions consist of parallel questions concerning other topics (e.g., watching television, eating a meal). Participants then (typically in a purportedly unrelated study) evaluate others who bolster or undermine their cultural worldview.

3. Independent researchers have obtained mortality-salience effects in the United States, Canada, Germany, The Netherlands, and Israel, using a variety of manipulations (e.g., gory accident footage and subliminal reminders of death) and dependent measures. Additional studies have demonstrated that the mortality-salience induction does not produce negative affect or arousal, and the effects are not mediated by self-awareness, affect, or arousal. The effects of mortality salience are also apparently unique to thoughts of death: Thoughts of exams, public speaking, pain, paralysis, or social exclusion do not replicate the effects (see Greenberg et al., 1997, for a review of this research).

4. This effect was reproduced in Colorado. In both studies, exaggerated consensus estimates were exhibited only by participants holding minority positions on the issue in question; presumably they had a greater need for social validation of their views.

References

Becker, E. (1975). *Escape from evil*. New York: Free Press.

Goldenberg, J., McCoy, S., Pyszczynski, T., Greenberg, J., & Solomon, S. (2000). The body as a source of self-esteem: The effect of mortality salience on identification with one's body, interest in sex, and appearance monitoring. *Journal of Personality and Social Psychology, 79*, 118-130.

Greenberg, J., Pyszczynski, T., & Solomon, S. (1986). The causes and consequences of the need for self-esteem: A terror management theory. In R.F. Baumeister (Ed.), *Public self and private self* (pp. 189-212). New York: Springer-Verlag.

Greenberg, J., Solomon, S., & Pyszczynski, T. (1997). Terror management theory of self-esteem and cultural worldviews: Empirical assessments and conceptual refinements. In M.P. Zanna (Ed.), *Advances in experimental social psychology* (Vol. 29, pp. 61-139). San Diego: Academic Press.

Greenberg, J., Solomon, S., Pyszczynski, T., Rosenblatt, A., Burling, J., Lyon, D., & Simon, L. (1992). Assessing the terror management analysis of self-esteem: Converging evidence of an anxiety-buffering function. *Journal of Personality and Social Psychology, 63*, 913-922.

Harmon-Jones, E., Simon, L., Greenberg, J., Pyszczynski, T., Solomon, S., & McGregor, H. (1997). Terror management theory and self esteem: Evidence that increased self-esteem reduces mortality salient effects. *Journal of Personality and Social Psychology, 72*, 24-36.

McGregor, H., Leiberman, J., Greenberg, J., Solomon, S., Arndt, J., Simon, L., & Pyszczynski, T. (1998). Terror management and aggression: Evidence that mortality salience promotes aggression against worldview threatening individuals. *Journal of Personality and Social Psychology, 74*, 590-605.

Pyszczynski, T., Greenberg, J., & Solomon, S. (1999). A dual process model of defense against conscious and unconscious death-related thoughts: An extension of terror management theory. *Psychological Review, 106*, 835-845.

Schimel, J., Simon, L., Greenberg, J., Pyszczynski, T., Solomon, S., Waxmonsky, J., & Arndt, J. (1999). Stereotypes and terror management: Evidence that mortality salience enhances stereotypic thinking and preferences. *Journal of Personality and Social Psychology, 77*, 905-926.

Simon, L., Greenberg, J., Arndt, J., Pyszczynski, T., Clement, R., & Solomon, S. (1997). Perceived consensus, uniqueness, and terror management: Compensatory responses to threats to inclusion and distinctiveness following mortality salience. *Personality and Social Psychology Bulletin, 23*, 1055-1065.

Taubman-Ben-Ari, O., Florian, V., & Mikulincer, M. (1999). The impact of mortality salience on reckless driving: A test of terror management mechanisms. *Journal of Personality and Social Psychology, 76,* 35-45.

Critical Thinking Questions

1. Describe two lines of research that support the hypothesis that self-esteem acts as a buffer for death anxiety. How might the construct of "worldview" relate to these findings?

2. Describe how damaging an American flag, using a crucifix as a hammer, and spiking breakfast with Tabasco have been used in experiments to demonstrate the influence of mortality-salience. How do these findings support the hypothesis that our worldview acts as a buffer for death anxiety?

3. The authors suggest that coming to terms with death or dealing with death anxiety through therapy may decrease one's tendency to use worldview defense as a buffer. Explain how they reached this conclusion and indicate why this would be beneficial.

The Psychology of Sexual Prejudice

Gregory M. Herek[1]

Department of Psychology, University of California, Davis, California

Abstract

Sexual prejudice refers to negative attitudes toward an individual because of her or his sexual orientation. In this article, the term is used to characterize heterosexuals' negative attitudes toward (a) homosexual behavior, (b) people with a homosexual or bisexual orientation, and (c) communities of gay, lesbian, and bisexual people. Sexual prejudice is a preferable term to *homophobia* because it conveys no assumptions about the motivations underlying negative attitudes, locates the study of attitudes concerning sexual orientation within the broader context of social psychological research on prejudice, and avoids value judgments about such attitudes. Sexual prejudice remains widespread in the United States, although moral condemnation has decreased in the 1990s and opposition to antigay discrimination has increased. The article reviews current knowledge about the prevalence of sexual prejudice, its psychological correlates, its underlying motivations, and its relationship to hate crimes and other antigay behaviors.

Keywords

attitudes; homosexuality; prejudice; homophobia; heterosexism

In a 6-month period beginning late in 1998, Americans were shocked by the brutal murders of Matthew Shepard and Billy Jack Gaither. Shepard, a 21-year-old Wyoming college student, and Gaither, a 39-year-old factory worker in Alabama, had little in common except that each was targeted for attack because he was gay. Unfortunately, their slayings were not isolated events. Lesbians, gay men, and bisexual people—as well as heterosexuals perceived to be gay—routinely experience violence, discrimination, and personal rejection. In all, 1,102 hate crimes based on sexual orientation were tallied by law-enforcement authorities in 1997. Because a substantial proportion of such crimes are never reported to police, that figure represents only the tip of an iceberg (Herek, Gillis, & Cogan, 1999).

People with homosexual or bisexual orientations have long been stigmatized. With the rise of the gay political movement in the late 1960s, however, homosexuality's condemnation as immoral, criminal, and sick came under increasing scrutiny. When the American Psychiatric Association dropped homosexuality as a psychiatric diagnosis in 1973, the question of why some heterosexuals harbor strongly negative attitudes toward homosexuals began to receive serious scientific consideration.

Society's rethinking of sexual orientation was crystallized in the term *homophobia*, which heterosexual psychologist George Weinberg coined in the late 1960s. The word first appeared in print in 1969 and was subsequently discussed at length in a popular book (Weinberg, 1972).[2] Around the same time, *heterosexism* began to be used as a term analogous to sexism and racism, describing an ideological system that casts homosexuality as inferior to heterosexuality.[3] Although usage of the two words has not been uniform, homophobia has typically been employed to describe individual antigay attitudes and behaviors, whereas heterosexism has referred to societal-level ideologies and patterns of institutionalized oppression of non-heterosexual people.

By drawing popular and scientific attention to antigay hostility, the creation of these terms marked a watershed. Of the two, homophobia is probably more widely used and more often criticized. Its critics note that homophobia implicitly suggests that antigay attitudes are best understood as an irrational fear and that they represent a form of individual psychopathology rather than a socially reinforced prejudice. As antigay attitudes have become increasingly central to conservative political and religious ideologies since the 1980s, these limitations have become more problematic. Yet, heterosexism, with its historical macro-level focus on cultural ideologies rather than individual attitudes, is not a satisfactory replacement for homophobia.

Thus, scientific analysis of the psychology of antigay attitudes will be facilitated by a new term. I offer *sexual prejudice* for this purpose. Broadly conceived, sexual prejudice refers to all negative attitudes based on sexual orientation, whether the target is homosexual, bisexual, or heterosexual. Given the current social organization of sexuality, however, such prejudice is almost always directed at people who engage in homosexual behavior or label themselves gay, lesbian, or bisexual. Thus, as used here, the term sexual prejudice encompasses heterosexuals' negative attitudes toward (a) homosexual behavior, (b) people with a homosexual or bisexual orientation, and (c) communities of gay, lesbian, and bisexual people. Like other types of prejudice, sexual prejudice has three principal features: It is an attitude (i.e., an evaluation or judgment); it is directed at a social group and its members; and it is negative, involving hostility or dislike.

Conceptualizing heterosexuals' negative attitudes toward homosexuality and bisexuality as sexual prejudice—rather than homophobia—has several advantages. First, sexual prejudice is a descriptive term. Unlike homophobia, it conveys no a priori assumptions about the origins, dynamics, and underlying motivations of antigay attitudes. Second, the term explicitly links the study of antigay hostility with the rich tradition of social psychological research on prejudice. Third, using the construct of sexual prejudice does not require value judgments that antigay attitudes are inherently irrational or evil.

PREVALENCE

Most adults in the United States hold negative attitudes toward homosexual behavior, regarding it as wrong and unnatural (Herek & Capitanio, 1996; Yang, 1997). Nevertheless, poll data show that attitudes have become more favorable over the past three decades. For example, whereas at least two thirds of respondents to the General Social Survey (GSS) considered homosexual behavior "always wrong" in the 1970s and 1980s, that figure declined noticeably in the 1990s. By 1996, only 56% of GSS respondents regarded it as always wrong (Yang, 1997).

Much of the public also holds negative attitudes toward individuals who are homosexual. In a 1992 national survey, more than half of the heterosexual respondents expressed disgust for lesbians and gay men (Herek, 1994). Respondents to the ongoing American National Election Studies have typically rated lesbians and gay men among the lowest of all groups on a 101-point feeling thermometer, although mean scores increased by approximately 10 points between 1984 and 1996 (Yang, 1997).

Despite these examples of negative attitudes, most Americans believe that a gay person should not be denied employment or basic civil liberties. The public is reluctant to treat homosexuality on a par with heterosexuality, however. Most Americans favor giving same-sex domestic partners limited recognition (e.g., employee health benefits, hospital visitation rights), but most oppose legalizing same-sex marriages. And whereas the public generally supports the employment rights of gay teachers, they do not believe that lesbians and gay men should be able to adopt children (Yang, 1997).

Unfortunately, most studies have not distinguished between lesbians and gay men as targets of prejudice. The available data suggest that attitudes toward gay men are more negative than attitudes toward lesbians, with the difference more pronounced among heterosexual men than women (Herek & Capitanio, 1996; Kite & Whitley, 1998). This pattern may reflect sex differences in the underlying cognitive organization of sexual prejudice (Herek & Capitanio, 1999).

CORRELATES

Laboratory and questionnaire studies have utilized a variety of measures to assess heterosexuals' attitudes toward gay men and lesbians (e.g., Davis, Yarber, Bauserman, Schreer, & Davis, 1998). Consistent with findings from public opinion surveys, they have revealed higher levels of sexual prejudice among individuals who are older, less educated, living in the U.S. South or Midwest, and living in rural areas (Herek, 1994). In survey and laboratory studies alike, heterosexual men generally display higher levels of sexual prejudice than heterosexual women (Herek & Capitanio, 1999; Kite & Whitley, 1998; Yang, 1998).

Sexual prejudice is also reliably correlated with several psychological and social variables. Heterosexuals with high levels of sexual prejudice tend to score higher than others on authoritarianism (Altemeyer, 1996; Haddock & Zanna, 1998). In addition, heterosexuals who identify with a fundamentalist religious denomination and frequently attend religious services typically manifest higher levels of sexual prejudice than do the nonreligious and members of liberal denominations (Herek & Capitanio, 1996). Since the 1980s, political ideology and party affiliation have also come to be strongly associated with sexual prejudice, with conservatives and Republicans expressing the highest levels (Yang, 1998).

Sexual prejudice is strongly related to whether or not a heterosexual knows gay people personally. The lowest levels of prejudice are manifested by heterosexuals who have gay friends or family members, describe their relationships with those individuals as close, and report having directly discussed the gay or lesbian person's sexual orientation with him or her. Interpersonal contact and prejudice are reciprocally related. Not only are heterosexuals with gay friends or relatives less prejudiced, but heterosexuals from demographic groups with low levels of sexual prejudice (e.g., women, highly educated people) are more likely to experience personal contact with an openly gay person (Herek & Capitanio, 1996).

Relatively little empirical research has examined racial and ethnic differences. Sexual prejudice may be somewhat greater among heterosexual African Americans than among heterosexual whites, mainly because of white women's relatively favorable attitudes toward lesbians and gay men. The correlates of sexual prejudice may vary by race and ethnicity. Interpersonal contact may be more important in shaping the attitudes of whites than of blacks, for example, whereas the belief that homosexuality is a choice may be a more influential predictor of heterosexual blacks' sexual prejudice (Herek & Capitanio, 1995).

UNDERLYING MOTIVATIONS

Like other forms of prejudice, sexual prejudice has multiple motivations. For some heterosexuals, it results from unpleasant interactions with gay individuals, which are then generalized to attitudes toward the entire group. This explanation probably applies mainly to cases in which interpersonal contact has been superficial and minimal. For other heterosexuals, sexual prejudice is rooted in fears associated with homosexuality, perhaps reflecting discomfort with their own sexual impulses or gender conformity. For still others, sexual prejudice reflects influences of in-group norms that are hostile to homosexual and bisexual people. Yet another source of prejudice is the perception that gay people and the gay community represent values that are directly in conflict with one's personal value system.

These different motivations can be understood as deriving from the psychological functions that sexual prejudice serves, which vary from one individual to another. One heterosexual's sexual prejudice, for example, may reduce the anxiety associated with his fears about sexuality and gender, whereas another heterosexual's prejudice might reinforce a positive sense of herself as a member of the social group "good Christians." Such attitudes are functional only when they are consistent with cultural and situational cues, for example, when homosexuality is defined as inconsistent with a masculine identity or when a religious congregation defines hostility to homosexuality as a criterion for being a good Christian (Herek, 1987).

PREJUDICE AND BEHAVIOR

Hate crimes and discrimination are inevitably influenced by complex situational factors (Franklin, 1998). Nevertheless, sexual prejudice contributes to antigay behaviors. In experimental studies, sexual prejudice correlates with antigay behaviors, although other factors often moderate this relationship (Haddock & Zanna, 1998; Kite & Whitley, 1998). Voting patterns on gay-related ballot measures have been generally consistent with the demographic correlates of sexual prejudice described earlier (Strand, 1998). Recognizing the complex relationship between sexual prejudice and antigay behavior further underscores the value of anchoring this phenomenon in the scientific literature on prejudice, which offers multiple models for understanding the links between attitudes and behavior.

CONCLUSION AND DIRECTIONS FOR RESEARCH

Although more than a quarter century has passed since Weinberg first presented a scholarly discussion of the psychology of homophobia, empirical research on sexual prejudice is still in its early stages. To date, the prevalence and correlates of sexual prejudice have received the most attention. Relatively little research has been devoted to understanding the dynamic cognitive processes associated with antigay attitudes and stereotypes, that is, how heterosexuals think about lesbians and gay men. Nor has extensive systematic inquiry been devoted to the underlying motivations for sexual prejudice or the effectiveness of different interventions for reducing sexual prejudice. These represent promising areas for future research.

In addition, there is a need for descriptive studies of sexual prejudice within different subsets of the population, including ethnic and age groups. Given the tendency for antigay behaviors to be perpetrated by adolescents and young adults, studies of the development of sexual prejudice early in the life span are especially needed. Finally, commonalities and convergences in the psychology of sexual prejudice toward different targets (e.g., men or women, homosexuals or bisexuals) should be studied. Much of the empirical research in this area to date has been limited because it has focused (implicitly or explicitly) on heterosexuals' attitudes toward gay men.

Stigma based on sexual orientation has been commonplace throughout the 20th century. Conceptualizing such hostility as sexual prejudice represents a step toward achieving a scientific understanding of its origins, dynamics, and functions. Perhaps most important, such an understanding may help to prevent the behavioral expression of sexual prejudice through violence, discrimination, and harassment.

Recommended Reading

Herek, G.M. (Ed.). (1998). *Stigma and sexual orientation: Understanding prejudice against lesbians, gay men, and bisexuals.* Newbury Park, CA: Sage.
Herek, G.M., & Berrill, K. (Eds.). (1992). *Hate crimes: Confronting violence against lesbians and gay men.* Thousand Oaks, CA: Sage.
Herek, G.M., Kimmel, D.C., Amaro, H., & Melton, G.B. (1991). Avoiding heterosexist bias in psychological research. *American Psychologist, 46,* 957-963.
Herman, D. (1997). *The antigay agenda: Orthodox vision and the Christian Right.* Chicago: University of Chicago Press.
Rothblum, E., & Bond, L. (Eds.). (1996). *Preventing heterosexism and homophobia.* Thousand Oaks, CA: Sage.

Acknowledgments—Preparation of this article was supported in part by an Independent Scientist Award from the National Institute of Mental Health (K02 MH01455).

Notes

1. Address correspondence to Gregory Herek, Department of Psychology, University of California, Davis, CA 95616-8775.

2. Although Weinberg coined the term homophobia, it was first used in print in 1969 by Jack Nichols and Lige Clarke in their May 23rd column in *Screw* magazine (J. Nichols, personal communication, November 5, 1998; G. Weinberg, personal communication, October 30, 1998).

3. Heterosexism was used as early as July 10, 1972, in two separate letters printed in the *Great Speckled Bird,* an alternative newspaper published in Atlanta, Georgia. I thank Joanne Despres of the Merriam Webster Company for her kind assistance with researching the origins of this word.

References

Altemeyer, B. (1996). *The authoritarian specter.* Cambridge, MA: Harvard University Press.

Davis, C.M., Yarber, W.L., Bauserman, R., Schreer, G., & Davis, S.L. (Eds.). (1998). *Handbook of sexuality-related measures.* Thousand Oaks, CA: Sage.

Franklin, K. (1998). Unassuming motivations: Contextualizing the narratives of antigay assailants. In G.M. Herek (Ed.), *Stigma and sexual orientation: Understanding prejudice against lesbians, gay men, and bisexuals* (pp. 1-23). Newbury Park, CA: Sage.

Haddock, G., & Zanna, M. (1998). Authoritarianism, values, and the favorability and structure of antigay attitudes. In G.M. Herek (Ed.), *Stigma and sexual orientation: Understanding prejudice against lesbians, gay men, and bisexuals* (pp. 82-107). Newbury Park, CA: Sage.

Herek, G.M. (1987). Can functions be measured? A new perspective on the functional approach to attitudes. *Social Psychology Quarterly, 50,* 285-303.

Herek, G.M. (1994). Assessing attitudes toward lesbians and gay men: A review of empirical research with the ATLG scale. In B. Greene & G.M. Herek (Eds.), *Lesbian and gay psychology* (pp. 206-228). Thousand Oaks, CA: Sage.

Herek, G.M., & Capitanio, J. (1995). Black heterosexuals' attitudes toward lesbians and gay men in the United States. *Journal of Sex Research, 32,* 95-105.

Herek, G.M., & Capitanio, J. (1996). "Some of my best friends": Intergroup contact, concealable stigma, and heterosexuals' attitudes toward gay men and lesbians. *Personality and Social Psychology Bulletin, 22,* 412-424.

Herek, G.M., & Capitanio, J.P. (1999). Sex differences in how heterosexuals think about lesbians and gay men: Evidence from survey context effects. *Journal of Sex Research, 36,* 348-360.

Herek, G.M., Gillis, J., & Cogan, J. (1999). Psychological sequelae of hate crime victimization among lesbian, gay, and bisexual adults. *Journal of Consulting and Clinical Psychology, 67,* 945-951.

Kite, M.E., & Whitley, B.E., Jr. (1998). Do heterosexual women and men differ in their attitudes toward homosexuality? A conceptual and methodological analysis. In G.M. Herek (Ed.), *Stigma and sexual orientation: Understanding prejudice against lesbians, gay men, and bisexuals* (pp. 39-61). Newbury Park, CA: Sage.

Strand, D. (1998). Civil liberties, civil rights, and stigma: Voter attitudes and behavior in the politics of homosexuality. In G.M. Herek (Ed.), *Stigma and sexual orientation: Understanding prejudice against lesbians, gay men, and bisexuals* (pp. 108-137). Newbury Park, CA: Sage.

Weinberg, G. (1972). *Society and the healthy homosexual.* New York: St. Martin's.

Yang, A. (1997). Trends: Attitudes toward homosexuality. *Public Opinion Quarterly, 61,* 477-507.

Yang, A. (1998). *From wrongs to rights: Public opinion on gay and lesbian Americans moves toward equality.* Washington, DC: National Gay and Lesbian Task Force Policy Institute.

Critical Thinking Questions

1. The author makes the argument that the term homophobia should be replaced with sexual prejudice. Explain the history of this terminology. What are some examples of other terminology that has changed over time in our society? Speculate on why language and terminology is so important to consider.

2. Describe the major reasons that the author has for replacing the term homophobia with sexual prejudice. What does he mean when he states that this change would anchor this phenomenon "in the scientific literature on prejudice." Why would this be advantageous for research or for efforts toward social change?

3. Describe some of the correlates of sexual prejudice. The author indicates that most of the work on sexual prejudice has focused on these correlates. Speculate on why researchers would have started their work examining these.

Ethnicity-Related Sources of Stress and Their Effects on Well-Being

Richard J. Contrada,[1] Richard D. Ashmore, Melvin L. Gary, Elliot Coups, Jill D. Egeth, Andrea Sewell, Kevin Ewell, Tanya M. Goyal, and Valerie Chasse

Department of Psychology, Rutgers-The State University of New Jersey, Piscataway, New Jersey (R.J.C., R.D.A., M.L.G., E.C., J.D.E., A.S., K.E., T.M.G.), and Social Sciences Area, Warren County Community College of New Jersey, Washington, New Jersey (V.C.)

Abstract

Early research on ethnicity focused on the stereotyped thinking, prejudiced attitudes, and discriminatory actions of Euro-Americans. Minority-group members were viewed largely as passive targets of these negative reactions, with low self-esteem studied as the main psychological outcome. By contrast, recent research has increasingly made explicit use of stress theory in emphasizing the perspectives and experiences of minority-group members. Several ethnicity-related stressors have been identified, and it has been found that individuals cope with these threats in an active, purposeful manner. In this article, we focus on ethnicity-related stress stemming from discrimination, from stereotypes, and from conformity pressure arising from one's own ethnic group. We discuss theory and review research in which examination of ethnicity-related outcomes has extended beyond self-esteem to include psychological and physical well-being.

Keywords

ethnicity; stress; coping; discrimination; stereotypes; well-being

Racial and ethnic categories, such as "white," "black," "Asian," and "Hispanic," reflect complex sets of sociocultural and historical factors (Williams, Spencer, & Jackson, 1999). The meaning and impact of these factors at an individual psychological level are not well understood. Of the many aspects of ethnicity[2] that appear to influence psychological processes, several may be conceptualized as psychological stressors, that is, as perceived threats to physical or psychological well-being. A number of qualitatively distinct ethnicity-related stressors have recently been subject to intensified investigation; we discuss three of them in this review.

ETHNIC DISCRIMINATION

Ethnic discrimination involves unfair treatment that a person attributes to his or her ethnicity. We discuss discrimination at some length because it has been given increased attention recently in journalistic accounts and in analyses involving systematic coding of the content of interviews with victims of discrimination. Discrimination also has been recognized in recent quantitative research and theoretical analyses as a psychological stressor and a possible risk factor for physical illness. These efforts have sparked new interest in the topic and identified some major issues. They represent a shift away from an emphasis on determinants of discriminatory behavior toward a focus on the perception and experience of discrimination by minority-group members. In another shift, by contrast with earlier accounts that emphasized major, often institutional, forms of discrimination (e.g., hiring practices), more recent accounts have highlighted subtle forms of discrimination that are embedded in everyday life (e.g., being followed in a store as a suspected shoplifter).

There have been several efforts to delineate the various forms of ethnic discrimination. For example, in a recent study (Contrada et al., in press), we identified five: (a) *verbal rejection*: insults, ethnic slurs; (b) *avoidance*: shunning; (c) *disvaluation*: actions that express negative evaluations; (d) *inequality-exclusion*: denial of equal treatment or access; and (e) *threat-aggression*: actual or threatened harm. This set of distinctions accords well with Allport's (1954) suggestion that the behavioral expression of prejudice may be described in terms of a continuum of increasing intensity.

Explicit conceptualization of discrimination as a psychological stressor has guided several recent theoretical analyses. This work suggests that members of ethnic minority groups form expectations regarding the likelihood that discrimination will be encountered in certain settings, decide whether to approach or avoid situations in which it is anticipated, and prepare for its occurrence (Swim, Cohen, & Hyers, 1998). Thus, the ever-present possibility of discrimination itself constitutes a stressor, requiring vigilance and other proactive coping responses.

Minority-group members also must judge whether specific events constitute discrimination. Feldman Barrett and Swim (1998) have conceptualized this process in terms of signal detection theory. This theory was developed as a way to distinguish between noticing a stimulus and responding to it once it is noticed, using the concepts of *sensitivity* and *response bias*. In the present context, sensitivity involves the ability to detect the presence or absence of cues indicating discrimination. It is determined, in part, by properties of discriminatory events or conditions. Acts of discrimination are often ambiguous because they can be subtle or involve treatment that is of borderline acceptability ("The waiter seemed to be ignoring me . . ."), the ethnicity-related motives that define them as discriminatory (". . . because I am black . . .") are often unobservable, and the behavior in question may be subject to alternative explanations (" . . . though the restaurant was extremely busy"). Sensitivity also may reflect attributes of the person, such as general knowledge, previous experience, and social awareness. Response bias involves the tendency either to underestimate or to overestimate the occurrence of discrimination. It is influenced by general beliefs about the probability that individuals are prejudiced, and by the goals a person has (e.g., self-protection) when judging whether discrimination has occurred.

When subjected to possible discriminatory behavior, members of ethnic minorities may be motivated to protect themselves against unfair treatment, but they also may wish to avoid false alarms (i.e., perceiving discrimination when it did not in fact occur). False alarms can disrupt social relations, cause members of ethnic minority groups to be identified as "thin-skinned," and undermine life satisfaction. One important task now being pursued by researchers is identifying conditions that favor minimizing false alarms, and those that favor being careful not to miss detecting acts of discrimination when they do occur (Feldman Barrett & Swim, 1998). There is accumulating evidence that when the situation is even just slightly ambiguous, members of ethnic minority groups may minimize the personal experience of discrimination. For example, they may attribute negative outcomes (e.g., unfavorable evaluations) to personal factors (e.g., the quality of their performance), which apparently serves to enhance their perception of personal control (Ruggiero & Taylor, 1997).

Coping with discrimination also requires decisions based on a complex set of factors (Swim et al., 1998). Different responses to perceived discrimination may serve different goals, some aimed at dealing with the initiating social situation, and some focusing on its emotional impact. Assertive reactions, such as the highly visible, confrontational communication of displeasure, may be directed at terminating the offensive behavior or at retaliation. Less assertive responses, such as trying to placate the perpetrator, may be aimed at self-protection or preservation of social relationships. Cognitive coping responses, such as reinterpreting the event as benign or as not ethnicity related, may preserve a positive, if illusory, view of the social consequences of one's ethnicity. Because discrimination can cause members of ethnic minority groups to feel badly about themselves personally, or about their group as a whole (Crocker, Major, & Steele, 1998), certain coping responses may be self- or identity-focused. They may, for example, involve either reduction or enhancement of psychological identification with one's ethnic group (Deaux & Ethier, 1998). Deciding whether and how to respond to discrimination appears to involve cost-benefit considerations, similar to those involved in the perception of discrimination, that have only recently begun to receive systematic attention (Swim et al., 1998).

STEREOTYPE THREAT AND STEREOTYPE-CONFIRMATION CONCERN

Stereotype threat has been defined, in part, as the condition of being at risk of appearing to confirm a negative stereotype about a group to which one belongs (Steele, 1997). Stereotype threat has been examined as a social psychological state created by situational cues in susceptible individuals. Much of this work has investigated stereotype threat associated with the American cultural beliefs that African Americans are low in intellectual ability and that women are not skilled in mathematics and physical sciences. One way stereotype threat is induced in this research is by instructing participants that their scores on tests that they are about to take will be diagnostic of their intellectual ability. Results have suggested that induction of stereotype threat activates relevant stereotypes in the thinking of participants, increases anxiety, and impairs test performance. In the long term, these experiences may promote *disidentification*, which, in this context, is a coping response of psychological disengagement from academic activity (Osborne, 1995). Thus, threat created by very subtle cues associated with ethnic stereotypes may have a negative impact with severe long-term implications.

Stereotype-confirmation concern arises from the relatively enduring or recurring experience of stereotype threat (Contrada et al., in press). It refers to a dimension defined at one extreme by chronic apprehension about appearing to confirm an ethnic stereotype, and at the other extreme by the absence of such concern. Stereotype-confirmation concern reflects both environmental factors (e.g., other people's ethnicity-related attitudes and behaviors) and personal attributes (e.g., one's ethnicity, the sensitivity and response bias constructs described earlier). Members of all ethnic groups are susceptible to stereotype-confirmation concern, and for each group, there are multiple stereotypes that may create such concern. For example, college undergraduates of diverse ethnicities have reported stereotype-confirmation concern with respect to a wide range of behaviors that might be linked to ethnic stereotypes (e.g., eating certain foods, dressing or speaking a certain way; Contrada et al., in press). Reports of stereotype-confirmation concern have been found to be only moderately correlated with reports of ethnic discrimination. Therefore, although not as widely recognized as ethnic discrimination, stereotype-confirmation concern appears to represent a distinct dimension of ethnicity-related stress.

OWN-GROUP CONFORMITY PRESSURE

Members of an ethnic group often have expectations about what is appropriate behavior for that group. For example, some African Americans who excel academically are accused by their peers of "acting white" (Fordham & Ogbu, 1986). This appears to be just one facet of a wider and more general form of stress originating in one's own ethnic group—what is called *own-group conformity pressure.*

Own-group conformity pressure is defined as the experience of being pressured or constrained by one's ethnic group's expectations specifying appropriate or inappropriate behavior for the group. This experience may be shaped by both internal and external factors, the former including one's ethnicity and perception of in-group norms and expectations, and the latter including explicit, overt sanctions for violating ethnic-group norms, as well as more subtle reminders about "how 'we' are supposed to behave." As with stereotype-confirmation concern, own-group conformity pressure is relatively enduring or recurring, and is potentially applicable to persons of all ethnic groups. Among ethnically diverse college students, reports of own-group conformity pressure relate to personal style and interests (e.g., pressure to dress a certain way, listen to particular music) and social relations (e.g., pressure to date or interact with members of one's own group only; Contrada et al., in press). Reports of own-group conformity pressure in these students are only moderately correlated with reports of ethnic discrimination and stereotype-confirmation concern. Thus, ethnicity-related stressors can arise from members of other ethnic groups, from societal stereotypes, and from members of one's own ethnic group, and these three categories of stressors are all relatively independent.

ETHNICITY-RELATED STRESSORS AND WELL-BEING

Until recently, research examining the impact of ethnicity-related stressors focused on the possibility that internalizing the pejorative stereotypes and prejudiced attitudes of the dominant majority might have a negative impact on the self-concepts of members of ethnic minority groups. However, the evidence does not suggest that being a member of an ethnic group that is devalued by the dominant majority leads inevitably, or even usually, to lower self-regard. For example, it has been found that African Americans do not score lower than whites on self-esteem measures (Crocker et al., 1998).

Regarding psychological outcomes other than self-esteem, there is evidence that members of certain minority groups experience higher rates of depressive symptoms than Euro-Americans (Crocker et al., 1998). However, simple comparisons of ethnic groups may reflect numerous causal determinants, including socioeconomic status and sociocultural norms, in addition to ethnicity-related stressors (Anderson & Armstead, 1995). The contributions of these factors to ethnic-group differences in well-being have yet to be teased apart. Nonetheless, several studies that have examined ethnic discrimination directly have reported that it is associated with negative psychological health outcomes (Williams et al., 1999).

A small but growing body of research has implicated ethnicity-related stressors as a determinant of physical health outcomes. Much of this work has focused on discrimination experienced by African Americans, whose rates of physical disease and mortality significantly exceed those of Euro-Americans (Williams et al., 1999). Some studies have focused directly on disease outcomes. For example, Krieger and Sidney (1996) found that higher blood pressure among African Americans, compared with whites, could be partially explained when blacks' experience of discrimination and their coping responses to such treatment were taken into account. Other work has examined physiological and behavioral factors that may increase risk of disease. Regarding the former, Armstead, Lawler, Gorden, Cross, and Gibbons (1989) demonstrated that when blacks viewed videotaped vignettes of situations involving discrimination, they showed cardiovascular responses thought to contribute to the development of cardiovascular disorders. In an example of research addressing cigarette smoking, a major behavioral risk factor for disease, it was found that African Americans with high scores on a measure of discrimination experienced in everyday life were significantly more likely to be smokers than those with low scores (Landrine & Klonoff, 1996).

CONCLUSION

Research on ethnic discrimination, stereotype threat and stereotype-confirmation concern, and own-group conformity pressure illustrates an emerging new perspective based on the premise that members of ethnic minority groups are not passive victims of prejudice and discrimination, but rather are active agents in making sense of and coping with multiple and distinct ethnicity-related threats. Among the many unresolved questions raised by this proposition are those pertaining to the features of social situations that give rise to ethnicity-related stress, and to the psychological factors that influence detection of these stressors and shape ensuing coping activities. Equally important is the need to isolate the effects of ethnicity-related stressors from the effects of other correlates of ethnic-group membership that may influence psychological and physical well-being, and to identify aspects of ethnic-group membership that may buffer the impact of these stressors. The concept of ethnicity-related stress provides new directions for investigating just some of the many psychological ramifications of ethnic-group membership.

Recommended Reading

Cose, E. (1993). *The rage of a privileged class*. New York: HarperCollins.
Crocker, J., Major, B., & Steele, C. (1998). (See References)
Feagin, J.R., & Sikes, M.P. (1994). *Living with racism: The black middle-class experience*. Boston: Beacon Press.
Phinney, J.S. (1996). When we talk about American ethnic groups, what do we mean? *American Psychologist, 51*, 918-928.
Steele, C.M. (1997). (See References)

Notes

1. Address correspondence to Richard J. Contrada, Department of Psychology, Rutgers University, 53 Avenue E, Piscataway, NJ 08854-8040; e-mail: contrada@rci.rutgers.edu.
2. We use the term ethnicity to refer both to broad groupings of individuals based on culture of origin and to those social groupings conventionally referred to in terms of "race," without presupposing that these groupings reflect a single, fixed quality or essence, biological or otherwise.

References

Allport, G.W. (1954). *The nature of prejudice*. Garden City, NY: Doubleday.
Anderson, N.B., & Armstead, C.A. (1995). Toward understanding the association of socioeconomic status and health: A new challenge for the biopsychosocial approach. *Psychosomatic Medicine, 57*, 213-225.
Armstead, C.A., Lawler, K.A., Gorden, G., Cross, J., & Gibbons, J. (1989). Relationship of racial stressors to blood pressure responses and anger expression in Black college students. *Health Psychology, 8*, 541-556.
Contrada, R.J., Ashmore, R.D., Gary, M.L., Coups, E., Egeth, J.D., Sewell, A., Ewell, K., Goyal, T., & Chasse, V. (in press). Measures of ethnicity-related stress: Psychometric properties, ethnic group differences, and associations with psychological and physical well-being. *Journal of Applied Social Psychology*.
Crocker, J., Major, B., & Steele, C. (1998). Social stigma. In D.T. Gilbert, S.T. Fiske, & G. Lindzey (Eds.), *The handbook of social psychology* (4th ed., Vol. 2, pp. 504-553). Boston: McGraw-Hill.
Deaux, K., & Ethier, K.A. (1998). Negotiating social identity. In J.K. Swim & C. Stangor (Eds.), *Prejudice: The target's perspective* (pp. 301-323). New York: Academic Press.
Feldman Barrett, L., & Swim, J.K. (1998). Appraisals of prejudice and discrimination. In J.K. Swim & C. Stangor (Eds.), *Prejudice: The target's perspective* (pp. 11-36). New York: Academic Press.
Fordham, S., & Ogbu, J.U. (1986). Black students' school success: Coping with the "burden of acting White." *Urban Review, 18*, 176-206.
Krieger, N., & Sidney, S. (1996). Racial discrimination and blood pressure: The CARDIA study of young Black and White adults. *American Journal of Public Health, 86*, 1370-1378.
Landrine, H., & Klonoff, E.A. (1996). The Schedule of Racist Events: A measure of racial discrimination and a study of its negative physical and mental health consequences. *Journal of Black Psychology, 22*, 144-168.
Osborne, J.W. (1995). Academics, self-esteem, and race: A look at the underlying assumptions of the discrimination hypothesis. *Personality and Social Psychology Bulletin, 21*, 449-455.
Ruggiero, K.M., & Taylor, D.M. (1997). Why minority group members perceive or do not perceive the discrimination that confronts them: The role of self-esteem and perceived control. *Journal of Personality and Social Psychology, 72*, 373-389.
Steele, C.M. (1997). A threat in the air: How stereotypes shape intellectual identity and performance. *American Psychologist, 52*, 613-629.

Swim, J.K., Cohen, L.L., & Hyers, L.L. (1998). Experiencing everyday prejudice and discrimination. In J.K. Swim & C. Stangor (Eds.), *Prejudice: The target's perspective* (pp. 38-61). New York: Academic Press.

Williams, D.R., Spencer, M.S., & Jackson, J.S. (1999). Race, stress, and physical health: The role of group identity. In R.J. Contrada & R.D. Ashmore (Eds.), *Self, social identity, and physical health: Interdisciplinary explorations* (pp. 71-100). New York: Oxford University Press.

Critical Thinking Questions

1. Distinguish among the 5 forms of ethnic discrimination presented in this article. How might each of these be unique sources of ethnicity-related stress? Explain how even the possibility of discrimination might serve as a source of stress. Describe the links between ethnicity-related stress and physical health outcomes that have been shown in past research.

2. Describe the concepts of sensitivity and response bias. Explain why members of ethnic minorities would engage in a cost-benefit analysis when they encounter a situation that might be discriminatory. How might this analysis be a source of stress in and of itself?

3. Summarize the concept of stereotype threat. How can stereotype threat lead to disidentification? Use an example other than academic performance to illustrate your point.

Reducing Prejudice: Combating Intergroup Biases

John F. Dovidio[1] and Samuel L. Gaertner
Department of Psychology, Colgate University, Hamilton, New York (J.F.D.), and Department of Psychology, University of Delaware, Newark, Delaware (S.L.G.)

Abstract

Strategies for reducing prejudice may be directed at the traditional, intentional form of prejudice or at more subtle and perhaps less conscious contemporary forms. Whereas the traditional form of prejudice may be reduced by direct educational and attitude-change techniques, contemporary forms may require alternative strategies oriented toward the individual or involving intergroup contact. Individual-oriented techniques can involve leading people who possess contemporary prejudices to discover inconsistencies among their self-images, values, and behaviors; such inconsistencies can arouse negative emotional states (e.g., guilt), which motivate the development of more favorable attitudes. Intergroup strategies can involve structuring intergroup contact to produce more individualized perceptions of the members of the other group, foster personalized interactions between members of the different groups, or redefine group boundaries to create more inclusive, superordinate representations of the groups. Understanding the nature and bases of prejudice can thus guide, theoretically and pragmatically, interventions that can effectively reduce both traditional and contemporary forms of prejudice.

Keywords

attitude change; intergroup contact; prejudice; racism; social categorization

Prejudice is commonly defined as an unfair negative attitude toward a social group or a member of that group. Stereotypes, which are overgeneralizations about a group or its members that are factually incorrect and inordinately rigid, are a set of beliefs that can accompany the negative feelings associated with prejudice. Traditional approaches consider prejudice, like other attitudes, to be acquired through socialization and supported by the beliefs, attitudes, and values of friends and peer groups (see Jones, 1997). We consider the nature of traditional and contemporary forms of prejudice, particularly racial prejudice, and review a range of techniques that have been demonstrated empirically to reduce prejudice and other forms of intergroup bias. Bias can occur in many forms, and thus it has been assessed by a range of measures. These measures include standardized tests of prejudice toward another social group, stereotypes, evaluations of and feelings about specific group members and about the group in general, support for policies and individual actions benefiting the other group, and interaction and friendship patterns.

In part because of changing norms and the Civil Rights Act and other legislative interventions that made discrimination not simply immoral but also illegal, overt expressions of prejudice have declined significantly over the past 35 years. Contemporary forms of prejudice, however, continue to exist and affect the lives of people in subtle but significant ways (Dovidio & Gaertner, 1998;

Gaertner & Dovidio, 1986). The negative feelings and beliefs that underlie contemporary forms of prejudice may be rooted in either individual processes (such as cognitive and motivational biases and socialization) or intergroup processes (such as realistic group conflict or biases associated with the mere categorization of people into in-groups and out-groups). These negative biases may occur spontaneously, automatically, and without full awareness.

Many contemporary approaches to prejudice based on race, ethnicity, or sex acknowledge the persistence of overt, intentional forms of prejudice but also consider the role of these automatic or unconscious processes[2] and the consequent indirect expressions of bias. With respect to the racial prejudice of white Americans toward blacks, for example, in contrast to "old-fashioned" racism, which is blatant, aversive racism represents a subtle, often unintentional, form of bias that characterizes many white Americans who possess strong egalitarian values and who believe that they are nonprejudiced. Aversive racists also possess negative racial feelings and beliefs (which develop through normal socialization or reflect social-categorization biases) that they are unaware of or that they try to dissociate from their non-prejudiced self-images. Because aversive racists consciously endorse egalitarian values, they will not discriminate directly and openly in ways that can be attributed to racism; however, because of their negative feelings, they will discriminate, often unintentionally, when their behavior can be justified on the basis of some factor other than race (e.g., questionable qualifications for a position). Thus, aversive racists may regularly engage in discrimination while they maintain self-images of being non-prejudiced. According to symbolic racism theory, a related perspective that has emphasized the role of politically conservative rather than liberal ideology (Sears, 1988), negative feelings toward blacks that whites acquire early in life persist into adulthood but are expressed indirectly and symbolically, in terms of opposition to busing or resistance to preferential treatment, rather than directly or overtly, as in support for segregation.

Contemporary expressions of bias may also reflect a dissociation between cultural stereotypes, which develop through common socialization experiences and because of repeated exposure generally become automatically activated, and individual differences in prejudicial motivations. Although whites both high and low in prejudice may be equally aware of cultural stereotypes and show similar levels of automatic activation, only those low in prejudice make a conscious attempt to prevent those negative stereotypes from influencing their behavior (Devine & Monteith, 1993).

INDIVIDUAL PROCESSES AND PREJUDICE REDUCTION

Attempts to reduce the direct, traditional form of racial prejudice typically involve educational strategies to enhance knowledge and appreciation of other groups (e.g., multicultural education programs), emphasize norms that prejudice is wrong, and involve direct persuasive strategies (e.g., mass media appeals) or indirect attitude-change techniques that make people aware of inconsistencies in their attitudes and behaviors (Stephan & Stephan, 1984). Other techniques are aimed at changing or diluting stereotypes by presenting counter-stereotypic or non-stereotypic information about group members. Providing stereotype-disconfirming information is more effective when the information concerns a broad range of group members who are otherwise typical of their group rather than when the information concerns a single person who is not a prototypical representative of the group. In the latter case, people are likely to maintain their overall stereotype of the group while subtyping, with another stereotype, group members who disconfirm the general group stereotype (e.g., black athletes; Hewstone, 1996). The effectiveness of multicultural education programs is supported by the results of controlled intervention programs in the real world; evidence of the effectiveness of attitude- and stereotype-change approaches, and the hypothesized underlying processes, comes largely (but not exclusively) from experimental laboratory research.

Approaches for dealing with the traditional form of prejudice are generally less effective for combating the contemporary forms. With respect to contemporary racism, for example, whites already consciously endorse egalitarian, non-prejudiced views and disavow traditional stereotypes. Instead, indirect strategies that benefit from people's genuine motivation to be non-prejudiced may be more effective for reducing contemporary forms of prejudice. For example, techniques that lead people who possess contemporary prejudices to discover inconsistencies among their self-images, values, and behaviors may arouse feelings of guilt, tension about the inconsistencies, or other negative emotional states that can motivate the development of more favorable racial attitudes and produce more favorable intergroup behaviors (even nonverbal behaviors) several months later. Also, people who consciously endorse non-prejudiced attitudes, but whose behaviors may reflect racial bias, commonly experience feelings of guilt and compunction when they become aware of discrepancies between their potential behavior toward minorities (i.e., what they *would* do) and their personal standards (i.e., what they *should* do) during laboratory interventions. These emotional reactions, in turn, can motivate people to control subsequent spontaneous stereotypical responses and behave more favorably in the future (Devine & Monteith, 1993). People's conscious efforts to suppress stereotypically biased reactions can inhibit even the immediate activation of normally automatic associations, and with sufficient practice, these efforts can eliminate automatic stereotype activation over the long term.

Approaches oriented toward the individual, however, are not the only way to combat contemporary forms of prejudice. Strategies that emphasize intergroup processes, such as intergroup contact and social categorization and identity, are alternative, complementary approaches.

INTERGROUP CONTACT

Real-world interventions, laboratory studies, and survey studies have demonstrated that intergroup contact under specified conditions (including equal status between the groups, cooperative intergroup interactions, opportunities for personal acquaintance, and supportive egalitarian norms) is a powerful technique for reducing intergroup bias and conflict (Pettigrew, 1998). Drawing on these principles, cooperative learning and "jigsaw" classroom interventions (Aronson

& Patnoe, 1997) are designed to increase interdependence between members of different groups working on a designated problem-solving task and to enhance appreciation for the resources they bring to the task. Cooperation is effective for reducing subsequent intergroup bias when the task is completed successfully, group contributions to solving the problem are seen as different or complementary, and the interaction among participants during the task is friendly, personal, and supportive.

Recent research has attempted to elucidate how the different factors of intergroup contact (e.g., cooperation, personal interaction) operate to reduce bias. Engaging in activities to achieve common, superordinate goals, for instance, changes the functional relations between groups from actual or symbolic competition to cooperation. Through psychological processes to restore cognitive balance or reduce inconsistency between actions and attitudes, attitudes toward members of the other group and toward the group as a whole may improve to be consistent with the positive nature of the interaction. Also, the rewarding properties of achieving success may become associated with members of other groups, thereby increasing attraction.

SOCIAL CATEGORIZATION AND IDENTITY

Factors of intergroup contact, such as cooperation, may also reduce bias through reducing the salience of the intergroup boundaries, that is, through *decategorization*. According to this perspective, interaction during intergroup contact can individuate members of the out-group by revealing variability in their opinions (Wilder, 1986) or can produce interactions in which people are seen as unique individuals (personalization), with the exchange of intimate information (Brewer & Miller, 1984). Alternatively, intergroup contact may be structured to maintain but alter the nature of group boundaries, that is, to produce *recategorization*. One recategorization approach involves either creating or increasing the salience of crosscutting group memberships. Making interactants aware that members of another group are also members of one's own group when groups are defined by a different dimension can improve intergroup attitudes (Urban & Miller, 1998). Another recategorization strategy, represented by our own work on the Common In-Group Identity Model, involves interventions to change people's conceptions of groups, so that they think of membership not in terms of several different groups, but in terms of one, more inclusive group (Gaertner, Dovidio, Anastasio, Bachman, & Rust, 1993).

The Common In-Group Identity Model recognizes the central role of social categorization in reducing as well as in creating intergroup bias (Tajfel & Turner, 1979). Specifically, if members of different groups are induced to conceive of themselves more as members of a single, superordinate group rather than as members of two separate groups, attitudes toward former out-group members will become more positive through processes involving pro-in-group bias. Thus, changing the basis of categorization from race to an alternative dimension can alter who is a "we" and who is a "they," undermining a contributing force to contemporary forms of racism, such as aversive racism. The development of a superordinate identity does not always require people to abandon their previous group identities; they may possess dual identities, conceiving of themselves as belonging both to the superordinate group and to one of the original two groups included within the new, larger group. The model also recognizes that decategorization (seeing people as separate individuals) can also reduce bias. In contrast, perceptions of the groups as different entities (we/they) maintains and reinforces bias. The Common In-Group Identity Model is presented schematically in Figure 1.

In experiments in the laboratory and in the field, and in surveys in natural settings (a multi-ethnic high school, banking mergers, and blended families), we have found evidence consistent with the Common In-Group Identity Model and the hypothesis that intergroup contact can reduce prejudice. Specifically, we have found that key aspects of intergroup contact, such as cooperation, decrease intergroup bias in part through changing cognitive representations of the groups. The development of a common ingroup identity also facilitates helping behav-

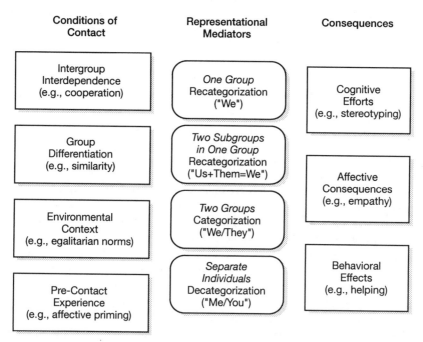

Fig. 1. The Common In-Group Identity Model. In this model, elements of an intergroup contract situation (e.g., intergroup interdependence) influence cognitive representations of the groups as one superordinate group (recategorization), as two subgroups in one group (recategorization involving a dual identity), as two groups (categorization), or as separate individuals (decategorization). Recategorization and decategorization, in turn, can both reduce cognitive, affective, and behavioral biases, but in different ways. Recategorization reduces bias by extending the benefits of in-group favoritism to former out-group members. Attitudes and behavior toward these former out-group members thus become more favorable, approaching attitudes and behaviors toward in-group members. Decategorization, in contrast, reduces favoritism toward original in-group members as they become perceived as separate individuals rather than members of one's own group.

iors and self-disclosing interactions that can produce reciprocally positive responses and that can further reduce intergroup prejudices through other mechanisms such as personalization.

Moreover, the development of a common in-group identity does not necessarily require groups to forsake their original identities. Threats to important personal identities or the "positive distinctiveness" of one's group can, in fact, exacerbate intergroup prejudices. The development of a dual identity (two subgroups in one group; see Fig. 1), in which original and superordinate group memberships are simultaneously salient, is explicitly considered in the model. Even when racial or ethnic identity is strong, perceptions of a superordinate connection enhance interracial trust and acceptance. Indeed, the development of a dual identity, in terms of a bicultural or multicultural identity, not only is possible but can contribute to the social adjustment, psychological adaptation, and overall well-being of minority-group members (LaFromboise, Coleman, & Gerton, 1993). Recognizing both different and common group membership, a more complex form of a common in-group identity, may also increase the generalizability of the benefits of intergroup contact for prejudice reduction. The development of a common in-group identity contributes to more positive attitudes toward members of other groups present in the contact situation, whereas recognition of the separate group memberships provides the associative link by which these more positive attitudes may generalize to other members of the groups not directly involved in the contact situation.

CONCLUSION

Prejudice can occur in its blatant, traditional form, or it may be rooted in unconscious and automatic negative feelings and beliefs that characterize contemporary forms. Whereas the traditional form of prejudice may be combated by using direct techniques involving attitude change and education, addressing contemporary forms requires alternative strategies. Individual-level strategies engage the genuine motivations of people to be non-prejudiced. Intergroup approaches focus on realistic group conflict or the psychological effects of categorizing people into in-groups and out-groups. The benefits of intergroup contact can occur through many routes, such as producing more individuated perceptions of out-group members and more personalized relationships. Intergroup contact can also produce more inclusive, superordinate representations of the groups, which can harness the psychological forces that contribute to intergroup bias and redirect them to improve attitudes toward people who would otherwise be recognized only as out-group members. Understanding the processes involved in the nature and development of prejudice can thus guide, both theoretically and pragmatically, interventions that can effectively reduce both traditional and contemporary forms of prejudice.

Recommended Reading

Brewer, M.B., & Miller, N. (1996). *Intergroup relations*. Pacific Grove, CA: Brooks/Cole.
Brown, R.J. (1995). *Prejudice*. Cambridge, MA: Blackwell.
Hawley, W.D., & Jackson, A.W. (Eds.). (1995). *Toward a common destiny: Improving race and ethnic relations in America*. San Francisco: Jossey-Bass.

Landis, D., & Bhagat, R.S. (Eds.). (1996). *Handbook of intercultural training*. Thousand Oaks, CA: Sage.

Stephan, W.G., & Stephan, C.W. (1996). *Intergroup relations*. Boulder, CO: Westview Press.

Acknowledgments—Preparation of this article was facilitated by National Institute of Mental Health Grant MH 48721.

Notes

1. Address correspondence to John F. Dovidio, Department of Psychology, Colgate University, Hamilton, NY 13346; e-mail: jdovidio@mail.colgate.edu.

2. For further information and a demonstration in which you can test the automaticity of your own racial attitudes using the Implicit Association Test, see Anthony Greenwald's World Wide Web site: http://weber.u.washington.edu/~agg/ (e-mail: agg@u.washington.edu).

References

Aronson, E., & Patnoe, S. (1997). *The jigsaw classroom*. New York: Longman.

Brewer, M.B., & Miller, N. (1984). Beyond the contact hypothesis: Theoretical perspectives on desegregation. In N. Miller & M.B. Brewer (Eds.), *Groups in contact: The psychology of desegregation* (pp. 281-302). Orlando, FL: Academic Press.

Devine, P.G., & Monteith, M.J. (1993). The role of discrepancy–associated affect in prejudice reduction. In D.M. Mackie & D.L. Hamilton (Eds.), *Affect, cognition, and stereotyping: Interactive processes in intergroup perception* (pp. 317-344). Orlando, FL: Academic Press.

Dovidio, J.F., & Gaertner, S.L. (1998). On the nature of contemporary prejudice: The causes, consequences, and challenges of aversive racism. In J. Eberhardt & S.T. Fiske (Eds.), *Confronting racism: The problem and the response* (pp. 3-32). Newbury Park, CA: Sage.

Gaertner, S.L., & Dovidio, J.F. (1986). The aversive form of racism. In J.F. Dovidio & S.L. Gaertner (Eds.), *Prejudice, discrimination, and racism* (pp. 61-89). Orlando, FL: Academic Press.

Gaertner, S.L., Dovidio, J.F., Anastasio, P.A., Bachman, B.A., & Rust, M.C. (1993). The Common Ingroup Identity Model: Recategorization and the reduction of intergroup bias. In W. Stroebe & M. Hewstone (Eds.), *European review of social psychology* (Vol. 4, pp. 1-26). London: Wiley.

Hewstone, M. (1996). Contact and categorization: Social psychological interventions to change intergroup relations. In N. Macrae, M. Hewstone, & C. Stangor (Eds.), *Foundations of stereotypes and stereotyping* (pp. 323-368). New York: Guilford Press.

Jones, J.M. (1997). *Prejudice and racism* (2nd ed.). New York: McGraw-Hill.

LaFromboise, T, Coleman, H.L.K., & Gerton, J. (1993). Psychological impact of biculturalism: Evidence and theory. *Psychological Bulletin, 114*, 395-412.

Pettigrew, T.F. (1998). Intergroup Contact Theory. *Annual Review of Psychology, 49*, 65-85.

Sears, D.C. (1988). Symbolic racism. In P.A. Katz & D.A. Taylor (Eds.), *Eliminating racism: Profiles in controversy* (pp. 53-84). New York: Plenum Press.

Stephan, W.G., & Stephan, C.W (1984). The role of ignorance in intergroup relations. In N. Miller & M.B. Brewer (Eds.), *Groups in contact: The Psychology of desegregation* (pp. 229-257). Orlando, FL: Academic Press.

Tajfel, H., & Turner, J.C. (1979). An integrative theory of intergroup conflict. In W.G. Austin & S. Worchel (Eds.), *The social psychology of intergroup relations* (pp. 33-48). Monterey, CA: Brooks/Cole.

Urban, L.M., & Miller, N. (1998). A theoretical analysis of crossed categorization effects: A meta-analysis. *Journal of Personality and Social Psychology, 74*, 894-908.

Wilder, D.A. (1986). Social categorization: Implications for creation and reduction of intergroup bias. In L. Berkowitz (Ed.), *Advances in experimental social psychology* (Vol. 19, pp. 291-355). Orlando, FL: Academic Press.

Critical Thinking Questions

1. Like the Fiske (2002) article in this section, this article distinguishes between two types of prejudice: intentional and subtle. Compare and contrast the information summarized in these two articles. What is the take-home point of each? How might Fiske in 2002 critique the main arguments that Dovidio and Gaertner made in 1999?

2. Distinguish between individual-level and intergroup approaches to reducing prejudice. Why might the approaches for dealing with traditional, intentional prejudice need to be different for more subtle prejudice?

3. Describe intergroup contact as a method of reducing prejudice. How does this lead to decategorization, and how does this relate to the Common In-Group Identity Model?

Applying Social Psychology:
Health and Justice

A passing glance through the preceding articles and sections quickly reveals that social psychology, although a basic research field, often is applicable to real-world issues and problems. Basic research speaks to cross-cultural understanding and intergroup relations (e.g., Elfenbein & Ambady, 2000; Fiske, 2002), lack of integrity in the workplace and job discrimination (e.g., Batson & Thompson, 2001; Dovidio & Gaertner, 1999), stress and health (e.g., Fincham, 2003; Contrada et al., 2000), violence in society (e.g., Baumeister, Bushman, & Campbell, 2000), and change through self-help, training, or therapy (e.g., Polivy & Herman, 2001). Like basic research, applied research relies upon theory and stringent methodology, but its primary goal is applicability. Some fields that are tightly tied to applied issues (e.g., organizational psychology, environmental psychology, health psychology, forensic psychology) have strong roots in social psychology. This final section introduces two areas that have remained important to both applied and basic social psychology researchers: psychosocial influences on health and the social psychological processes operating in the legal system.

Health psychology is by nature interdisciplinary, relying upon medical fields such as epidemiology and psychology fields such as clinical and social psychology. Social psychologists interested in health have addressed a number of issues, including self-regulation and attitude change. For example, individuals may engage in risky behaviors (e.g., taking amphetamines), fail to engage in preventative behaviors (e.g., using condoms or sun-screen), or avoid detecting health problems (e.g., not conducting breast or testicle self-exams). Applied social psychologists who are interested in health may endeavor to ascertain why people take risks, as well as how training, public service announcements, and other interventions can promote health. For instance, individuals may experience dissonance at the incongruity between their risky behavior and alternate behaviors, but may continue their risks if they are able to reduce the dissonance by adjusting beliefs. They can, for example, trivialize their risk (e.g., I've never had sex with someone who *looks* like she had a sexually transmitted disease) or poking holes in the argument reporting the risk (e.g., Who cares what a study in Australia says about skin cancer?). But if people cannot reduce dissonance through such mental gymnastics, dissonance ultimately may play a role in reducing risk behavior (cf. Tesser, 2001).

Researchers interested in health also may examine how social and personality factors are related to successful recovery. For example, people who are able to realize that the situation could be worse show better outcomes (i.e., they make downward social comparisons; cf. Suls, Martin, & Wheeler, 2002). Realistic optimism or resilience also may be associated with better health outcomes; individuals with these personality characteristics "bounce back" more quickly than less optimistic or less resilient individuals. Conversely, individuals who are lonely conceivably might have more difficulty recovering or fending off illness. Cacioppo, Hawkley, and Bernston (2003) suggest that loneliness adds one more stressor to life. Loneliness is associated with lowered immune functioning, inflated blood pressure, and less efficient sleep patterns. Along a similar vein, individuals who have limited social support also show reduced resistance to viruses (Uchino, Uno, & Holt-Lunstad, 1999).

Why is good social support and not being lonely so important to health? For starters, supportive friends and family members may discourage risky behaviors, assist in their reduction, and encourage healthy behaviors. Their presence also may mitigate other sources of stress in one's life. They can provide tangible support, such as relieving one of duties that currently are difficult to manage during illness or recovery (e.g., running errands, yard maintenance). Close others can provide emotional support, by allowing the person to express concerns and work through fears (i.e., rather than suppressing fears, which could act as an additional stressor). Even when one is not sick or recovering from illness, having supportive friends and family simply might make one happier. All things being equal, having a subjective sense of well-being may put less stress on one's physical person. Subjective well-being sometimes can translate to objective well-being.

As is evident from the readings thus far, subjective perceptions and objective reality are not always aligned, however. What people believe is true of themselves (Gilovich & Savitsky, 1999) or others (cf. Fincham, 2003; Fiske, 2002), is fair or justified (cf. Batson & Thompson, 2001), or is intended versus happenstance (Norenzayan & Nisbett, 2000) often is a matter of viewpoint. This disparity perhaps is most keenly noticed in social psychological research concerning justice and the legal system. For example, although artistic renditions of "Justice" depict her blindfolded, juries, witnesses, judges, attorneys, and victims fall prey to the same biases that plague most human social understanding. Witnesses and victims may be more likely to mis-identify individuals from racial or gender outgroups (cf. Elfenbein & Ambady, 2003). Juries may be influenced strongly by witnesses who exude confidence, even though confidence and accuracy may be poorly related (Wells, Olson, & Charman, 2002); juries also may be influenced by the demeanor of the judge, whom they regard as an expert. Does the defendant have supportive family members present, is he or she a member of one's own ingroup, is there a member of the defendant's ingroup on the jury, does the judge appear to dislike the prosecuting attorney, is the witness credible? All of these factors— in addition to the facts of the case—can influence the outcome.

In cases that go to trial, a jury deliberates upon the evidence presented. The ultimate goal of the jury is to determine whether a law has been broken and, sometimes, to recommend a punishment. Researchers interested in jury decision-making might consider the emergence of leadership, convergent thinking about a single plausible explanation, use of persuasive arguments, and pressures toward conformity. Behind all this gloriously complex and sometimes caustic group behavior remains the goal: determine if a law has been broken and recommend a punishment. As Darley (2001) observes, citizens' understanding of justice is not always in line with that of the legal system. What is recognized legally as rape, failure to help, or intent may not be viewed as such by the citizens whom the justice system presumably serves.

Social psychological research about the legal system and about psychosocial influences on health only scratch the surface of how social psychology is applied to real-world issues. Given that our most complex situations comprise interactions with other people, both research traditions duly reflect the heart of social psychology: the person in the situation. Be it lab or field research, the person in the situation must be studied with respect to understanding the basic processes underlying behavior, as well as articulating clearly the applications of such understanding.

Social Support, Physiological Processes, and Health

Bert N. Uchino,[1] Darcy Uno, and Julianne Holt-Lunstad
Department of Psychology and Health Psychology Program,
University of Utah, Salt Lake City, Utah

Abstract

Social relationships serve important functions in people's everyday lives. Epidemiological research indicates that supportive relationships may also significantly protect individuals from various causes of mortality, including cardiovascular disease. An important issue is how social support influences such long-term health outcomes. In this article, we review evidence indicating that social support may influence mortality via changes in the cardiovascular, endocrine, and immune systems. These data suggest that it may be worthwhile to incorporate social-support interventions in the prevention and treatment of physical health problems.

Keywords

social support; cardiovascular function; immune function; health

Relationships with others form a ubiquitous part of people's everyday lives. In the classic analysis by Durkheim (1897/1951), suicide rates were higher among individuals who were less socially integrated than among those who had many social ties. The loneliness and despair that characterize a lack of social connections may be responsible for such unfortunate outcomes. Less obvious, however, is the possibility that individuals with poor relationships may also be more at risk for physical illnesses, such as cardiovascular disease, cancer, or infectious diseases. Is there evidence that such an association exists? If so, how is it that social relationships influence such disease processes?

The answer to the first question is relatively well documented. A review of large prospective studies comparing groups with differing degrees of social integration found that less socially integrated individuals had higher mortality rates from all causes, including cardiovascular mortality (House, Landis, & Umberson, 1988). In fact, the evidence linking social relationships to mortality was comparable to the evidence linking standard risk factors such as smoking and physical activity to mortality. What is less known is the answer to the second question, that is, how social relationships influence such long-term health outcomes. In this article, we review the evidence linking positive aspects of social relationships (i.e., social support) to physiological processes. These associations are helping us to understand how relationships may influence physical health outcomes such as cardiovascular disease.

HOW MIGHT RELATIONSHIPS INFLUENCE PHYSICAL HEALTH OUTCOMES?

Relationships serve important functions. For instance, most people can recall times when others made a difference in their lives by giving good advice (informational support); helping them feel better about themselves (emotional support); directly providing aid, such as money (tangible support); or just "hanging out" with them (belonging support). The actual or perceived availability of these helpful behaviors by others is broadly defined as social support.

Figure 1 depicts a simplified model of how social support might influence physical health outcomes (see Cohen, 1988, for a detailed model). The major pathway depicted in the top portion of the figure suggests that social support may be beneficial because it protects individuals from the deleterious behavioral and physiological consequences of stress. In theory, social support may decrease how stressful an individual finds an event to be. For instance, a person who has supportive ties may experience less job stress because close others provide helpful information or reaffirm other aspects of that person's life (e.g., familial role). The decreased stress appraisal may in turn influence psychological processes such as negative mood states, feelings of personal control, and self-esteem. These psychological processes are thought to influence the cardiovascular, endocrine, and immune systems, with implications for relevant disease outcomes (Kiecolt-Glaser & Glaser,1995). For instance, over the long term, alterations in cardiovascular function (e.g., heart rate) may influence cardiovascular disorders such as high blood pressure, whereas a decrease in immune function may have implications for cancer and infectious diseases. However, even when individuals are not encountering stressful life events, it is possible that social support may affect physiological processes by directly influencing the psychological processes of self-esteem, feelings of personal control, and negative mood states. For instance, simply being in the company of close friends may elevate one's mood.

An additional pathway by which social support may be linked to physical health outcomes is through the modification of health behaviors, such as smoking, exercise, and diet (Umberson, 1987), that in turn influence relevant physiological processes (e.g., exercise decreases blood pressure). There are several ways in which social support may influence health behaviors. First, higher levels of stress have been linked to poorer health behaviors (Kiecolt-Glaser & Glaser, 1995). Social support may facilitate better health behaviors because it decreases

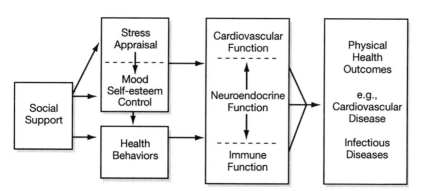

Fig. 1. Simplified model of how social support may influence physical health outcomes. Dotted lines within the boxes separate distinct pathways within the various systems.

the amount of stress that an individual experiences. Second, social support may directly motivate individuals to engage in more healthy practices. For instance, close family members may place pressures on an individual to exercise or stop smoking. It is also possible that having adequate social support communicates the fact that one is loved, and this may lead to better health behaviors by increasing the motivation to care for oneself.

IS SOCIAL SUPPORT RELATED TO PHYSIOLOGICAL PROCESSES?

The model shown in Figure 1 indicates that social support ultimately influences health outcomes via relevant biological pathways. In a recent review, we examined the evidence linking social support to physiological processes that might influence disease risk (Uchino, Cacioppo, & Kiecolt Glaser, 1996). In particular, we focused on the cardiovascular, endocrine, and immune systems as potential pathways by which social support might influence health.

Most of the studies we examined investigated the association between social support and cardiovascular function. There were more than 50 such studies, and most focused on blood pressure. Blood pressure is an important variable because over time, elevations in blood pressure can be a risk factor for cardiovascular diseases. In fact, there is increasing concern about the potential risk of elevated blood pressure even below the range that is normally considered hypertensive (MacMahon et al., 1990). Overall, we found in our review of studies that individuals with high levels of social support had lower blood pressure than individuals with lower levels of social support.

It is noteworthy that there was also evidence linking social support to better blood pressure regulation in hypertensive patients. Most of these studies were interventions that utilized the patient's spouse as a source of support to help the patient control his or her blood pressure. These intervention studies provide direct evidence for the health relevance of social support and suggest that recruiting familial sources of support may be a particularly effective (and cost-effective) intervention strategy.

Finally, recent studies suggest that social support can reduce the magnitude of cardiovascular changes during stressful circumstances, a finding consistent with the model in Figure 1. For instance, Gerin, Pieper, Levy, and Pickering (1992) compared physiological reactivity of subjects who participated in a debate task when a supportive person (an individual who agreed with the participant) was or was not present. The presence of the supportive person was associated with lower blood pressure and heart rate changes during the task. The ability of social support to reduce cardiovascular changes during stress is important because it has been hypothesized that heightened physiological reactivity to stress may increase the risk for the development of cardiovascular disorders (Manuck,1994). The finding of lowered cardiovascular reactivity when social support is available may also have implications for individuals who have existing cardiovascular disease, as heightened cardiovascular changes when psychological stressors are experienced can induce a temporary imbalance of oxygen supply and demand in the heart (Krantz et al., 1991). This imbalance can lead to potentially dangerous cardiac conditions in such at-risk populations.

In our review of the literature, we also examined 19 studies that tested the possibility that social support may be related to aspects of immune function. An association between social support and immunity would be important because the immune system is responsible for the body's defense against infectious and malignant (cancerous) diseases. In general, the available studies suggest that social support is related to a stronger immune response. For instance, natural killer cells are an important line of defense against virus-infected and some tumor cells. In our review, several studies found that individuals with high levels of social support had stronger natural killer cell responses (i.e., ability to kill susceptible tumor cells) than individuals with lower levels of social support.

The associations between social support and immune function are consistent with the results of a recent study by Cohen, Doyle, Skoner, Rabin, and Gwaltney (1997), who examined whether social support predicted susceptibility to the common-cold virus. In this study, consenting participants were directly exposed to common-cold viruses (i.e., via nasal drops) and quarantined for 5 days. Individuals who had more diverse social networks (i.e., relationships in a variety of domains, such as work, home, and church) were less likely to develop clinical colds than individuals with less diverse networks. The authors discussed the possibility that having a diverse social network may be particularly beneficial as support may be obtained from a variety of sources.

It is important to note that many of the studies that found an association between social support and immune function were conducted with older adult populations. Aging is associated with decreased immunity, and infectious diseases are a major source of morbidity and mortality in older adults. Thus, the lowered immune function in older individuals with low social support may be a finding with particular health relevance.

One important way in which social support may influence the immune system is via the release of endocrine hormones. Environmental factors such as stress can lead to the release of hormones (i.e., catecholamines and cortisol) that in turn influence the immune system. This is possible because many cells of the immune system have hormone receptors that can augment or inhibit the cells' function when activated by specific endocrine hormones. Unfortunately, there is not much research examining if social support is related to endocrine function. However, preliminary evidence from the MacArthur studies of successful aging suggests that higher levels of social support may be linked to lower levels of catecholamines and cortisol in men (Seeman, Berkman, Blazer, & Rowe, 1994). These data are consistent with the research linking social support to alterations in the cardiovascular system because endocrine hormones such as catecholamines directly influence cardiovascular function.

CONCLUSIONS

The available evidence is consistent with the possibility that social support may influence physical health outcomes via relevant physiological processes. What is less clear in this literature is exactly how these changes occur. As shown in

Figure 1, there are a number of potential pathways, including changes in negative mood states or health behaviors, but direct evidence bearing on the validity of these pathways is presently lacking. A few studies we reviewed did look for a health-behavior pathway, along with psychological pathways involving depression and perceived stress. Although preliminary, these studies found that these factors could not account for the association between social support and physiological function. Unfortunately, many of these studies utilized cross-sectional designs that provide a less sensitive test of the pathways linking social support to physiological function than do longitudinal designs. This point underscores the importance of conducting longitudinal studies that examine how these dynamic processes involving social support, physiology, and actual health outcomes unfold over time.

An additional issue that warrants further attention is the conditions under which social relationships are most beneficial. Not all close relationships are uniformly positive (consider, e.g., marital conflict). This is an important consideration because negative interactions can interfere with effective social support. In addition, having many supportive friends and family could be beneficial, but it may also entail obligations to be a support provider. At least in some circumstances, being a support provider can be a significant source of stress (e.g., the demands of caregiving activities). These issues highlight the importance of investigating how the relative balance of positive and negative aspects of close relationships influences physiological function and subsequent health outcomes.

Overall, however, we believe that the research reviewed has significant implications for present notions of health and well-being. Would it be possible to utilize this research in combination with standard medical approaches in preventing and treating physical disease? Several interventions suggest the promise of such an approach. Spiegel, Bloom, Kraemer, and Gottheil (1989) found that breast cancer patients randomly assigned to a support group lived almost twice as long as patients simply given routine oncological care. There is also indirect evidence of beneficial effects from general psychosocial interventions that include social-support intervention (Linden, Stossel, & Maurice, 1996). For instance, Fawzy et al. (1993) evaluated the effects of a 6-week structured group intervention that provided education, problem-solving skills, stress management, and social support to cancer patients. A 6-year follow-up revealed that only 9% of individuals in the structured group intervention had died, compared with 29% of individuals in the no-intervention condition. These studies suggest the potential promise of future interventions aimed at utilizing social relationships to promote positive health outcomes.

Recommended Reading

Berkman, L.F. (1995). The role of social relations in health promotion. *Psychosomatic Medicine, 57*, 245-254.
House, J.S., Landis, K.R., & Umberson, D. (1988). (See References)
Kiecolt-Glaser, J.K., & Glaser, R. (1995). (See References)
Uchino, B.N., Cacioppo, J.T., & Kiecolt-Glaser, K.G. (1996). (See References)

Wills, T.A. (1997). Social support and health. In A. Baum, S. Newman, J. Weinman, R. West, & C. McManus (Eds.), *Cambridge handbook of psychology, health, and medicine* (pp. 168-171). New York: Cambridge University Press.

Acknowledgments—Preparation of this article was generously supported by National Institute on Aging Grant No. 1 R55 AG13968 and National Institute of Mental Health Grant No. 1 RO1MH58690. We would like to thank our supportive spouses, Heather M. Llenos, Sean Fujioka, and Nathan Lunstad, for their helpful suggestions on this manuscript. This article is dedicated to the memory of Sean K. Okumura.

Note

1. Address correspondence to Bert N. Uchino, Department of Psychology, 390 S. 1530 E., Room 502, University of Utah, Salt Lake City, UT 84112; e-mail: uchino@psych.utah.edu.

References

Cohen, S. (1988). Psychological models of the role of social support in the etiology of physical disease. *Health Psychology, 7,* 269-297.

Cohen, S., Doyle, W.J., Skoner, D.P, Robin, B.S., & Gwaltney, J.M. (1997). Social ties and susceptibility to the common cold. *Journal of the American Medical Association, 277,* 1940-1944.

Durkheim, E. (1951). *Suicide* (J.A. Spaulding & G. Simpson, Trans.). New York: Free Press. (Original work published 1897)

Fawzy, F.I., Fawzy, N.W., Hyun, C.S., Gutherie, D., Fahey, J.L., & Morton, D. (1993). Malignant melanoma: Effects of an early structured psychiatric intervention, coping, and affective state on recurrence and survival six years later. *Archives of General Psychiatry, 50,* 681-689.

Gerin, W., Pieper, C., Levy, R., & Pickering, T.G. (1992). Social support in social interactions: A moderator of cardiovascular reactivity. *Psychosomatic Medicine, 54,* 324-336.

House, J.S., Landis, K.R., & Umberson, D. (1988). Social relationships and health. *Science, 241,* 540-545.

Kiecolt-Glaser, J.K., & Glaser, R. (1995). Psychoneuroimmunology and health consequences: Data and shared mechanisms. *Psychosomatic Medicine, 57,* 269-274.

Krantz, D.S., Helmers, K.F., Bairey, N., Nebel, L.E., Hedges, S.M., & Rozanski, A. (1991). Cardiovascular reactivity and mental stress-induced myocardial ischemia in patients with coronary artery disease. *Psychosomatic Medicine, 53,*142.

Linden, W., Stossel, C., & Maurice, J. (1996). Psychosocial interventions for patients with coronary artery disease. *Archives of Internal Medicine, 156,* 745-752.

MacMahon, S., Peto, R., Cutler, J., Collins, R., Sorlie, P., Neaton, J., Abbott, R., Godwin, J., Dyer, A., & Stamler, J. (1990). Blood pressure, stroke, and coronary heart disease. Part 1, prolonged differences in blood pressure: Prospective observational studies corrected for the regression dilution bias. *Lancet, 335,* 765-774.

Manuck, S.B. (1994). Cardiovascular reactivity in cardiovascular disease: "Once more unto the breach." *International Journal of Behavioral Medicine, 1,* 4-31.

Seeman, T.E., Berkman, L.E, Blazer, D., & Rowe, J.W. (1994). Social ties and support and neuroendocrine function: The MacArthur studies of successful aging. *Annals of Behavioral Medicine, 16,* 95-106.

Spiegel, D., Bloom, J.R., Kraemer, H.C., & Gottheil, E. (1989). Effect of psychosocial treatment on survival of patients with metastatic breast cancer. *Lancet, 334,* 888-891.

Uchino, B.N., Cacioppo, J.T., & Kiecolt-Glaser, K.G. (1996). The relationships between social support and physiological processes: A review with emphasis on underlying mechanisms and implications for health. *Psychological Bulletin, 119,* 488-531.

Umberson, D. (1987). Family status and health behaviors: Social control as a dimension of social integration. *Journal of Health and Social Behavior, 28,* 306-319.

Critical Thinking Questions

1. Briefly describe the model predicted in Figure 1. According to this model, how does social support relate to physical health outcomes such as cardiovascular disease and infectious diseases?

2. Stress emerges as an important variable in the relation between social support and physical health outcomes, and the authors mention several examples of stress as it relates to social support. How might ethnicity-related stress (as discussed in the Contrada et al. article in the previous section) be influential in this relation?

3. The authors suggest that future research should consider different conditions under which social relationships are beneficial. Speculate on some circumstances in which social relationships might not be beneficial to physical health. Does the existence of these circumstances discredit the model presented in Figure 1? Explain.

The Anatomy of Loneliness

John T. Cacioppo,[1] Louise C. Hawkley, and Gary G. Berntson

Department of Psychology, University of Chicago, Chicago, Illinois (J.T.C., L.C.H.), and Department of Psychology, Ohio State University, Columbus, Ohio (G.G.B.)

Abstract

Loneliness is a potent but little understood risk factor for broad-based morbidity and mortality. We review five social neurobehavioral mechanisms that may account for this association. The evidence suggests that different mechanisms explain short-term and long-term effects, and that the long-term effects operate through multiple pathways. Implications for the design of interventions are discussed.

Keywords

loneliness; stress; physiology; health

Dramatic changes have occurred in the age distribution of the population and the structure of social relationships in the United States. Within the past decade, for instance, the proportion of single-parent households rose 21%, while the number of people living alone increased by 20% (Hobbs & Stoops, 2002). As objective social isolation increases, the likelihood that intimate and social needs are met decreases, and the prevalence of loneliness increases (de Jong-Gierveld, 1987). In light of epidemiological research showing that loneliness is a risk factor for broad-based morbidity and mortality (Seeman, 2000), identifying the mechanisms underlying this association may be important.

TRANSDUCTION PATHWAYS

We have examined five mechanisms through which loneliness, or related factors, may contribute to broad-based morbidity and mortality across the life span: (a) evolutionary fitness, (b) medical decision making, (c) health behaviors and lifestyles, (d) stressful lives, and (e) repair and maintenance physiology.

Evolutionary Fitness

The evolutionary-fitness account, which derives from evolutionary psychology, posits that non-lonely individuals are healthier and more physically appealing and intelligent than lonely individuals are. Buss and Schmitt (1993) have argued that features judged to be physically attractive are also features associated with health and fertility. To assess this hypothesis, we used scores on the UCLA Loneliness Scale to categorize young adults as either lonely or non-lonely. Contrary to the hypothesis, the two groups did not differ significantly in physical attractiveness, height, weight, body mass index, education, age, scholastic aptitude, grade-point average, or number of roommates (Cacioppo et al., 2000).

Medical Decision Making

According to this account, the health care system provides better medical care for obviously non-lonely individuals than for lonely individuals. Developments in medicine have made it possible to maintain an individual's life for extended periods of time, but the cost of doing so demands strategies more rational than "maximum care for all" when making decisions about the allocation of limited health resources. Therefore, the association between loneliness and health may arise subtly from differences in medical decisions and care provisions for patients who appear socially connected versus those who appear isolated.

To address this possibility, we conducted a national study, randomly sampling physicians whose practice would place them in frequent contact with patients who were over 55 years of age and therefore more likely than average to be facing serious health concerns. The results were clear: Physicians reported not only that they themselves provided better or more complete medical care to patients who had supportive families than to patients who appeared to be socially isolated, but also that, in their experience, other doctors, nurses, and ancillary staff did the same.

Health Behaviors

If people simply avoid smoking, a sedentary lifestyle, and obesity, they add years to their life expectancy (Committee on Future Directions for Behavioral and Social Sciences Research, 2001). According to the health-behavior (or social-control) account of the association between loneliness and health, compared with people who are socially connected, those who are lonely are exposed to weaker pressures from and control by friends and loved ones to perform healthy behaviors and to access health care when needed.

In our survey of more than 2,600 young adults and our more intensive study of 135 of these individuals, we found that individuals who scored high versus low on the UCLA Loneliness Scale did not differ in the amount of weekly exercise in which they engaged, their use of tobacco, or their consumption of caffeine and soda; high scorers consumed slightly more alcohol than individuals who scored average or low on this loneliness scale. The comparability of health behaviors does not appear to be limited to a sample of young adults, either; a study of older adults in south Chicago revealed comparable levels of daily tobacco use, weekly caffeine consumption, weekly alcohol consumption, medical compliance, use of seat belts, and healthiness of diet across the full range of scores on the UCLA Loneliness Scale (Cacioppo et al., 2000; Cacioppo, Hawkley, Berntson, et al., 2002; cf. Cacioppo, Hawkley, Crawford, et al., 2002). Epidemiological studies, too, find health behaviors account for only a small portion of the association between loneliness and health (Seeman, 2000).

Unlike the health behaviors typically examined—such as exercise, diet, and smoking—suicide is a deliberate behavior that has a short rather than long time course from the time of the act to the point of death. Does suicide contribute to higher death rates in lonely than non-lonely individuals? The extant evidence, though limited, suggests it does. In the United States, suicide rates are highest among individuals aged 65 years and older, and within this group, suicide rates are highest for those who are divorced or widowed. Social isolation and bereavement are also risk factors for suicide for young people ages 15 to 24, for whom suicide is the third leading cause of death. Overall, living alone increases the risk of suicide across the life span (Goldsmith, Pellmar, Kleinman, & Bunney, 2002).

Cumulative Stress

A third family of mechanisms through which loneliness may operate to affect health involves stress. The notion is that lonely individuals have higher levels of stress in their lives than non-lonely individuals do, and that this stress contributes to wear and tear on individual organs (e.g., the heart) and deterioration of regulatory mechanisms (e.g., homeostasis) in the brain and body. As a consequence, the health of lonely individuals fails sooner than the health of non-lonely individuals.

Stress has tended to be treated as if it represented a single mechanism, although, in fact, it represents a family of mechanisms that serve to mobilize and defend the body (e.g., fight or flight). Each mechanism comprises a different set of operations that could contribute to higher levels of stress in the lives of lonely than non-lonely individuals. According to the *added-stress hypothesis,* loneliness is associated with perceptions of social rejection and exclusion, which are themselves stressors that produce negative affect and lowered feelings of self-worth and, in turn, promote chronic elevations in activity in the sympathetic nervous, sympathetic adrenomedullary (SAM), and hypothalamic-pituitary-adrenocortical (HPA) systems.[2] According to the *differential-exposure hypothesis,* lonely individuals are exposed to stressful events more frequently than non-lonely individuals, so that they experience more frequent sympathetic, SAM, and HPA activation; over time, the greater wear and tear on the regulatory mechanisms of lonely individuals promotes chronic elevations in sympathetic, SAM, and HPA activity. The *differential-reactivity hypothesis* posits that the stressors to which lonely individuals are exposed may not be more frequent than the stressors non-lonely individuals experience, but are more intense, eliciting stronger sympathetic, SAM, and HPA activation and, over time, chronic elevations in such activation. Finally, the *differential-stress-buffering hypothesis* posits that lonely individuals are less likely than non-lonely individuals to have other people to whom they can turn for assistance. Therefore, the stressors to which lonely individuals are exposed, even if objectively comparable in frequency and intensity, tend to be perceived as more severe.

We have collected evidence from four sources to test these hypotheses: (a) questionnaires about life events, major life stressors, daily uplifts and hassles, and perceived stress (Cacioppo et al., 2000; Cacioppo, Hawkley, Crawford, et al., 2002); (b) participants' reports about the people and events to which they were exposed and the stresses they were feeling when queried at random times during a normal day (a method referred to as experience sampling; Hawkley, Burleson, Berntson, & Cacioppo, in press); (c) physiological measures taken before, during, and after participants were exposed to acute psychological stressors and postural adjustments (e.g., the transition from sitting to standing; Cacioppo, Hawkley, Crawford, et al., 2002); and (d) physiological measurements taken at random times as participants went about their activities during the course of a normal day (Hawkley et al., in press). Our results were consistent with the added-stress hypothesis, in that lonely individuals reported higher levels of perceived stress than non-lonely individuals even when the frequency and intensity of the stressors did not differ and even when they were relaxing. However, little evidence for the differential-exposure hypothesis was found in the experience-sampling study, and lonely and non-lonely participants did not differ in the reported number of major life stressors, number of life events the prior year, and number of daily hassles or uplifts.

Despite the similarities in the frequency of exposure to objective stressors, analyses indicated that lonely, relative to non-lonely, individuals reported more severe hassles, less intense uplifts, and more stressful everyday events—a pattern consistent with the differential-reactivity hypothesis. Some support for the operation of stress buffering was found, as well. Lonely and non-lonely individuals were just as likely to interact with other people, but for lonely individuals the interactions were of poorer quality and provided less support and comfort (Hawkley et al., in press). The detrimental effects of loneliness were only partly attributable to weaker buffers in times of stress, however. In the experience-sampling study, the difference between lonely and non-lonely individuals' ratings of the severity of stressors did not vary as a function of the presence of other people; instead, social interactions, themselves a potential uplift and a source of pleasure for most individuals, were experienced less positively by lonely than by non-lonely individuals, as might be expected from the added-stress hypothesis.

In healthy, resilient young adults, physiological regulation is robust to a variety of assaults. We therefore expected regulated end points such as blood pressure to be normal in lonely young adults but to rise in lonely older adults as physiological resilience declines with age. Blood pressure reflects two component processes, the amount of blood per minute flowing from the heart into the circulatory system (cardiac output) and the total resistance to blood flow from the heart throughout the circulatory system (total peripheral resistance). The greater the total peripheral resistance or the cardiac output, the greater the blood pressure. Total peripheral resistance and cardiac output are components of a regulatory feedback system that serves to maintain normal blood pressure, so they may show signs of cumulative stress before blood pressure does.

As expected, among young people blood pressure was comparable in lonely and non-lonely individuals, but lonely individuals had higher total peripheral resistance and lower cardiac output than did non-lonely individuals. These differences were apparent when participants were at rest and when they performed postural adjustments and psychological stressors (Cacioppo, Hawkley, Crawford, et al., 2002), and both during the course of a normal day and in the laboratory (Hawkley et al., in press).

Chronic elevations in total peripheral resistance mean not only that the heart muscle must work harder to distribute the same amount of blood through the circulatory system, but also that the vasculature may become damaged by blood flow turbulence induced by blood vessels with a reduced diameter. Further, physiological mechanisms in the brain and in the body that serve to maintain normal blood pressure may undergo wear and tear over time, leading to elevated blood pressure. Consistently elevated levels of vascular resistance, coupled with age-related decreases in vascular compliance (e.g., elasticity), may set the stage for the development of hypertension—a risk factor for a variety of diseases. We hypothesized that lonely older adults would, on average, have higher blood pressure than non-lonely older adults. Our study in south Chicago confirmed this hypothesis: Age was positively and significantly correlated with blood pressure in the group of lonely participants, but age and blood pressure were unrelated in the non-lonely group (Cacioppo, Hawkley, Crawford, et al., 2002).

Kiecolt-Glaser et al. (1984) reported that lonely, relative to non-lonely, individuals had higher urinary measures of cortisol, a powerful steroid secreted by the body, for instance, in response to stress. Using measures that reflected more momentary levels of cortisol than the measures Kiecolt-Glaser et al. used, and a momentary measure of the precursor of cortisol (adrenocorticotrophic hormone, or ACTH), we found that lonely individuals had higher morning levels of ACTH than non-lonely individuals, and slightly but nonsignificantly higher levels of cortisol (Cacioppo, Hawkley, Crawford, et al., 2002).

Repair and Maintenance Physiology

The final general transduction pathway, termed the *repair-and-maintenance hypothesis,* posits that loneliness weakens constructive or restorative processes that serve to repair, maintain, recover, and enhance physiological capacities. Sleep is the quintessential restorative behavior, and sleep deprivation has dramatic effects on metabolic, neural, and hormonal regulation that mimic those of aging. In one study (Cacioppo, Hawkley, Berntson, et al., 2002), lonely and non-lonely young adults had their sleep recorded during a night in the hospital and during several subsequent nights in their residence. At both sites, total time in bed did not differ as a function of loneliness, but the time in bed spent asleep was lower and wake time after sleep onset was higher for lonely than non-lonely individuals. Moreover, on the Pittsburgh Sleep Quality Inventory, lonely young adults reported poorer sleep quality, longer time in bed before falling asleep, longer perceived sleep duration, and greater daytime dysfunction due to sleepiness compared with non-lonely participants. These effects were replicated in our study of older adults in Chicago (Cacioppo, Hawkley, Crawford, et al., 2002, Study 2). Together, these results indicate that the restorative act of sleep is more efficient and effective—that is, salubrious—in non-lonely individuals than in lonely individuals.

CONCLUSION

The research on loneliness suggests that different mechanisms operate to explain short-term and long-term effects of loneliness on health and well-being. We have further found that slowly unfolding pathophysiological processes triggered by loneliness are the consequence of multiple physiological systems. An important question for future research is whether the specific disease that develops from the higher levels of cumulative wear and tear in lonely, compared with non-lonely, individuals reflects each individual's diathesis.

An important implication for intervention studies is that careful attention needs to be given to the different time courses of an intervention's effects on behavioral versus health outcomes. In a recent large multi-site intervention study (Sheps, Freedland, Golden, & McMahon, 2003), patients who had had a myocardial infarction received standard medical care or standard care plus treatment for depression and social deprivation. Despite improvements in depression and social support in the latter group, no differences in survival were found. Our review suggests that post-intervention measurement periods of weeks or months may allow time to detect changes in people's feelings but too little time for societal, community, interpersonal, and mental events to filter down to measurable pathophysiological and health outcomes.

Recommended Reading

Berscheid, E., & Reis, H. (1998). Attraction and close relationships. In D.T. Gilbert, S.T. Fiske, & G. Lindzey (Eds.), *The handbook of social psychology* (4th ed., pp. 193-281). New York: McGraw-Hill.
Cacioppo, J.T., Hawkley, L.C., Crawford, L.E., Ernst, J.M., Burleson, M.H., Kowalewski, R.B., Malarkey, W.B., Van Cauter, E., & Berntson, G.G. (2002). (See References)
House, J.S., Landis, K.R., & Umberson, D. (1988). Social relationships and health. *Science, 241,* 540-545.

Acknowledgments—Support for this research was provided by the John D. and Catherine T. MacArthur Foundation Network and National Institute of Aging Grant No. POI AG18911.

Notes

1. Address correspondence to John T. Cacioppo, Department of Psychology, University of Chicago, 5848 S. University Ave., Chicago, IL 60637; e-mail: cacioppo@uchicago.edu.

2. The sympathetic nervous system is a major division of the autonomic nervous system that prepares the body for action and responding to stressors. Both the SAM axis and the HPA axis are components of the endocrine system that also prepare the body for action and responding to stressors, but they do so through different hormones. The effects of the SAM system are similar to those of the sympathetic nervous system, but are typically slower and longer lasting. The effects of the HPA system take longer to occur, apply more generally, and require more time to dissipate than the effects of the SAM system or the sympathetic nervous system.

References

Buss, D.M., & Schmitt, D.P. (1993). Sexual strategies theory: An evolutionary perspective on human mating. *Psychological Review, 100,* 204-232.
Cacioppo, J.T., Ernst, J.M., Burleson, M.H., McClintock, M.K., Malarkey, W.B., Hawkley, L.C., Kowalewski, R.B., Paulsen, A., Hobson, J.A., Hugdahl, K., Spiegel, D., & Berntson, G.G. (2000). Lonely traits and concomitant physiological processes: The MacArthur Social Neuroscience Studies. *International Journal of Psychophysiology, 35,* 143-154.
Cacioppo, J.T., Hawkley, L.C., Berntson, G.G., Ernst, J.M., Gibbs, A.C., Stickgold, R., & Hobson, J.A. (2002). Do lonely days invade the nights? Potential social modulation of sleep efficiency. *Psychological Science, 13,* 384-387.
Cacioppo, J.T., Hawkley, L.C., Crawford, L.E., Ernst, J.M., Burleson, M.H., Kowalewski, R.B., Malarkey, W.B., Van Cauter, E., & Bemtson, G.G. (2002). Loneliness and health: Potential mechanisms. *Psychosomatic Medicine, 64,*407-417.

Committee on Future Directions for Behavioral and Social Sciences Research at the National Institutes of Health. (2001). *Health and behavior.* Washington, DC: National Academy Press.

de Jong-Gierveld, J. (1987). Developing and testing a model of loneliness. *Journal of Personality and Social Psychology, 53,* 119-128.

Goldsmith, S.K., Pellmar, T.C., Kleinman, A.M., & Bunney, W.E. (2002). *Reducing suicide: A national imperative.* Washington, DC: National Academy Press.

Hawkley, L.C., Burleson, M.H., Bemtson, G.G., & Cacioppo, J.T. (in press). Loneliness in everyday life: Cardiovascular activity, psychosocial context, and health behaviors. *Journal of Personality and Social Psychology.*

Hobbs, F., & Stoops, N. (2002). *Demographic trends in the 20th century* (U.S. Census Bureau, Census 2000 Special Reports, Series CENSR-4). Washington, DC: U.S. Government Printing Office.

Kiecolt-Glaser, J.K., Richer, D., George, J., Messick, G., Speicher, C.E., Garner, W., & Glaser, R. (1984). Urinary cortisol levels, cellular immunocompetency, and loneliness in psychiatric inpatients. *Psychosomatic Medicine, 46,* 15-23.

Seeman, T.E. (2000). Health promoting effects of friends and family on health outcomes in older adults. *American Journal of Health Promotion, 14,* 362-370.

Sheps, D.S., Freedland, K.E., Golden, R.N., & McMahon, R.P. (2003). ENRICHD and SADHART: Implications for future biobehavioral intervention efforts. *Psychosomatic Medicine, 65,* 1-2.

Critical Thinking Questions

1. Describe each of the five mechanisms that may explain why loneliness is a risk factor for poor physical health and mortality. Evaluate the empirical research support for each possible mechanism.

2. Once again, stress emerges as an important factor when considering the association between loneliness and health. Describe the four specific hypotheses related to stress that the authors present (e.g., added stress hypothesis), and discuss the research that either confirms or disconfirms each hypothesis.

3. Discuss the repair and maintenance hypothesis regarding the relationship between loneliness and physical health. What is the role of sleep in this theory? Could sleep disturbances also be related to stress? Explain.

Citizens' Sense of Justice and the Legal System

John M. Darley[1]

Psychology Department, Princeton University, Princeton, New Jersey

Abstract

When an actor commits a wrong action, citizens have perceptions of the kind of responsibility the actor incurs, the degree to which the act was mitigated or justified, and the appropriate punishment for the actor. The legislatively mandated law of criminal courts, statutes, and criminal codes deals with the same issues. Experimental evidence shows that there are important discrepancies between the principles that people and legal codes use to assign responsibility. That is, the moral retributive-justice principles that people use are sometimes in conflict with the directions in which modern code drafters are taking criminal law. These discrepancies may cause citizens to feel alienated from authority, and to reduce their voluntary compliance with legal codes.

Keywords

justice; morality; criminal responsibility; legal decisions

There are many contributions that psychology can make to the criminal justice system. For instance, psychological studies and theories are relevant to the distortions that can affect eyewitness testimony, or whether an individual is competent to stand trial. Other possible contributions are more controversial, in that they might require some considerable rethinking of significant aspects of the legal system. One such area centers around citizens' perceptions of justice, and the relation between those notions of justice and the rules of justice written into the various legal codes.

Why should we care about "commonsense justice?"[2] The reason is that if a legal system's rules for assigning blame and punishment diverge in important ways from the principles that the citizens believe in, then those citizens may lose respect for the legal system. They may continue to obey the rules that the "justice" system imposes, but will do so largely to avoid punishment. No society can continue to exist if its citizens take that attitude toward its legal system.

Does the system of justice in the United States have this problem? Are there important discrepancies between the laws and the citizens' sense of justice?

MAPPING THE CONTOURS OF THE CITIZENS' SENSE OF JUSTICE

A number of investigations have elucidated the outlines of U.S. citizens' sense of just procedures. A landmark series of studies (Thibaut & Walker, 1975) demonstrated Americans' preference for procedures that give all participants repeated opportunities to express "their side" of the case, rather than more court-guided inquisitorial procedures. Continuing this tradition, Tyler (1990) studied persons who had gone through court proceedings. If they felt the proceedings were fair and impartial, and that they had been treated with respect, they were willing to accept the verdict even when it went against them. There is less research on citizens' sense of retributive justice, punishments for acts of wrongdoing, but researchers recently have been turning to this area as well. The criminal code in force is decided in the United States on a state-by-state basis, but a large majority of states have based their criminal code on the Model Penal Code (MPC; American Law Institute, 1962), which was drafted by the American Law Institute in the 1950s. It is useful to contrast citizens' intuitions with this code both because it is likely to be the code in force in most jurisdictions and because the code set forth general principles of justice. We can therefore ask whether those principles, thought by the code drafters to be modem and rational, accord with the citizens' sense of just principles.

Attempted Crimes

In one such study (Darley, Sanderson, & LaMantha, 1996), my colleagues and I examined the MPC treatment of the concept of criminal attempt. The question at issue was this: When has a person come close enough toward committing a crime that he or she has committed a criminal action, and what should the penalty for that action be? The MPC holds that a person deserves punishment when he or she has "formed a settled intent" to commit a crime; this is a subjectivist standard that focuses on the person's criminal intent. In keeping with the view that intent is what matters, the MPC assigns the same penalty to attempt as it does to the completed offense. The MPC, in other words, criminalizes taking the early steps leading up to committing a crime and punishes taking those steps as severely as it punishes the completed crime. The older common-law standard was vastly different: It did not criminalize attempt until the actor was in what was called "dangerous proximity" to the crime (e.g., the would-be burglar had broken into the store), and it punished attempt to a lesser degree than the completed offense.

How do ordinary people think about attempt? Do they follow the subjectivist stance of the MPC, or do they hold the older common-law view? Pause for a moment and think about how to research this. One could ask people whether they agree with a series of statements, such as "A person's intent to commit a crime is what should determine his or her punishment." The problem with doing this is that the researcher is likely to find general agreement with a number of potentially contradictory principles. For this reason, researchers generally use what is called a policy-capturing approach, in which respondents are asked to judge a set of cases that differ along dimensions suggested by the competing theories being tested.

That is how my colleagues and I examined the competing principles that determine how attempts should be punished: We asked respondents to assign punishment after reading short scenarios involving agents who had taken one or more steps toward committing either robbery or murder. The pattern of results corresponded far more closely with the older common-law formulation than with the MPC. For the cases in which the agent had taken action preliminary to the crime (e.g., examining the premises that he planned to burgle), most respondents judged the person not guilty of any offense, and a few assigned a mild penalty.

179

The punishments showed a sharp increase in severity when the person reached the point of dangerous proximity to the crime, and even then they were only half as severe as the penalties assigned to the completed offense. The results of this and other studies (Robinson & Darley, 1998) indicate that people do not share the subjectivist perspective that forming the intent to take an action is the moral equivalent of taking the action.

Rape and Sexual Intercourse

In other studies, we have found other areas in which the code and the community disagree in important ways. In some cases, it seems intuitively plausible that the code-community differences might be due to a change in community standards over the years (although we do not think this is the cause of the differences regarding attempted crimes). For example, the MPC, drafted during the 1950s, assigns a very serious punishment to consensual intercourse with an underage partner, but our respondents saw this offense as much less serious (Robinson & Darley, 1995). However, the code mitigates the sentence if the underage partner has a history of promiscuity, and our respondents did not. The code also mitigates the penalty for forcible rape if a previous relationship existed between the rapist and the victim, or if the victim was a voluntary social companion of the rapist at the time of the rape. Our respondents, questioned in the 1990s, focused on whether the victim was the non-consenting victim of sexual assault; if she was, then they did not care whether a previous sexual relationship existed or the victim had been on a date with the rapist (many state codes have moved in this direction; Robinson & Darley, 1995, p. 204).

Omissions: Failing to Help

In Anglo-American law, no penalty is imposed for failing to help a stranger, even if that stranger's life is at risk and the help could be given at no risk to the helper. Macauley (1837), busily drafting the penal code for India, remarked, "It is evident that to attempt to punish men by law for not rendering to others all the service which is their [moral] duty to render to others would be preposterous" (note M, pp. 53-54). But why would this be preposterous? Macauley was making a disguised appeal to what people think. Do people think there should be no criminal liability assigned to a person who fails to rescue? Certainly, the MPC imposes no punishment for failure to rescue, even when the rescue could be accomplished without much inconvenience to the rescuer.

To test people's thoughts about failure to help, we presented subjects with a scenario in which a person was pushed into the deep water off a pier and called out that he was drowning (Robinson & Darley, 1995). A person who witnessed this could not swim, but saw that there was a life-saving flotation device that he could throw to the drowning man. He did not throw it, and the man died. Later, he reported that he did not want the man to drown, but "just didn't want to get too involved."

Respondents assigned an average punishment of about 2 months in jail to this person. When we varied how inconvenient it was for the person to intervene, respondents still gave about the same level of punishment. Only by creating a danger for a person who intervened did we begin to cancel the liability assigned to the non-helper. Thus, people expect strangers to intervene to help when a person's life is in danger, and think that failure to do so is criminal and deserves a penalty.

THE POSSIBLE CONSEQUENCES OF CITIZEN-CODE DISAGREEMENTS

Why should anyone care about discrepancies between legal codes and the community's commonsense notions of justice? One reason is that the people of the state are citizens, who have some right to have their voices heard when important moral issues are being turned into laws. A second reason concerns what happens to the community's respect for the legal system if the code violates citizens' consensus. Examples such as prohibition suggest that in such cases, the community moves toward contempt for the legal system. Initial contempt for the specific laws in question soon spreads to the criminal justice system enforcing those laws, the police force and the judges, and finally the legal code in general. When this happens, the law loses its most powerful force for keeping order: the citizens' belief that the laws are to be obeyed because they represent the moral consensus of the community, and therefore the moral views that all citizens should hold.

This is not only a conclusion of psychologists. Legal theorists have argued the same point. Lately, disturbingly, Congress has "criminalized" many actions that do not fit Americans' prototype of a wrongful action, intentionally committed. A number of these prototypically innocent or thoughtless actions are now treated as crimes that require the heavy punishments available within the criminal justice system. Coffee (1991), a leading legal commentator, commented that "this blurring . . . will weaken the efficacy of the criminal law as an instrument of social control" because "the criminal law is obeyed not simply because there is a legal threat underlying it, but because the public perceives its norms to be legitimate and deserving of compliance" (pp. 193-194). That is, people think of criminal conduct as immoral conduct, so if the law criminalizes actions that people do not think of as immoral, it loses credibility. Such a law is obeyed, if it is obeyed, only to avoid jail. Other legal scholars agree. Pound (1907) remarked that in "all cases of divergence between the standard of the common law and the standard of the public, it goes without saying that the latter will prevail in the end" (p. 615). Holmes (1881) wrote that the "first requirement of a sound body of law is, that it should correspond with the actual feelings and demands of the community" (pp. 41-42).

CONCLUSIONS

The psychological study of citizens' perceptions of what counts as wrongdoing and the appropriate punishments for wrongdoing is quite a recent activity. Still, two sorts of discoveries have been made. The first are procedural. Studies have shown that a useful technique is to ask people to assign innocence or guilt and punishment to agents in a set of vignettes that differ in ways that correspond to legal distinctions. Using this technique has enabled researchers to trace the chains of reasoning that respondents follow to judge blame and responsibility.

Other discoveries have been substantive: First, the community does have coherent and consistent views of what counts as criminal behavior. Second, there are important differences between legal codes and citizens' intuitions about just punishments. For example, the MPC adopts a subjectivist definition of the essence of a crime, and Americans do not. This finding suggests that it may be useful to investigate whether there are other doctrines incorporated in the MPC that violate the modal citizen's perceptions of justice.

I have argued that contradictions between criminal codes and the moral views of the community put people's respect for the legal system at risk. But this speculation requires research, and if it is found to be valid, additional work will be needed to uncover the processes by which these divergences affect citizens' perceptions of the justness of the legal system and willingness to voluntarily make the code's standards their own. What are the psychological processes of alienation involved? Because it is inevitable that occasionally, for policy reasons, legal codes will deviate from the moral intuitions of the citizens, it is imperative to discover how this alienation and disobedience can be avoided.

Fundamental questions often emerge as a research project progresses, and this happened in our work on the citizen's sense of justice. Why is it, when an actor knowingly commits an offense, that an observer feels that punishment is objectively required? What is the justification for punishment? Psychologists have been quite silent about this, although philosophers have suggested answers: deterrence for Bentham, "just desserts" for Kant. But what does the ordinary citizen take to be the justification for punishment of wrongdoing? This is perhaps the most intriguing remaining question about retributive justice.

Recommended Reading

Finkel, N. (1997). *Common sense justice: Jurors' notions of the law.* Cambridge, MA: Harvard University Press.
Finkel, N., & Sales, B. (Eds.). (1997). Common sense justice [Special issue]. *Psychology, Public Policy, and Law, 3*(2/3).
Hamilton, V.L., & Sanders, J. (1992). *Everyday justice: Responsibility and the individual in Japan and the United States.* New Haven, CT: Yale University Press.
Robinson, P.H., & Darley, J.M. (1995). (See References)
Robinson, P.H., & Darley, J.M. (1997). The utility of desert. *Northwestern University Law Review, 91,* 453-499.

Notes

1. Address correspondence to John Darley, Psychology Department, Princeton University, Princeton, NJ 08544; e-mail: jdarley@princeton.edu.

2. "Common sense justice" is Norman Finkel's term for ordinary people's perceptions of just rules for determining such matters as a perpetrator's degree of responsibility for a harm. Finkel has been one of the leaders in discovering these naive psychological rules. Lee Hamilton, often working with Joseph Sanders, has been another. Volume 3, number 2/3, of *Psychology, Public Policy, and Law* (1997) is entirely on aspects of commonsense justice.

References

American Law Institute. (1962). *Model Penal Code official draft, 1962*. Philadelphia: Author.

Coffee, J.D. (1991). Does 'unlawful' mean 'criminal'? Reflections on the disappearing tort/ crime distinction in American law. *Boston University Law Review, 71*, 193-246.

Darley, J., Sanderson, C., & LaMantha, P. (1996). Community standards for defining attempt: Inconsistencies with the Model Penal Code. *American Behavioral Scientist, 39*, 405-420.

Holmes, O.W., Jr. (1881). *The common law*. Boston: Little, Brown.

Macauley, T. (1837). *A penal code prepared by the Indian law commissioners*. Calcutta, India: Bengal Military Orphans Press.

Pound, R. (1907). The need of a sociological jurisprudence. *Green Bag, 19*, 607-615.

Robinson, P.H., & Darley, J.M. (1995). *Justice, liability, and blame: Community views and criminal laws*. Boulder, CO: Westview Press.

Robinson, P.H., & Darley, J.M. (1998). Objective vs. subjectivist views of criminality: A study in the role of social science in criminal law theory. *Oxford Journal of Legal Studies, 18*, 409-447.

Thibaut, J., & Walker, L. (1975). *Procedural justice: A psychological analysis*. Mahwah, NJ: Erlbaum.

Tyler, T. (1990). *Why people obey the law*. New Haven, CT: Yale University Press.

Critical Thinking Questions

1. This article presents an empirical look at "common sense justice." Explain why it might be important for citizens' sense of justice to match legal codes. Why is social psychology uniquely positioned to address this question?

2. The authors argue that the policy capturing approach is superior to simple self reports as a data collection technique in this area. Drawing on your knowledge of research methods, discuss some reasons why this approach would be preferable.

3. Discuss how the author uses historical quotes to back up his idea that consistency between citizens' sense of justice and the legal system is vital. Provide some other examples (past or present) to illustrate this point.

The Confidence of Eyewitnesses in Their Identifications From Lineups

Gary L. Wells,[1] Elizabeth A. Olson, and Steve D. Charman
Psychology Department, Iowa State University, Ames, Iowa

Abstract

The confidence that eyewitnesses express in their lineup identifications of criminal suspects has a large impact on criminal proceedings. Many convictions of innocent people can be attributed in large part to confident but mistaken eyewitnesses. Although reasonable correlations between confidence and accuracy can be obtained under certain conditions, confidence is governed by some factors that are unrelated to accuracy. An understanding of these confidence factors helps establish the conditions under which confidence and accuracy are related and leads to important practical recommendations for criminal justice proceedings.

Keywords

eyewitness testimony; lineups; eyewitness memory

Mistaken identification by eyewitnesses was the primary evidence used to convict innocent people whose convictions were later overturned by forensic DNA tests (Scheck, Neufeld, & Dwyer, 2000; Wells et al., 1998). The eyewitnesses in these cases were very persuasive because on the witness stand they expressed extremely high confidence that they had identified the actual perpetrator. Long before DNA exoneration cases began unfolding in the 1990s, however, eyewitness researchers in psychology were finding that confidence is not a reliable indicator of accuracy and warning the justice system that heavy reliance on eyewitness's confidence in their identifications might lead to the conviction of innocent people.

Studies have consistently demonstrated that the confidence an eyewitness expresses in an identification is the major factor determining whether people will believe that the eyewitness made an accurate identification. The confidence an eyewitness expresses is also enshrined in the criteria that the U.S. Supreme Court used 30 years ago (and that now guide lower courts) for deciding the accuracy of an eyewitness's identification in a landmark case. Traditionally, much of the experimental work examining the relation between confidence and accuracy in eyewitness identification tended to frame the question as "What is the correlation between confidence and accuracy?" as though there were some single, true correlation value. Today, eyewitness researchers regard the confidence-accuracy relation as something that varies across circumstances. Some of these circumstances are outside the control of the criminal justice system, but some are determined by the procedures that criminal justice personnel control.

A GENERAL FRAMEWORK FOR CONFIDENCE-ACCURACY RELATIONS

It has been fruitful to think about eyewitness accuracy and eyewitness confidence as variables that are influenced by numerous factors, some of which are the same and some of which are different. We expect confidence and accuracy to be more closely related when the variables that are influencing accuracy are also influencing confidence than when the variables influencing accuracy are different from those influencing confidence. Consider, for instance, the variable of exposure duration (i.e., how long the eyewitness viewed the culprit while the crime was committed). An eyewitness who viewed the culprit for a long time during the crime should be more accurate than one who had only a brief view. Furthermore, the longer view could be a foundation for the eyewitness to feel more confident in the identification, either because the witness has a more vivid and fluent memory from the longer duration or because the witness infers his or her accuracy from the long exposure duration. Hence, the correlation between confidence and accuracy should be higher the more variation there is in the exposure duration across witnesses (Read, Vokey, & Hammersley, 1990). Suppose, however, that some eyewitnesses were reinforced after their identification decision (e.g., "Good job. You are a good witness."), whereas others were given no such reinforcement. Such postidentification reinforcement does nothing to make witnesses more accurate, but dramatically inflates their confidence (Wells & Bradfield,1999).

Eyewitness confidence can be construed simply as the eyewitness's belief, which varies in degree, about whether the identification was accurate or not. This belief can have various sources, both internal and external, that need not be related to accuracy. Shaw and his colleagues, for example, have shown that repeated questioning of eyewitnesses about mistaken memories does not make the memories more accurate but does inflate the eyewitnesses' confidence in those memories (Shaw, 1996; Shaw & McLure, 1996). Although the precise mechanisms for the repeated-questioning effect are not clear (e.g., increased commitment to the mistaken memory vs. increased fluidity of the response), these results illustrate a dissociation between variables affecting confidence and variables affecting accuracy.

It is useful to think about broad classes of variables that could be expected to drive confidence and not accuracy, or to drive accuracy and not confidence, or to drive both variables. It is even possible to think about variables that could decrease accuracy while increasing confidence. Consider, for instance, coincidental resemblance. Mistaken identifications from lineups occur primarily when the actual culprit is not in the lineup. Suppose there are two such lineups, one in which the innocent suspect does not highly resemble the real culprit and a second in which the innocent suspect is a near clone (coincidental resemblance) of the real culprit. The second lineup will result not only in an increased rate of mistaken identification compared with the first lineup, but also in higher confidence in that mistake. In this case, a variable that decreases accuracy (resemblance of an innocent suspect to the actual culprit) serves to increase confidence.

THE CORRELATION, CALIBRATION, AND INFLATION OF CONFIDENCE

Although many individual studies have reported little or no relation between eyewitnesses' confidence in their identifications and the accuracy of their identifications, an analysis that statistically combined individual studies indicates that the confidence-accuracy correlation might be as high as +.40 when the analysis is restricted to individuals who make an identification (vs. all witnesses; see Sporer, Penrod, Read, & Cutler, 1995). How useful is this correlation for predicting accuracy from confidence? In some ways, a correlation of .40 could be considered strong. For instance, when overall accuracy is 50%, a .40 correlation would translate into 70% of the witnesses with high confidence being accurate and only 30% of the witnesses with low confidence being accurate. As accuracy deviates from 50%, however, differences in accuracy rates between witnesses with high and low confidence will diminish even though the correlation remains .40.

Another way to think about a .40 correlation is to compare it with something that people experience in daily life, namely the correlation between a person's height and a person's gender. Extrapolating from males' and females' average height and standard deviation (69.1, 63.7, and 5.4 in., respectively; Department of Health and Human Services, n.d.) yields a correlation between height and gender of +.43. Notice that the correlation between height and gender is quite similar to the correlation between eyewitnesses' identification confidence and accuracy. Thus, if eyewitnesses' identifications are accurate 50% of the time, we would expect to encounter a highly confident mistaken eyewitness (or a non-confident accurate eyewitness) about as often as we would encounter a tall female (or a short male).

Although the eyewitness-identification literature has generally used correlation methods to express the statistical association between confidence and accuracy, it is probably more forensically valid to use calibration and overconfidence/underconfidence measures rather than correlations (Brewer, Keast, & Rishworth, 2002; Juslin, Olson, & Winman, 1996). In effect, the correlation method (specifically, point-biserial correlation) expresses the degree of statistical association by calculating the difference in confidence (expressed in terms of the standard deviation) between accurate and inaccurate witnesses. Calibration, on the other hand, assesses the extent to which an eyewitness's confidence, expressed as a percentage, matches the probability that the eyewitness is correct. Overconfidence reflects the extent to which the percentage confidence exceeds the probability that the eyewitness is correct (e.g., 80% confidence and 60% probability correct), and underconfidence reflects the extent to which the percentage confidence underestimates the probability that the eyewitness is correct (e.g., 40% confidence and 60% probability correct). Juslin et al. pointed out that the confidence-accuracy correlation can be quite low even when calibration is high.

Work by Juslin et al. (1996) indicates that eyewitnesses can be well calibrated at times, but recent experiments (Wells & Bradfield, 1999) illustrate a problem that can arise when trying to use percentage confidence expressed by witnesses to infer the probability that their identifications are accurate. In a series of experiments, eyewitnesses were induced to make mistaken identifications from lineups in which the culprit was absent and were then randomly assigned to receive confirming "feedback" telling them that they identified the actual suspect or to receive no feedback at all. Later, these witnesses were asked how certain they were at the time of their identification (i.e., how certain they were before the feedback). Those who did not receive confirming feedback gave average confidence ratings of less than 50%, but those receiving confirming feedback gave average confidence ratings of over 70%. Because all of these eyewitnesses had made mistaken identifications, even the no-feedback witnesses were overconfident, but the confirming-feedback witnesses were especially overconfident. Confidence inflation is a difficult problem in actual criminal cases because eyewitnesses are commonly given feedback about whether their identification decisions agree with the investigator's theory of the case. In these cases, it is the detective, rather than the eyewitness, who determines the confidence of the eyewitness.

Confirming feedback not only inflates confidence, thereby inducing overconfidence, but also harms the confidence-accuracy correlation. When eyewitnesses are given confirming feedback following their identification decisions, the confidence of inaccurate eyewitnesses is inflated more than is the confidence of accurate eyewitnesses, and the net result is a reduction in the confidence-accuracy correlation (Bradfield, Wells, & Olson, 2002). Hence, although the confidence of an eyewitness can have utility if it is assessed independently of external influences (e.g., comments from the detective, learning about what other eyewitnesses have said), the legal system rarely assesses confidence in this way.

IMPACT ON POLICIES AND PRACTICES

What impact has research on the confidence-accuracy problem had on the legal system? Until relatively recently, the impact has been almost nil. However, when DNA exoneration cases began unfolding in the mid-1990s, U.S. Attorney General Janet Reno initiated a study of the causes of these miscarriages of justice. More than three fourths of these convictions of innocent persons involved mistaken eyewitness identifications, and, in every case, the mistaken eyewitnesses were extremely confident and, therefore, persuasive at trial (Wells et al., 1998). A Department of Justice panel used the psychological literature to issue the first set of national guidelines on collecting eyewitness identification evidence (Technical Working Group for Eyewitness Evidence, 1999). One of the major recommendations was that the confidence of the eyewitness be assessed at the time of the identification, before there is any chance for it to be influenced by external factors.

The state of New Jersey has gone even further in adopting the recommendations of eyewitness researchers. Based on findings from the psychological literature, guidelines from the attorney general of New Jersey now call for double-blind testing with lineups. Double-blind lineup testing means that the person who administers the lineup does not know which person in the lineup is the suspect and which ones are merely fillers. Under the New Jersey procedures, the confidence expressed by the eyewitness will be based primarily on the eyewitness's memory, not on the expectations of or feedback from the lineup administrator.

There is growing evidence that the legal system is now beginning to read and use the psychological literature on eyewitnesses to formulate policies and procedures. The 2002 report of Illinois Governor George Ryan's Commission on Capital Punishment is the latest example of this new reliance on the psychological literature. The commission specifically cited the literature on the problem with confidence inflation and recommended double-blind testing and explicit recording of confidence statements at the time of the identification to prevent or detect confidence inflation (Illinois Commission on Capital Punishment, 2002).

NEW DIRECTIONS

Although the psychological literature on eyewitness identification has done much to clarify the confidence-accuracy issue and specify some conditions under which confidence might be predictive of accuracy, research has started to turn to other indicators that might prove even more predictive of accuracy. One of the most promising examples is the relation between the amount of time an eyewitness takes to make an identification and the accuracy of the identification. Eyewitnesses who make their identification decision quickly (in 10 s or less) are considerably more likely to be accurate than are eyewitnesses who take longer (e.g., Dunning & Perretta, in press). Confidence is a self-report that is subject to distortion (e.g., from post-identification feedback), whereas decision time is a behavior that can be directly observed. Hence, decision time might prove more reliable than confidence as an indicator of eye-witness accuracy. Yet another new direction in eyewitness identification research concerns cases in which there are multiple eyewitnesses. Recent analyses show that the behaviors of eyewitnesses who do not identify the suspect from a lineup can be used to assess the likely accuracy of the eyewitnesses who do identify the suspect from a lineup (Wells & Olson, in press). The future of eyewitness identification research is a bright one, and the legal system now seems to be paying attention.

Recommended Reading

Cutler, B.L., & Penrod, S.D. (1995). *Mistaken identification: The eyewitness, psychology, and the law.* New York: Cambridge University Press.
Scheck, B., Neufeld, P., & Dwyer, J. (2000). (See References)
Wells, G.L., Malpass, R.S., Lindsay, R.C.L., Fisher, R.P., Turtle, J.W., & Fulero, S. (2000). From the lab to the police station: A successful application of eyewitness research. *American Psychologist, 55,* 581-598.

Note

1. Address correspondence to Gary L. Wells, Psychology Department, Iowa State University, Ames, IA 50011; e-mail: glwells@iastate.edu.

References

Bradfield, S.L., Wells, G.L., & Olson, E.A. (2002). The damaging effect of confirming feedback on the relation between eyewitness certainty and identification accuracy. *Journal of Applied Psychology, 87,* 112-120.
Brewer, N., Keast, A., & Rishworth, A. (2002). Improving the confidence-accuracy relation in eyewitness identification: Evidence from correlation and calibration. *Journal of Experimental Psychology: Applied, 8,* 44-56.
Department of Health and Human Services, National Center for Health Statistics. (n.d.). *National Health and Nutrition Examination Survey.* Retrieved May 22, 2002, from http:// www.cdc.gov/ nchs/about/major/nhanes/ datatblelink.htm#unpubtab

Dunning, D., & Perretta, S. (in press). Automaticity and eyewitness accuracy: A 10 - to -12 second rule for distinguishing accurate from inaccurate positive identifications. *Journal of Applied Psychology.*

Illinois Commission on Capital Punishment. (2002, April). *Report of the Governor's Commission on Capital Punishment.* Retrieved April 23, 2002, from http://www.idoc.state.il.us/ccp/ccp/reports/commission_report/

Juslin, P., Olson, N., & Winman, A. (1996). Calibration and diagnosticity of confidence in eyewitness identification: Comments on what can and cannot be inferred from a low confidence-accuracy correlation. *Journal of Experimental Psychology: Learning, Memory, and Cognition, 5,* 1304-1316.

Read, J.D., Vokey, J.R., & Hammersley, R. (1990). Changing photos of faces: Effects of exposure duration and photo similarity on recognition and the accuracy-confidence relationship. *Journal of Experimental Psychology: Learning, Memory, and Cognition, 16,* 870-882.

Scheck, B., Neufeld, P., & Dwyer, J. (2000). *Actual innocence.* New York: Random House.

Shaw, J.S., III. (1996). Increases in eyewitness confidence resulting from post-event questioning. *Journal of Experimental Psychology: Applied, 2,* 126-146.

Shaw, J.S., III, & McClure, K.A. (1996). Repeated post-event questioning can lead to elevated levels of eyewitness confidence. *Law and Human Behavior, 20,* 629-654.

Sporer, S., Penrod, S., Read, D., & Cutler, B.L. (1995). Choosing, confidence, and accuracy: A meta-analysis of the confidence-accuracy relation in eyewitness identification studies. *Psychological Bulletin, 118,* 315-327.

Technical Working Group for Eyewitness Evidence. (1999). *Eyewitness evidence: A guide for law enforcement.* Washington, DC: U.S. Department of Justice, Office of Justice Programs.

Wells, G.L., & Bradfield, A.L. (1999). Distortions in eyewitnesses' recollections: Can the post-identification-feedback effect be moderated? *Psychological Science, 10,* 138-144.

Wells, G.L., & Olson, E.A. (in press). Eyewitness identification: Information gain from incriminating and exonerating behaviors. *Journal of Experimental Psychology: Applied.*

Wells, G.L., Small, M., Penrod, S., Malpass, R.S., Fulero, S.M., & Brimacombe, C.A.E. (1998). Eyewitness identification procedures: Recommendations for lineups and photo-spreads. *Law and Human Behavior, 22,* 603-647.

Critical Thinking Questions

1. Explain the point that the authors are trying to make in comparing the height/weight correlation to the accuracy/confidence correlation. What conclusions can you draw from this? Based on your conclusion, is the accuracy/confidence relationship good enough to be used in a court of law?

2. What do the authors mean when they state that in some cases "it is the detective, rather than the eyewitness, who determines the confidence of the eyewitness." Describe the research that supports this statement.

3. Discuss some of the implications of this line of research on legal policies and practices. What have some courts already done to incorporate these findings? Based on this growing body of research, speculate on other measures that the legal system might take to improve its effectiveness.

Topic Index